A Taste Of The South

·

TERRY THOMPSON

HPBooks
a division of
PRICE STERN SLOAN
Los Angeles

Published by HPBooks, a division of Price Stern Sloan, Inc.
360 North La Cienega Boulevard, Los Angeles, California 90048

© Copyright HPBooks 1988
1st Printing
Printed in U.S.A.

Illustrations by Christy Sheets Mull

Library of Congress Cataloging-in-Publication Data

Thompson, Terry, 1946-
    A taste of the South / Terry Thompson.
        p.   cm.
    Includes index.
    ISBN 0-89586-555-6
    1. Cookery, American—Southern style. I. Title.
TX715.2.S68T48   1988   88-17745
641.5975—dc19   CIP

CONTENTS

TERRY THOMPSON

Terry Thompson is a nationally known cooking school teacher and restaurant consultant. She has taught over 10,000 students in cooking schools and seminars all over the United States. She has created recipes that grace restaurant menus from coast to coast. Terry is also a food writer and has written for several major food magazines. She is a member of the International Association of Cooking Professionals and has attained the highest distinction that the organization offers—that of Certified Food Professional.

Terry's first and very successful book, **Cajun-Creole Cooking,** demonstrated her ability to seek out the secrets of regional cuisine from her home base in Southern Louisiana. She now lives in Bay St. Louis, Mississippi, a natural spawning ground for this comprehensive book on Southern foods.

Terry researched the foods of the South, tracing their development from the earliest settlement at Jamestown. This book presents an in-depth look at Southern home cooking, prepared according to time-honored methods, preserving the tastes that have given it the reputation as being among the world's finest food.

INTRODUCTION

Think of the mind as having an attic. Not just a complex neurological databank, but an actual compartment where we store reminiscences so real we can feel their dust. These are the memorabilia of a million yesterdays and their trappings. In the minds of born-and-bred Southerners, this attic is crowded with the richest of such recollections—with the aroma of baking breads and pastries, the scent of sizzling pork roasts and the sensuous, musky perfume of freshly boiled seafood, and with tastes so profoundly wonderful they cannot be described by mere words: the flavors of dark and mysterious gumbos, steaming bread puddings with heady rum sauces, hot corn bread dripping with butter. Every Southerner is born with such a secret attic, an inherent nostalgia toward his heritage, and he will defend this heritage with an undying pride.

"As God is my witness, I'm never going to be hungry again!" These were the immortal words of Scarlett O'Hara, heroine of Margaret Mitchell's classic tale of the South, *Gone with the Wind*.

In the epic film based on Ms. Mitchell's work, this poignant scene portrayed a disheveled Miss Scarlett silhouetted against a vast blue sky, scratching at the dry earth with her bare hands. Digging up a handful of radishes, she held them aloft as she spat out the now famous words. A meager meal for the distraught young planter's daughter finding herself reduced to paltry circumstances, but salvation from hunger to Scarlett and her peers throughout the war-ravaged South. What had been was to be no more. The forces which brought about the upheaval and those that would shape the future forever changed the face of the South and left their indelible mark on all its people, regardless of color or class. The way of life was over, ended in a thousand bloody battles staged in once idyllic meadows, primeval forests and sleepy back road towns. The war and the humiliating period of Reconstruction which followed left wounds, which would persist for generations. But still the South had to go on, to grow and to progress. Yet its past would never be forgotten: The New South would be built upon the cornerstone of deeply-rooted traditions.

The South has long been an enigma, a contradiction about which hundreds of books were written. Scholarly intellectuals have penned weighty tomes attempting to explain the South and Southerners—people who jump to their feet with fierce loyalty at the first strains of "Dixie," no matter where they are.

Southerners are special in their fervid love of place. They are Southerners first, and Americans second. They are a people to whom duty, honor and obligation are strongly held virtues. Southern writers such as William Faulkner, Tennessee Williams, Flannery O'Connor, Carson McCullers, Walker Percy and many others have written raw and earthy tales of Southern life and the odd characters who give it breath. Tales of religion and church revivals. Tales of ancient pick-up trucks held together with baling wire, bumping over dusty back roads with cargoes of moonshine. Tales of eating hoppin' John and fried chicken and hush puppies. Even the vocabulary of the South is a rich and complex tapestry woven from the remnants of its past—from the Cajun-French patois of South Louisiana to the Gullah Low Country tongue of South Carolina to the Elizabethan dialects of North Carolina's Outer Banks. The accents range from the Mississippi "good old boy" twang to Georgia's 30-minutes-per-word drawl to New Orleans's Ninth Ward "Wotcher want dawlin'," the very sound of which would make you swear you were in Brooklyn.

Mention Southern cooking to most people and visions of crispy fried chicken, grits, hush puppies, lighter-than-air biscuits and assorted pies fill their minds. But Southern cuisine is much more complex and varied than is generally realized. It represents the resplendent union of three powerful cultures—native American, African and Western European—with a healthy dash of Caribbean-Creole ingredients and methodology thrown into the pot.

As early as the colonial days, Southerners were concerned with fine cuisine and the struggle to provide it in the new world. Thomas Jefferson, the world-traveled Virginia statesman, could easily be called the South's first gourmet. A student of French cooking, he is credited with merging many of the classic dishes and ingredients of France into the developing American cuisine. One such dish is ice cream—and Jefferson even constructed a thick-walled brick building at Monticello for storing ice. Jefferson prided himself on importing the finest breeds of hogs and varieties of exotic foodstuffs from Europe. He planted vegetable crops previously unknown in America, keeping meticulous records of seed varieties.

The South began on May 16, 1607, when Christopher Newport sailed his three ships—*Susan Constant, Godspeed* and *Discovery*—into the mouth of a river he named the James, after the King of England. He disembarked with 104 British settlers at a point which he claimed for England and christened Jamestown. They were, however, totally unable to cope with the unfamiliar new world. These would-be colonists were city dwellers with no experience in hunting, fishing and trapping. Nor did they know how to farm. By October they had run out of supplies and half of them had perished.

The event which saved the colony from total extinction was also the first culinary merger of cultures in America. Deprived of the wheat flour to which they were accustomed, the colonists adopted the cultivation of corn, a staple of the American Indian diet for centuries. This versatile grain was used in many dishes and corn bread in particular quickly became a Southern institution.

From their beginnings as primitive backwoods communities, Jamestown and the other 17th-century settlements in the Virginia Tidewater region eventually gave birth to the Southern aristocracy. Over the next 200 years Southern society began to refine itself and by 1800 the Plantation South of popular literature was well advanced. The landed country gentry became the ruling class. Theirs was a totally agrarian society which scorned any type of industry except that necessary to the efficient operation of the plantation.

The South of the Eastern seacoast retained strong English traditions, but as new settlers arrived and pushed inland, the Southern society became more diluted by other European influences. In Florida, the Spanish established lasting traditions, as they did along the Gulf Coast and especially in the Louisiana Territory. Here, Spanish and French culture merged to form an entire class—the Creoles.

In most regions of the South, society remained largely rural, with the exception of the great port cities such as Charleston, New Orleans, Mobile and Savannah. Even where cities were established, they existed mainly as places where money could be spent, but not necessarily made! To the Southerner of this rapidly developing society, making money was not the end goal, but simply a means by which to accomplish a pleasurable lifestyle wherein each moment could be enjoyed to the fullest.

Black Americans had a profound effect on the food of the South. Many slaves who came to work the plantations of the South had previously worked on Caribbean plantations, and brought with them a Caribbeanized version of African cooking as well as many exotic spices and ingredients from the Far East. Indeed, they introduced some of the most traditional Southern ingredients—eggplant, peanuts, peas, sesame seeds and sesame oil. They brought seeds of a strange, podlike vegetable they called *kingumbo;* we know it today as okra, but the vegetable gave its African name to gumbo, the rich, thick, roux-based soup for which the Cajuns and Creoles are famous. Red pepper, too, came from Africa with the slaves and became a central ingredient in Southern cooking.

As slavery became an established system indigenous African ingredients and cooking methods were integrated into Southern cuisine, spawning the "soul food" for which the South is still famous. In fact, soul food has changed very little since its origin. Slaves were issued weekly rations of salt pork and cornmeal; on some plantations, they received seasonal fresh vegetables, and most were allowed to plant small gardens adjacent to their quarters and keep a few chickens. They also hunted, trapped and fished for the American wild game which became an integral part of soul food. Opossum, squirrel, raccoon, rabbit and groundhog were common game which the slaves added to their weekly rations, with opossum being the favorite. It was generally skinned and parboiled, then roasted with fatback, seasoned with red pepper and persimmon beer and eaten with sweet potatoes. Young opossum was often fried, as was rabbit. Squirrel pie with dumplings was a soul food delicacy. Chickens were stuffed with dressing, greased with lard and wrapped in cabbage leaves, then roasted in the fireplace, and completely covered by hot coals.

The "secret" of soul food—and anyone who has tasted it will agree that it is so good it must have a secret—lies in its imaginative and assertive use of spices and herbs. The skill of the Black cook in seasoning produces a flavor at once subtle and intense, the type of flavor that makes jambalaya, hoppin' John and gumbo almost worth dying for! Sarah Hicks Williams, a New Yorker living in the South, wrote to her parents in 1853, "Red pepper is much used to flavor meat and the famous 'barbecue' of the South—roasted pig dressed with red pepper and vinegar—a dish I believe they esteem above all others." The Black preference for highly spiced food was subtly transmitted to the whites through the Black command of the "Big House" kitchens.

Great wealth existed in the antebullum South and the large planters spared no expense in procuring the finest ingredients for grand multi-course meals featuring dozens of dishes. William Howard Russell, a *London Times* correspondent in America in 1861, wrote of a breakfast he enjoyed on a visit to a Louisiana plantation: "There is on the table a profusion of dishes—grilled fowl, prawns, eggs and ham, fish from New Orleans, potted salmon from England, preserved meats from France, claret, iced water, coffee and tea, varieties of hominy, mush and African vege-table preparations." But the really big meal of the day was dinner, served around 2:00 p.m. One such meal at a Low Country South Carolina plantation consisted of turtle soup, boiled mutton, turtle steaks, macaroni pie, oysters, boiled ham, venison, roast turkey, bread pudding, ice cream, pie and fruit. Madeira, sherry and champagne were generally served with the meal; cordials and ratafias would follow dessert.

Likewise, no expense was spared in training cooks for the plantation kitchens. Wealthy plantation owners often sent male house slaves to Paris to be trained as cooks. During the height of the plantation era, it was customary for the planters to take their families on grand European tours. They often brought the house staff along. On these lavish trips the slaves learned to prepare the classic dishes of Europe, then "translated" them into their own Southern style back home in the plantation kitchen.

Restaurants in the great cities of New Orleans, Mobile and Charleston gained the attention of world travelers for the outstanding quality of their food. Shortly after the close of the Civil War, Mark Twain commented, "New Orleans food is as delicious as the less criminal forms of sin."

Even as the tattered remnants of the South struggled to rebuild some semblance of society during the dark days of Reconstruction, determined Southerners successfully upheld their reputation for fine, distinctive foods.

Until 25 to 30 years ago, the South remained largely rural and agrarian, sheltered from the trends toward processed, "standardized" foods which began to take root in the North and Midwest in the late 1800s. Family structure has remained tight in the South, and religious values are important—both factors which tend to maintain strong ties to home and the family table. Southern home cooks take pride in a heritage of good cooking that began to develop with the first colonist's campfire in Virginia. Indeed, for many young Southern brides, the most prized possession—even above the Cuisinart and the toaster oven—is grandmother's recipe file. Southern home-style cooking today is a link to the past, perhaps even the mind's link to an imaginary past before the Civil War. It is comfortable food that makes you feel as warm and secure as the flannel nightgown of your childhood memories.

Legions of talented Southern chefs are spreading the gospel of Southern food throughout the land, drawing from the culinary reminiscences of their childhood. And the hallmarks of the Southern style of cooking—profound quality of taste, liberal and innovative use of seasonings, reliance upon fresh, premium-grade ingredients—are making a definitive impact on the development of the "new American cuisine." A few years ago, collard greens were the subject of slurs and jokes in Manhattan. Today, they are a side dish on dinner party menus in that same city.

Real Southern food will never languish into obscurity to be replaced by pasteurized, processed, more convenient foods—either in the home or the restaurant. Southern eaters are just too spoiled to allow such a thing to happen! The cuisine will continue to evolve, using the freshest and best ingredients available and drawing inspiration from its delicious tradition of good food. No, Southern food will never lose its very special character, but rather, like a slowly simmering pot of catfish courtbouillon, it will become better with the passing of time and the loving tending of the pot.

APPETIZERS

Southern hospitality. The phrase itself sketches an inviting scene in the mind. To those who live in the South, it is a way of life. To those who enjoy it as visitors, it is a revelation—an experience described as "gracious," "overwhelming," "certainly more than expected." Some speak of feeling transported to an earlier, less hectic time. Mr. Webster defines hospitality as "the reception and entertainment of guests or strangers with liberality and kindness," and I am certain that he penned that definition after a stay in a Southern home. In the South, there are no strangers, and friendships are often lifetime relationships.

Being a guest in a Southern home is a treat that everyone should experience. Southerners just have a magical way of seeing that their guests are comfortable and well fed, and making sure they leave with pleasant memories. You can

unwind, slow down and by all means, stop to smell the magnolias! When you leave, chances are you'll still have the same problems you arrived with, but you'll also have a new peace of mind to help deal with them. As to the extra ten pounds you will carry away with you—well, I can assure you it will be worth it to have dined for a while on Southern food.

"Socializing" has always been a very important aspect of Southern life. Historically, families were large—having ten or twelve children was not unusual—and close-knit. In many areas of the Deep South, folks rarely moved very far from where they were born. But even when visiting family or friends meant traveling for many miles or days, the trip was spent in joyful anticipation of the warm fellowship waiting at journey's end. And no small part of that anticipation centered on the food that would be shared, whether the fare was collard greens cooked with smoked hog jowl in a one-room cabin or a grand banquet of dozens of dishes served at a wealthy planter's estate.

In the South, there is food to fit any occasion, and you can bet your grits that no Southerner will come up short when it comes to food for entertaining. The cocktail as we know it today—a mixed drink usually containing alcohol—was actually invented in the South, in New Orleans, a city known far and wide for its exuberant imbibing. Appetizers as we know them today—bite-size foods often eaten with the fingers—are legion in the South. Many Southern hostesses could effortlessly quote you recipes for hundreds of delicious finger foods and other munchies. The appearance of a tasty new appetizer at a party can make that party the talk of the town, and the other ladies won't sleep well until they have pried the recipe from the clever hostess.

One reason Southerners have such a wide repertoire of party foods is that we have so many parties! We seem to have built our entire society around events designed for having fun. Mardi Gras involves an entire month of revelry and overeating; Derby Day in Louisville is built around grand brunches and buffets. Literally hundreds of country festivals occur at all times of the year throughout the South, all celebrating a local crop, game, fish or meat. And all of them are based on eating. The social level of the event may vary. The location may range from a French Quarter courtyard or mansion garden in New Orleans to "down by the creek" on the family farm in Mississippi; from the intimate parlor of a grand city home on Peachtree Street in Atlanta to the veranda of an antebellum plantation-turned-thoroughbred farm in Louisville's countryside. The invitation may arrive in the mail, engraved on fine paper; it may contain an identification card which must be presented for admittance, as an invitation to a Mardi Gras ball would, or it may be as simple as the South's universal call to fellowship: "Y'all come!" But the promise is always the same—good friends, great food, bountiful drink and precious memories.

Garlic-Cheddar Cheese Cones

A real attention-getter at a party, this molded cheese spread is so attractive that you'll probably have to be the first to assault it! The zesty flavor is right in line with America's current infatuation with seasoning pizzazz. Serve with your favorite crackers.

>   2 large garlic cloves, peeled
>   1 pound pasteurized process cheese, cut into chunks
>   1 (3-oz.) package cream cheese, room temperature
>   3/4 teaspoon red (cayenne) pepper
>   1/2 cup coarsely chopped pecans
>   1 teaspoon Worcestershire sauce
>   2 (6-oz.) cans whole smoked almonds
>   2 pine tree sprigs, if desired, washed, patted dry

❦ In a food processor with the steel blade and with machine running, drop garlic through feed tube. Stop machine and add process cheese, cream cheese, red pepper, pecans and Worcestershire sauce. Process until smooth, stopping once or twice to scrape down side of bowl. Divide mixture into 2 equal portions. Form each into the shape of a pine cone and place on a small serving tray or cutting board. Starting at bottom of cone, press rows of whole almonds into cheese, with each row slightly overlapping the row beneath it. Place 1 pine sprig at top of each completed cone, if desired. Makes 2 cheese cones.

Garlic-Tomato Bread
with Mozzarella & Sun-Dried Tomatoes

A very trendy and irresistible finger food! This recipe was inspired by the South's bounty of tomatoes and basil that grows to bush size. Each appetizer is topped with mild mozzarella and a fresh basil leaf tucked beneath a sun-dried tomato piece.

> 1 cup peeled, coarsely chopped fresh tomatoes
> 2 teaspoons sugar
> 1 (1/4-oz.) package active dry yeast (about 1 tablespoon)
> 4 green onions (including tops), coarsely chopped
> 4 large garlic cloves, peeled
> 1 teaspoon celery seeds
> 1 teaspoon salt
> 1/2 teaspoon freshly ground black pepper
> 2 tablespoons unsalted butter or margarine, room temperature
> 3 cups bread flour
> 1 pound sliced mozzarella cheese
> About 60 fresh basil leaves
> 2 cups sun-dried tomatoes packed in olive oil, well drained

❦ Lightly grease bottom and sides of a large bowl; set aside. Lightly grease a double-trough French bread pan and set aside. In a food processor fitted with the steel blade, process fresh tomatoes and sugar until pureed. Transfer to a small saucepan and heat until a thermometer registers 115F (45C). Stir in yeast; set aside. In a clean food processor bowl, combine green onions, garlic, celery seeds, salt, pepper, butter and flour. Process to blend. When yeast is dissolved and tomato mixture is bubbly, add mixture to processor work bowl; process to form a smooth, slightly sticky dough. If dough is too dry, add more warm water, a tablespoon at a time, processing just to blend after each addition, until consistency is correct. If dough is too wet, add more flour, a tablespoon at a time, processing just to blend after each addition, until consistency is correct. Process 15 seconds longer to knead dough. Place dough in greased bowl and turn to coat all surfaces. Cover bowl with plastic wrap; let rise in a warm place until dough is doubled in bulk (about 1-1/2 hours). Punch down dough and divide in half. Shape each half into a round rope about 13 inches long; lay ropes in troughs of greased bread pan. Cover loosely with plastic wrap and let rise until doubled in bulk (about 1 hour). Twenty minutes before loaves have finished rising, preheat oven to 375F (190C). When loaves have doubled, carefully remove plastic wrap. Bake in preheated oven until loaves are browned and sound hollow when tapped (about 30 minutes). Remove from pans and cool on wire racks. When ready to make appetizers, position oven rack 4 inches below heat source and preheat broiler. To assemble appetizers, use a serrated knife to slice loaves into rounds about 1/4 inch thick. Place rounds on baking sheets. On each round, place a piece of cheese cut to fit bread (use scraps too). Place a whole basil leaf on cheese and top with a 2-inch piece of sun-dried tomato. Place baking sheets under preheated broiler and broil until cheese is melted and bubbly (2 to 3 minutes). Serve hot. Makes about 60 appetizers.

Assorted Canapé Spreads

Appropriate for just about any type of social gathering the canapé tray is an institution in the South. Canapés are prepared ahead of time, then passed on trays by servers or arranged on serving tables for guests to serve themselves, depending upon the occasion. Serve the following spreads with a variety of French bread or brioche slices; melba toasts; zucchini, yellow squash or cucumber rounds. Or, using a pastry bag fitted with a star tip, pipe the spreads into celery sticks or even snow pea pods.

Roquefort & Walnut Spread

1 (3-oz.) package cream cheese, room temperature
1/2 cup walnuts
3 tablespoons crumbled blue cheese
3 tablespoons Poire William (pear-flavored liqueur)

❦ In a food processor fitted with the steel blade, process all ingredients until smooth. Cover and refrigerate until ready to use. Makes about 1-1/4 cups.

Zucchini & Ham Spread

1 medium zucchini (about 1/4 lb.), sliced
2 medium garlic cloves, peeled
1 (3-oz.) package cream cheese, room temperature
2 tablespoons dairy sour cream
2 tablespoons minced chives
1-1/2 tablespoons prepared horseradish
1/4 teaspoon dried leaf oregano
1/2 teaspoon dried leaf basil
1/4 teaspoon dried leaf rosemary, minced
1/2 teaspoon freshly ground black pepper
Salt to taste
2 ounces smoked ham, cut into small chunks

❦ In a food processor fitted with the steel blade, process all ingredients until smooth. Cover and refrigerate until ready to use. Makes about 1-1/2 cups.

Caviar & Onion Spread

3 ounces red lumpfish caviar
2 ounces cream cheese, room temperature
1/3 cup whipping cream, stiffly whipped
1/4 cup finely minced red onion

❦ Place caviar in a fine strainer and rinse several times with ice-cold water; drain well. In a small bowl, combine cream cheese, whipped cream and onion, folding to blend. Gently fold in drained caviar. Cover and refrigerate until ready to use. Makes about 1-1/4 cups.

Poor Man's Caviar

Southerners love mushrooms, and we put them into almost everything. This simple spread doesn't really taste anything like caviar, but it's so good that the effect upon the senses is much the same! Serve hot or chilled, as a spread for melba toasts.

1/4 cup unsalted butter or margarine
3/4 pound mushrooms (including stems), finely chopped
2 large garlic cloves, minced
2 tablespoons finely chopped pecans
3 green onions (including tops), minced
1/4 cup minced onion
1 tablespoon minced parsley, preferably flat-leaf
1/4 cup dry white wine
3 tablespoons dairy sour cream
1-1/2 teaspoons finely ground black pepper
Salt to taste

❦ Melt butter or margarine in a heavy 10-inch skillet over medium heat. Add mushrooms, garlic, pecans, green onions, onion and parsley. Cook, stirring constantly, until mixture is dry and vegetables are thoroughly cooked (8 to 10 minutes). Add wine, sour cream, pepper and salt; stir to blend. Cook until thickened and creamy (about 4 minutes). Makes about 1-1/2 cups.

Golden Nuggets with Plum Sauce

These delicious tidbits were popular in the South long before Chicken McNuggets™ became the rage.

1-1/2 cups buttermilk
2 tablespoons fresh lemon juice
2 teaspoons Worcestershire sauce
2 teaspoons good-quality soy sauce
1 teaspoon paprika
1 teaspoon dried leaf basil
1 teaspoon dried leaf oregano
1/2 teaspoon salt
1 teaspoon freshly ground black pepper
2 medium garlic cloves, minced
2 pounds skinned, boned chicken breasts, cut into 1-1/2-inch pieces
1/4 cup unsalted butter or margarine
1/4 cup solid vegetable shortening
4 cups fresh bread crumbs
2/3 cup sesame seeds
Plum Sauce, see below

Plum Sauce:
1-1/2 cups red plum jam
1-1/2 tablespoons ballpark-style mustard
1-1/2 tablespoons prepared horseradish
1-1/2 teaspoons fresh lemon juice

❦ In a large bowl, combine buttermilk, lemon juice, Worcestershire sauce, soy sauce, paprika, basil, oregano, salt, pepper and garlic. Add chicken and toss to coat well. Cover with plastic wrap and refrigerate overnight. Preheat oven to 375F (190C). Lightly grease two 13″ x 9″ baking dishes and set aside. In a small saucepan, melt butter or margarine and shortening together. Set aside. Drain chicken thoroughly. In a medium bowl, combine bread crumbs and sesame seeds, mixing well. Add chicken and toss to coat well. Shake off excess topping. Place chicken in a single layer in greased baking dishes and drizzle butter-shortening mixture over top. Bake in preheated oven until golden brown and crisp (30 to 35 minutes). Meanwhile, prepare Plum Sauce. Set bowl of sauce in center of a platter. Place nuggets in circles around bowl and serve hot. Makes 50 to 60 pieces.
Plum Sauce: In a medium saucepan, combine all ingredients and cook over medium heat until hot. Transfer sauce to small serving bowl.

Almond Chicken Nibbles

These crispy, nut-crunchy, delectable little finger foods have been around at Southern parties longer than I care to remember! One thing is for sure—no one can eat just one.

4 egg whites
2/3 cup dry sherry
1/4 cup good-quality soy sauce
1 tablespoon sugar
3 tablespoons cornstarch
2 pounds skinned, boned chicken breasts, cut into 1-1/2-inch pieces
Vegetable oil for deep-frying
1-1/2 cups chopped sliced almonds (about 8 oz.)
2-1/2 tablespoons cornstarch

❦ In a medium bowl, combine egg whites, sherry, soy sauce, sugar and 3 tablespoons cornstarch; beat until very frothy. Place chicken in a single layer in a large baking dish. Pour egg white mixture over chicken; cover with plastic wrap and refrigerate overnight, turning pieces several times. In a deep-sided 12-inch skillet, heat 1 inch of oil until a 1-inch bread cube turns golden brown in 60 seconds. In a small bowl, combine almonds with 2-1/2 tablespoons cornstarch, blending. Remove chicken pieces from marinade and dredge in almond mixture, turning to coat all sides. Add pieces to hot oil, 4 or 5 at a time being careful not to crowd pan. Deep-fry until golden brown (2 to 3 minutes). Take care to maintain a correct oil temperature. Remove chicken from oil with a slotted spoon and drain on paper towels. Serve hot. Makes 50 to 60 pieces.

TIP The chicken pieces may be frozen after frying. To serve, thaw and reheat 15 minutes in a 350F (175C) oven.

Sweet & Sour Olives

A must for the party appetizer tray—and a tasty topping for your favorite homemade pizza. Store tightly covered in refrigerator. Serve at room temperature.

1/3 cup good-quality olive oil
2 medium onions, halved lengthwise, sliced
4 cups pitted ripe olives, drained
1/2 cup red wine vinegar
2 tablespoons sugar

❦ Heat oil in a heavy 12-inch skillet over medium heat, add onions and cook until thoroughly wilted and transparent (about 10 minutes). Stir in olives. Add vinegar and sugar; bring mixture to a boil, then reduce heat; simmer, uncovered, until liquid has thickened slightly to form a thin syrup (10 minutes). Cool completely before serving. Makes 6 cups.

Bacon & Onion Quichelettes

When you hear the raves they produce from your guests, you'll consider the preparation time for these tiny quiches well spent. The best part is that they can be done completely ahead of time, frozen and reheated directly from the freezer.

Pastry, see below
3/4 cup shredded Gruyère cheese (3 oz.)
2 eggs, beaten
3/4 cup whipping cream
4 crisp-cooked bacon slices, minced
3 tablespoons minced onion
1/2 teaspoon dry mustard

Pastry:
1 cup all-purpose flour
1/4 cup frozen unsalted butter, cut into 1-inch cubes
Dash of salt
1/4 cup ice water

❦ Prepare Pastry; refrigerate. Preheat oven to 400F (205C). In a medium bowl, combine all remaining ingredients and whisk to blend. Divide Pastry into 24 equal balls. Press balls into miniature (1-3/4-inch) muffin cups, being careful to press Pastry evenly onto sides and bottom. Fill each shell 3/4 full of filling mixture. Bake 8 minutes in preheated oven; reduce oven temperature to 350F (175C). Continue to bake until puffy and golden brown (10 to 15 minutes longer). Remove from muffin cups and serve hot. Makes 24 appetizers.
Pastry: In a food processor fitted with the steel blade, process flour, butter and salt until butter is broken into pea-size bits. With machine running, pour ice water through feed tube and process until dough holds together. Turn out dough onto a work surface and knead gently once or twice to form a ball. Wrap tightly in plastic wrap and refrigerate at least 30 minutes before using.

Cheese Beignets

This variation on classic choux pastry produces lighter-than-air puffs, which will disappear almost as soon as they are served.

1/4 cup unsalted butter
1 cup water
1 cup all-purpose flour
4 eggs
2/3 cup shredded Emmenthaler cheese (2-2/3 oz.)
1/2 teaspoon salt
1/2 teaspoon Tabasco sauce
Vegetable oil for deep-frying

Melt butter in a heavy medium saucepan over medium heat. Add water and bring to a full boil. Add flour all at once and stir constantly until dough is smooth and leaves sides of pan completely; a very light crust should begin to form on pan bottom. Transfer dough to a food processor fitted with the steel blade. With machine running, add eggs through feed tube, 1 at a time; when all have been added, process 60 seconds. Add cheese, salt and Tabasco sauce. Process just until blended. In a deep-sided 12-inch skillet, heat 2 inches of oil to 375F (190C) or until a 1-inch bread cube turns golden brown in 50 seconds. Drop rounded tablespoons of batter into hot oil, 3 or 4 at a time, being careful not to crowd pan. Deep-fry until golden brown on all sides (2 to 3 minutes); take care to maintain correct oil temperature. Drain on paper towels and serve hot. Makes about 35 beignets.

Puff Pastry Cheese Straws

I suspect that cheese straws were served at the first party ever given in the South. There are as many variations on the recipe as there are hostesses—but the real, honest-to-goodness, crispy Southern cheese straws are made from genuine puff pastry and have a subtle "nip" from red (cayenne) pepper. They are a delicious standby and I'm never without an ample supply in my freezer.

1 (17-1/4-oz.) box frozen puff pastry, thawed, or 1 pound homemade puff pastry
1-1/4 cups grated Parmesan cheese (about 3-3/4 oz.)
1-1/2 teaspoons red (cayenne) pepper
1-1/4 teaspoons salt

❦ If using commercial puff pastry, spread sheets out on work surface and flatten them. If using homemade puff pastry, roll out pastry to a 1/16-inch-thick rectangle on a lightly floured work surface. Combine cheese, red pepper and salt, tossing to blend. Cover surface of pastry with a sprinkling of cheese mixture; set remaining cheese mixture aside. Fold top edge of pastry down to meet bottom edge, then turn pastry so that folded edge is to your left. Roll out pastry again to a 1/16-inch-thick rectangle. Again sprinkle with cheese mixture and fold top down; turn folded edge to your left again. Repeat the entire process 2 more times, for a total of 4 folds and turns with cheese mixture. After the final turn, roll out pastry to a 1/16-inch-thick rectangle; cut rectangle in half horizontally, making a decisive cut with a long, sharp knife. Now cut each half lengthwise into slices about 1/2 inch wide, using all pastry. Separate slices; hold each slice at both ends and twist tightly. Place twists on a baking sheet, positioning them right up against each other to keep them from un-twisting. Place baking sheet in freezer 15 minutes to chill pastry. Meanwhile, preheat oven to 425F (220C). Place baking sheet in preheated oven and immediately reduce heat to 400F (205C). Bake until tops of cheese straws are light golden brown (15 to 20 minutes). Remove from oven, quickly separate straws and turn them over. Return to oven and continue to bake just until browned on bottoms (about 6 minutes longer). When straws are browned and crisp on all sides, remove from baking sheets and cool on wire racks. If desired, freeze baked cheese straws. To serve, place frozen straws in a preheated 350F (175C) oven and bake 15 minutes. Cool and serve. Makes about 60 cheese straws.

Crabmeat Crisps

Southerners find so many innovative uses for the wonderfully sweet meat of the blue crab. This recipe is one of my party favorites: the delectable crabmeat is tucked into flaky sheets of phyllo pastry. The pastries can be made up to a day ahead of time and popped in the oven as needed throughout a party.

1 pound claw crabmeat
1 pound phyllo pastry sheets, thawed if frozen
3 tablespoons unsalted butter or margarine
2 medium garlic cloves, minced
4 green onions (including tops), finely chopped
1/2 teaspoon Tabasco sauce
1/4 teaspoon freshly ground black pepper
2 (3-oz.) packages cream cheese, room temperature, cut into 1-inch cubes
1/4 cup dry white wine
1 cup shredded Monterey Jack cheese (4 oz.)
1 cup unsalted butter or margarine, melted

❦ Carefully pick through crabmeat and remove any bits of shell and cartilage. Set aside. Unroll phyllo sheets on a work surface. Cover stacked pastry sheets with a slightly damp towel and set aside. Melt 3 tablespoons butter or margarine in a heavy 12-inch skillet over medium heat. Add garlic and green onions; cook until onions are slightly wilted (2 to 3 minutes). Add crabmeat and toss gently. Mix in Tabasco sauce, pepper, cream cheese and wine. Simmer gently over low heat just until cream cheese is melted (about 8 minutes); stir 3 or 4 times just to blend ingredients and prevent sticking. Remove from heat and fold in Monterey Jack cheese. Set aside to cool. Preheat oven to 400F (205C). Lightly grease a baking sheet and set aside. Using a sharp knife, cut stack of pastry sheets lengthwise into 3 equal strips. Work with 1 (single-thickness) strip at a time, keeping remainder covered with damp towel. To shape each pastry, place 1 tablespoon of crabmeat mixture in lower right-hand corner of a pastry strip. Fold pastry over from right corner until it is lined up with left edge, forming a triangle. Using a pastry brush, brush rest of pastry strip with melted butter or margarine. Fold triangle up, again lining it up with left side of pastry. Now fold triangle over to meet right edge of pastry. Continue folding in this way until you reach top of pastry. Use melted butter or margarine to seal end of pastry. Place completed triangle on greased baking sheet. Repeat to shape remaining pastries, using remaining pastry strips and filling. Bake completed triangles in preheated oven until puffed and golden brown (about 15 minutes). Serve hot. Makes about 150 pastries.

Marinated Crab Fingers

Many of my favorite Southern restaurants serve marinated crab fingers (the cracked claws of the blue crab) by the pound or half-pound. What a treat it is to feast on these sweet little delicacies before dinner or throughout the evening!

2 cups red wine vinegar
3 tablespoons minced garlic
1/2 cup fresh lemon juice
1 tablespoon dried leaf oregano
1 teaspoon salt
1 teaspoon freshly ground black pepper
1/4 cup sugar
1/4 cup minced parsley, preferably flat-leaf
3 cups good-quality olive oil
3/4 cup chopped pimento-stuffed green olives
3/4 cup chopped ripe olives
2 tablespoons minced capers
1/2 cup chopped green onions (including tops)
1 cup minced onion
2 pounds cracked crab claws

❦ In a large bowl, combine vinegar, garlic, lemon juice, oregano, salt, pepper, sugar and parsley; whisk to blend. Slowly pour in oil in a steady stream, whisking constantly to form a smooth dressing. Stir in green and ripe olives, capers, green onions and onion until blended. Place crab claws in a large baking dish and pour marinade mixture over top. Cover with plastic wrap and refrigerate at least 3 hours before serving. Makes 14 to 16 servings.

Chandeleur Island Crab Dip

This heavenly dip always brings back memories of my first trip to the Chandeleur Islands, a small, uninhabited chain off the Louisiana/Mississippi coast and a paradise for boaters and fishermen. We caught dozens of blue crabs, boiled them in a big pot and ate them until we could barely breathe! The next day, once again able to face the rest of the iced-down crabs, I picked out the meat and created a dip named for these beautiful islands. Serve with your favorite crackers or with cucumber and zucchini rounds.

1 medium garlic clove, peeled
1 egg
2 tablespoons fresh lemon juice
1/2 teaspoon Creole mustard or other whole-grain mustard
1/2 teaspoon paprika
1 tablespoon grated Parmesan cheese
1/4 teaspoon freshly ground black pepper
1/4 teaspoon red (cayenne) pepper
1 tablespoon red wine vinegar
2 tablespoons minced green bell pepper
3 green onions (including tops), coarsely chopped
1 tablespoon prepared horseradish
1-1/2 teaspoons Worcestershire sauce
1 cup vegetable oil
1 pound plain white crabmeat

❦ In a food processor with the steel blade, and with machine running, drop garlic through feed tube. Stop machine and add remaining ingredients except oil and crabmeat; process until smooth. With machine running, pour oil through feed tube in a slow, steady stream, processing to form a smooth emulsion. Transfer mixture to a medium bowl. Carefully pick through crabmeat and remove any bits of shell and cartilage. Fold crabmeat into dip, cover and refrigerate until ready to serve. Makes about 2-1/2 cups.

Potted Pickled Shrimp Pâté

This flavorful pâté is typical of the "potted" ground meat and fish spreads served in the South. Before the days of refrigeration, such dishes, sealed under a layer of solidified fat, could be kept in the spring house for extended periods of time. For best flavor, make the pâté with butter—don't use margarine. Serve with melba toasts and/or cucumber rounds.

1/2 recipe Pickled Shrimp, page 83, marinated 24 hours
3/4 cup unsalted butter
1/4 teaspoon salt
1/2 teaspoon finely ground black pepper
1/8 teaspoon ground mace

❦ Drain Pickled Shrimp well and discard bay leaf. Melt 1/2 cup butter in a heavy 12-inch skillet over medium heat. Add drained Pickled Shrimp, salt, pepper and mace. Cook, stirring often, until onion is slightly wilted (about 5 minutes). Scrape mixture (including butter) into a blender or food processor fitted with the steel blade; process until pureed. Pack into a 1-cup cheese crock or mold, pressing down hard to compress. In a small saucepan, melt remaining 1/4 cup butter and pour over top. Refrigerate until very firm (6 to 8 hours) before serving. Makes about 1 cup.

Smoked Oyster Log

An innovative and tasty party food, sure to please all oyster lovers—and maybe a few oyster haters! Before serving, arrange crackers on the platter alongside the log.

> **1 (8-oz.) package cream cheese, room temperature**
> **2 teaspoons Worcestershire sauce**
> **1 (1/2-inch-thick) slice medium red onion**
> **1 medium garlic clove, minced**
> **3 green onions (including tops), coarsely chopped**
> **1/4 teaspoon salt**
> **1/2 teaspoon freshly ground black pepper**
> **1/2 teaspoon Tabasco sauce**
> **1 tablespoon fresh lemon juice**
> **1 (3-2/3-oz.) can smoked oysters**
> **1/2 cup minced parsley, preferably flat-leaf**
> **Pimento-stuffed green olive slices**

❦ In a food processor fitted with the steel blade, process cream cheese, Worcestershire sauce, red onion, garlic, green onions, salt, pepper, Tabasco sauce and lemon juice until smooth. On a piece of waxed paper, spread mixture out to make a 13″ x 9″ rectangle. Place waxed paper on a baking sheet. Drain oysters and pat dry on paper towels. Mince oysters and sprinkle over cream cheese mixture; press oysters into mixture. Place baking sheet in freezer 10 to 15 minutes to firm cheese, then roll up cheese jelly-roll fashion, beginning with a long side. Gently roll log in parsley to cover outside and place on a serving tray. Garnish top of log with olive slices. Refrigerate until ready to serve. Makes 15 to 20 servings.

Baked Ham Balls

A delicious hot party food, at its best when prepared with slow-smoked Southern ham. Serve in a bowl, with wooden picks for spearing.

> 1 cup fine dry bread crumbs
> 3 tablespoons milk
> 1 pound ground pork
> 1/2 pound smoked ham, ground
> 1 tablespoon ballpark-style mustard
> 1 tablespoon minced parsley, preferably flat-leaf
> 1 egg, lightly beaten
> 1/2 teaspoon freshly ground black pepper
> Salt to taste
> 2 tablespoons unsalted butter or margarine
> 1/4 cup vegetable oil
> 3/4 cup Cabernet Sauvignon or Burgundy wine
> 2/3 cup red currant jelly

❦ In a medium bowl, combine bread crumbs, milk, pork, ham, mustard, parsley, egg, pepper and salt. Blend and form into 40 balls. Place on a baking sheet, then freeze 30 minutes. Preheat oven to 350F (175C). Melt butter or margarine with oil in a heavy 12-inch skillet over medium heat. Add ham balls, a portion at a time, and cook until browned on all sides (about 5 minutes). Transfer to a 13" x 9" baking dish. Drain all fat from skillet; return skillet to heat. Add wine and stir to scrape up all browned bits from bottom of skillet. Add jelly and cook until melted. Pour glaze over ham balls. Bake in preheated oven 30 minutes, basting every 10 minutes. Drain and serve hot. Makes 40 ham balls.

Little Smokies in Bourbon Sauce

If you have a large Christmas party in the South and you don't serve Little Smokies cocktail sausages in one guise or another, you, my dear, are simply not a hostess with the mostest! Little Smokies are a part of Southern life and harried mothers often use them as "hush puppies": a handful of Little Smokies can calm fussing children at once. And in Cajun grocery stores in central Louisiana, the French-speaking butchers hand them out to children who are less than thrilled over being included in the weekly shopping. It isn't only the little ones who like Little Smokies, though; if you meet a Southern adult who won't own up to loving them equally well, you know he's fibbing to save face. In fact, the following recipe was created by a bachelor friend of mine who gives the greatest parties in Louisiana.

1 cup good-quality Kentucky bourbon whiskey
1 cup bottled chili sauce
1 teaspoon Tabasco sauce
1 cup firmly packed light brown sugar
2 pounds Little Smokies cocktail sausages, such as Hormel brand

❦ Combine bourbon, chili sauce, Tabasco sauce and brown sugar in a medium saucepan over medium heat. Stir to blend, then simmer 15 minutes. Add sausages and cook until heated through (about 10 minutes). When ready to serve, transfer to a chafing dish. Place wooden picks nearby for spearing sausages. Makes 15 to 20 servings.

Artichoke Squares

Southerners adore bottled marinated artichoke hearts and use them in dozens of culinary creations. I first tasted this spicy custard at a party given by Patricia Andrus, a Southern hostess known far and wide for the wonderful food she serves. It's been one of my favorites ever since.

2 (6-oz.) jars marinated artichoke hearts
1 small onion, coarsely chopped
1 large garlic clove, peeled
4 eggs
1/4 cup fine dry bread crumbs
1/2 teaspoon freshly ground black pepper
1/4 teaspoon dried leaf oregano
1/2 teaspoon Tabasco sauce
Salt to taste
2 tablespoons minced parsley, preferably flat-leaf
1/2 pound Cheddar cheese, shredded

❦ Preheat oven to 325F (165C). Grease a 13" x 9" baking dish and set aside. In a food processor fitted with the steel blade, process artichoke hearts with half of their liquid, onion, garlic, eggs, bread crumbs, pepper, oregano, Tabasco sauce, salt and parsley until smooth. Add cheese; pulse on-off 3 or 4 times just to combine well. Spread mixture evenly in greased baking dish. Bake in preheated oven until mixture is firm and feels set in center (about 30 minutes). Cool until lukewarm. Cut into 1-inch squares and serve. Makes about 117 pieces.

The Rib-Eye Sloop

This novel and delicious appetizer will be the hit of your party buffet table. If you wish to replenish the "sloop" several times throughout the party, just prepare extra filling.

1 (18-inch) loaf Italian bread
2 pounds rib-eye steaks, cut 1/2 inch thick
1 teaspoon freshly ground black pepper
Salt
1/4 cup unsalted butter or margarine
1/4 cup brandy
1 cup Brown Stock, page 38, or canned beef broth
1-1/2 cups whipping cream
2 medium garlic cloves, minced
3 tablespoons minced parsley, preferably flat-leaf
1 teaspoon dried leaf thyme

❦ Preheat oven to 350F (175C). To make sloop, cut a slice from top of bread that runs full length of loaf, leaving a 1/2-inch border of crust on sides and ends. Carefully scoop out interior of loaf, leaving a 1/2-inch-thick shell. Reserve scooped-out bread for another use. Bake shell in preheated oven until hardened (about 20 minutes). Line cavity of loaf with foil, bringing foil up sides of shell. Assemble frilled wooden picks in a row down each side of loaf to resemble oars. Set loaf aside. To prepare filling, trim all fat from steaks; cut meat into bite-size pieces. Sprinkle with pepper, pressing pepper in with your fingers. Sprinkle lightly with salt. Melt butter or margarine in a heavy 12-inch skillet over medium-high heat. Add meat cubes and brown quickly on all sides to produce an evenly seared crust. Remove meat and set aside; drain all fat from skillet and return skillet to heat. Add brandy and cook until reduced to a glaze, stirring to scrape up all browned bits from bottom of skillet (3 to 4 minutes). Add stock and again reduce to a glaze (5 to 6 minutes). Add cream, garlic, parsley and thyme and stir to blend. Return meat to skillet and cook over medium-high heat, stirring constantly, to reduce and thicken cream (about 7 minutes). To serve, pour filling into sloop. Use "oars" to spear pieces of meat. Makes 10 to 12 servings.

SALADS & SOUPS

S outherners love salads of all sorts. It wouldn't surprise me in the least if I were told that the ubiquitous "salad bar" concept began in the South. At any rural community supper or church covered-dish dinner in the South, you will find the ultimate salad bar, an entire table filled with nothing but salads—molded salads, tossed salads with every type of dressing, fruit salads, seafood salads, marinated salads, layered salads. There are so many salads, it's often hard to make it to the meat table! Each time I attend such a function, I find a new category of salad.

Salads play an important role in the Southern lifestyle as well as in our diet. For those who have not experienced August in the Deep South, let me tell you how hot it gets. It gets so hot that when you try to breathe outside—just to get enough oxygen to keep your brain functioning—

you feel as though an elephant were sitting on your chest. The air is so thick you can almost grab it, and though Southern ladies do not perspire (we "glow"), some of us still get mighty sticky. On such a day, you won't find many of us volunteering to tend a hot stove to prepare dinner! But salads come to the rescue of Southern belles in such distress. Cool and refreshing, they even seem to soothe frayed tempers and revitalize a wilted body.

The South is a virtual garden of lush, nutritious greens for the salad bowl. Wild greens with names like lamb's quarters and rocket were widely used in the Old South; today, we know them by their trendier names—mâche and arugula. Watercress grows wild in shallow cold streams and springs, and Southerners have long enjoyed a variety known as "winter cress," now available by mail order from herb farms as "upland cress." There's no shortage of vegetables for salads, either, and even some rather unlikely choices—eggplant, for example—play starring roles in memorable Southern salads.

In the early South, there was no such thing as vegetable oil, and only the wealthy could afford imported olive oils. But the lack of oil for dressings did not discourage creative Southern housewives—or diminish the popularity of salads. A hot dressing made from bacon drippings and vinegar was poured over fresh greens to make the "wilted salad" that is still common fare at family tables. Since oil was not available, there was also no mayonnaise; potato salad, coleslaw and other vegetable salads were dressed with an all-purpose "boiled dressing" (actually a variation of hollandaise sauce) that remains a Southern favorite.

Molded salads were enjoyed in the South even before the days of Jell-O and Knox gelatin. The gelatin used in the early days came from boiled calves' feet; it was sometimes combined with isinglass, a jelly obtained from fish. With the advent of refrigeration and the introduction of colored commercial gelatins, though, the popularity of the molded salad skyrocketed. Salad could now be prepared in colors to coordinate with the table linens and china! I must admit that molded salads are not one of the front-runners in today's food trends, but perhaps that makes them more enticing—not everyone is serving them. A very elegant and tasty luncheon or light supper can be planned around individual molded salads with very little effort.

Combined with a salad and bread, soup often makes a meal in the South, and we take our soups very seriously. Indeed, some of the country's best-known soups are of Southern origin—who has not heard of turtle soup or shrimp bisque or Creole gumbo?

The first soups were probably concocted as a means of stretching a little bit of food a long way—when cooked in lots of broth, a small amount of meat would seem like more. Gumbo was (and still is) put together from whatever bits of this and that that might be on hand; some gumbos are made entirely from greens, with perhaps a bit of salt pork for seasoning. At the opposite extreme, of course, you'll find gumbos served in Creole restaurants that contain five or six different types of fish and shellfish—a very pricey bowl of soup!

The soups served in different parts of the South can tell you a lot about the folks who live there, and each region has its favorites. Black Bean Soup, page 47, at its best in the Cuban-American communities of south Florida, reflects the Caribbean influence on Southern cooking. Rich, costly seafood soups such as Charleston She-Crab Soup, page 41, express the opulence of wealthy and sophisticated Southern cities. Georgia Peanut Soup, page 48, is a fine and tasty example of the country food prepared by Black cooks of the Old South. In every state, there are hearty, rib-sticking concoctions for cold winter days and cool, refreshing soups for spring and steamy Southern summers. One guarantee: whatever your preference, there's a Southern soup to titillate your senses and please your palate.

Velvety Egg Salad

This positively divine molded salad was created by a truly accomplished Southern hostess, Sarah Belle November of Richmond, Virginia. Easy to prepare and very striking in appearance, it's a much-requested item at covered-dish, buffet-style get-togethers.

> 1 (1/4-oz.) envelope unflavored gelatin
> 1/4 cup dry white wine
> 1 cup boiling Poultry Stock, page 38, or canned chicken broth
> 1 cup rich mayonnaise, preferably homemade, page 36
> 1 tablespoon fresh lemon juice
> 2 tablespoons minced green onion (including top)
> 1 tablespoon minced parsley, preferably flat-leaf
> 1/4 teaspoon Tabasco sauce
> 12 hard-cooked eggs, grated
> Salt and freshly ground white pepper to taste
> 2 (2-oz.) jars black lumpfish caviar
> Melba toast rounds or thin-sliced rye bread

❧ Lightly grease a flat-topped, 6-cup gelatin mold and set aside. In a medium bowl, stir gelatin into wine; set aside until all liquid is absorbed and gelatin feels spongy to the touch. Add boiling stock and stir until gelatin is completely dissolved. Add mayonnaise, lemon juice, green onion, parsley and Tabasco sauce. Gently stir in eggs, then add salt and white pepper. Pour into greased mold and refrigerate until set (about 8 hours). Unmold onto a serving platter. Place caviar in a fine strainer; rinse several times with ice-cold water. Drain well; spread over top of salad. Accompany with melba toasts or rye bread. Makes 6 to 8 servings.

Apple & Fennel Salad with Celery Seed Dressing

One bite of this salad will have your guests asking, "Wow, what is this crunchy stuff?" The crunch comes from fennel, an often overlooked vegetable with a marvelously refreshing, licoricelike flavor. It grows well in most regions of the South, though it is generally available throughout the country. I first discovered fennel in the Georgia kitchen of Nathalie Dupree.

Celery Seed Dressing, see below
1 (10-oz.) package fresh spinach
1 small head fennel, thinly sliced, feathery tops reserved
3 medium apples (about 1-1/4 lbs. *total*), cored, cubed
1 small red onion, halved lengthwise, thinly sliced

Celery Seed Dressing:
1/2 cup sugar
1/2 teaspoon dry mustard
1/2 teaspoon salt
1/4 cup raspberry-flavored vinegar
1-1/2 teaspoons pureed onion
1/2 cup vegetable oil
1-1/2 teaspoons celery seeds

❧ Prepare dressing; refrigerate. Thoroughly wash spinach and remove fibrous stems and midribs; dry leaves well and place in a salad bowl. Add fennel, apples and onion; drizzle with desired amount of dressing and toss well. Garnish with reserved fennel tops. Makes 6 to 8 servings.
Celery Seed Dressing: Combine sugar, mustard, salt, vinegar and pureed onion in a food processor fitted with the steel blade. Process until smooth. With machine running, pour oil through feed tube in a slow, steady stream. Add celery seeds and process just until blended. Place dressing in a jar with a tight-fitting lid and refrigerate until ready to use.

West Indies Crab Salad

No one can explain the name of this popular Southern marinated crab salad; certainly nothing in its makeup particularly indicates a West Indian origin. There's nothing mysterious about its preparation, though: the recipe is ultimately simple. The secret to its perfection lies in using *absolutely fresh* crabmeat; I go so far as to insist on catching and picking the crabs myself!

I first tried West Indies Crab Salad many years ago, in a tiny seafood restaurant on Dauphin Island, off the coast of Alabama. Sadly, a hurricane later destroyed the restaurant, along with a sizable portion of the island.

> 1 pound backfin lump crabmeat
> Salt and freshly ground black pepper to taste
> 2 medium onions, finely chopped
> 1/2 cup vegetable oil
> 1/2 cup ice water
> 1/2 cup apple cider vinegar
> Iceberg lettuce leaves
> Minced parsley, preferably flat-leaf

❦ Carefully pick through crabmeat and remove any bits of shell and cartilage. Place a thin layer of crabmeat in a non-metal 13″ x 9″ baking dish, taking care not to break up lumps. Sprinkle with salt and pepper. Arrange a layer of chopped onions atop crabmeat; sprinkle with salt and pepper. Repeat until all crabmeat and onions have been used, salting and peppering each layer. In a jar with a tight-fitting lid, combine oil, ice water and vinegar. Shake to blend. Pour over layered crabmeat and onions; press down to moisten all layers. Cover very tightly (crabmeat is famous for picking up odors from the refrigerator); refrigerate 12 hours before serving. To serve, place lettuce leaves in sherbet bowls and spoon in a portion of the salad, scooping all the way to bottom of dish for each spoonful. Top with a sprinkling of parsley. Makes 4 to 6 servings.

Chicken Salad Véronique with Almonds

This refreshing variation on the standard chicken salad has been just what the doctor ordered on many lazy summer days at my house. Chances are that once you've served this dish, your family will never be satisfied with "plain old chicken salad" again!

> **4 chicken breast halves**
> **1 small onion, coarsely chopped**
> **2 teaspoons whole black peppercorns**
> **4 green onions (including tops), chopped**
> **2 hard-cooked eggs, chopped**
> **2 small celery stalks, finely chopped**
> **1 cup seedless green grapes, halved**
> **1/2 cup toasted sliced almonds**
> **2/3 cup rich mayonnaise, preferably homemade, page 36**
> **1/4 cup dairy sour cream**
> **1 teaspoon Dijon-style mustard**
> **2 tablespoons whipping cream**
> **1/8 teaspoon curry powder**
> **1/4 teaspoon freshly ground black pepper**
> **Salt to taste**
> **Red-leaf lettuce leaves**
> **Tomato wedges**

🌱 In a 4- to 5-quart saucepan, combine chicken, onion and peppercorns. Cover with water and bring to a boil, then reduce heat, cover and simmer until chicken is tender (25 to 30 minutes). Set aside to cool in cooking broth. When chicken is cool, drain, then remove and discard skin and bones. Cut meat into bite-size pieces and place in a medium bowl. Mix in green onions, eggs, celery, grapes and almonds. Set aside. In a small bowl, combine mayonnaise, sour cream, mustard, whipping cream, curry powder, pepper and salt. Whisk to blend. Fold dressing into chicken mixture, cover and refrigerate until ready to serve. Serve on lettuce leaves, garnished with tomato wedges. Makes 4 to 6 servings.

Shrimp & Cucumber Mousse
with Caviar Dressing

In the South, we could live on shrimp and never tire of it. Southern chefs and homemakers never run out of fresh new ways to use this bountiful shellfish; like veal, it is compatible with countless seasonings, companion ingredients and cooking methods. The combination of shrimp and cucumber in this delicate mousse is as refreshing as springtime. Topped with Caviar Dressing, it makes an elegant luncheon entree.

2 medium cucumbers
Dry white wine
2 tablespoons unflavored gelatin
1 pound shelled, deveined boiled shrimp, minced
1/2 teaspoon salt
1/4 teaspoon paprika
1/2 teaspoon Tabasco sauce
2 teaspoons fresh lemon juice
1 tablespoon prepared horseradish
1/4 teaspoon freshly ground black pepper
1 tablespoon minced fresh dill or 1/2 teaspoon dried dill weed
1 pint (2 cups) whipping cream
Caviar Dressing, see below
Boston lettuce leaves
Curly-leaf parsley sprigs or fresh dill sprigs

Caviar Dressing:
1/2 cup rich mayonnaise, preferably homemade, page 36
2 tablespoons pureed onion
1/3 cup herb-flavored vinegar
1 tablespoon fresh lemon juice
1/4 teaspoon freshly ground black pepper
1/2 teaspoon salt
1/3 cup good-quality olive oil
1 (2-oz.) jar red lumpfish caviar

❦ Peel and grate cucumbers. Place in a fine strainer over a bowl and let stand 30 minutes to drain. Press down on pulp to remove as much juice as possible; reserve juice. Set pulp aside. Add wine to cucumber juice to equal 3/4 cup. In a small pan, stir gelatin into wine mixture; set aside until all liquid is absorbed and gelatin feels spongy to the touch. Meanwhile, in a medium bowl, combine cucumber pulp with shrimp, salt, paprika, Tabasco sauce, lemon juice, horseradish, pepper and minced dill. Stir to blend. Set softened gelatin over simmering water and stir until completely dissolved, then stir into shrimp mixture. Refrigerate until slightly thickened (about 45 minutes). Whip cream until stiff peaks form. Fold in whipped cream; pour into 8 individual 4-ounce molds. Refrigerate until completely set (4 to 5 hours). Meanwhile, prepare Caviar Dressing and refrigerate. Unmold salads onto lettuce-lined plates; top with Caviar Dressing. Garnish with parsley or dill sprigs. Makes 8 servings.

Caviar Dressing: Combine mayonnaise, pureed onion, vinegar, lemon juice, pepper and salt in a food processor fitted with the steel blade. Process until smooth. With machine running, pour oil through feed tube in a slow, steady stream. Turn mixture out into a bowl. Place caviar in a fine strainer and rinse several times with ice-cold water. Drain well and fold into dressing. Cover and refrigerate until ready to use.

Shrimp Salad Pontchartrain

Here's a flavorful and very versatile dish: you can serve it as a small first course or a luncheon entree—or even as cocktail finger food, with the sauce as a dip for the chilled shrimp. Your guests will love you, no matter how you serve it!

> 1 cup rich mayonnaise, preferably homemade, page 36
> 1/2 pint (1 cup) dairy sour cream
> 1/4 cup bottled chili sauce
> 1/4 cup vegetable oil
> 2 tablespoons sherry wine vinegar
> 2 tablespoons prepared horseradish
> 1 tablespoon fresh lemon juice
> 3 tablespoons minced parsley, preferably flat-leaf
> 2 tablespoons grated onion
> 2 tablespoons chopped capers
> 2 green onions (including tops), minced
> 2 tablespoons Creole mustard or other whole-grain mustard
> 1/4 teaspoon freshly ground black pepper
> Salt to taste
> Boston lettuce leaves
> 3 pounds cooked medium shrimp, shelled, deveined, well chilled
> Curly-leaf parsley sprigs, lemon wedges, tomato wedges and hard-cooked egg
>   wedges

❦ In a medium bowl, blend mayonnaise, sour cream, chili sauce, oil, vinegar, horseradish, lemon juice, parsley, onion, capers, green onions, mustard, pepper and salt to taste. Refrigerate at least 4 hours before serving to allow flavors to meld. To serve, arrange lettuce leaves on individual serving plates and top with shrimp, fanning them out in an attractive pattern. Spoon some of sauce over each portion and garnish as desired with parsley sprigs and lemon, tomato and egg wedges. Makes 6 to 8 servings.

Greens & Mint Salad with Cheese Vinaigrette

Fresh mint has long been part of Southern cuisine, and no respectable Southern home would be without a little bed of mint somewhere. Even in city homes, I'll bet you'll find a little pot of it tucked under a leaky faucet in the courtyard. This delightful herb has myriad uses, and this salad is one of the best. It makes you feel good just to eat it.

1 (10-oz.) package fresh spinach, thoroughly washed, dried well
1/2 bunch watercress, thoroughly washed, dried well
8 to 10 large curly endive leaves, thoroughly washed, dried well
2/3 cup pitted calamata olives
1/2 cup loosely packed small whole fresh mint leaves
1 large tomato, cut into thin wedges
Cheese Vinaigrette, see below

Cheese Vinaigrette:
3 tablespoons red wine vinegar
1/2 teaspoon salt
1/4 teaspoon freshly ground black pepper
1 teaspoon minced fresh marjoram or 1/4 teaspoon dried leaf marjoram
1/2 teaspoon sugar
1/2 cup good-quality olive oil
2 ounces feta cheese, finely crumbled

❦ Remove fibrous stems and midribs from spinach, then tear leaves into bite-size pieces. Place in a large salad bowl. Tear leaves and tender tops from watercress; add to bowl. Tear endive into bite-size pieces and add to bowl along with olives, mint and tomato. Refrigerate while you prepare the vinaigrette or until ready to serve. To serve, pour vinaigrette over salad and toss to blend. Makes 4 to 6 servings.
Cheese Vinaigrette: Combine vinegar, salt, pepper, marjoram and sugar in a medium bowl and whisk to blend. Then pour in oil in a slow, steady stream; whisk until smooth. Stir in cheese.

Charleston Green Salad with Benne Seeds

The benne seed—or sesame seed, as we commonly know it—came to the Southern United States from the Orient by way of Africa. Sesame seeds were used in a variety of ways in Charleston; this unusual salad is one of my favorite dishes. The delicate balance of ingredients gives it a uniquely different taste.

1 small head romaine lettuce
2/3 cup sliced, pimento-stuffed green olives
1/4 cup lightly toasted sesame seeds
Dressing, opposite

Dressing:
1/4 cup white wine vinegar
1 tablespoon rich mayonnaise, preferably homemade, page 36
1/4 cup whipping cream
1 egg
2 teaspoons paprika
3 medium garlic cloves, peeled
1/4 teaspoon sugar
1/4 teaspoon freshly ground black pepper
1/2 teaspoon salt
1 cup good-quality olive oil

❦ Remove and discard fibrous midribs from lettuce leaves. Tear leaves into bite-size pieces and place in a large salad bowl. Add olives and sesame seeds; refrigerate until ready to serve. Prepare Dressing. To serve, drizzle desired amount of Dressing over salad and toss to coat all greens well. Makes 6 to 8 servings.

Dressing: Combine all ingredients except oil in a food processor fitted with the steel blade and process until smooth. With machine running, pour oil through feed tube in a slow, steady stream. Cover tightly and refrigerate until ready to use.

Southern Wilted Salad

Wilted salads were created in the mountainous poor rural regions of the early South. Olive oil for dressings was not available in these areas, but bacon drippings were always on hand, and inventive cooks used them in a simple hot dressing to pour over greens. The flavor of the ever-so-slightly wilted greens was so delightful that the salad is still a favorite in Southern homes today. As a child, I always loved to sop up the dressing left in the bottom of the bowl with a chunk of bread.

Remember: The salad must be served as soon as the greens have been tossed with the dressing!

8 bacon slices
1 small head red- or green-leaf lettuce
1/2 medium cucumber, peeled, chopped
5 green onions (including tops), chopped
1/4 cup distilled white vinegar
2 teaspoons sugar
1/2 teaspoon salt
1/2 teaspoon finely ground black pepper

❦ Cook bacon in a heavy 12-inch skillet until crisp. Remove and drain on paper towels; crumble and set aside. Reserve drippings in skillet to use for dressing. Remove fibrous midribs from lettuce leaves, then tear leaves into bite-size pieces. Place in a large salad bowl, add crumbled bacon and cucumber and toss well. When ready to serve, reheat bacon drippings over medium-high heat; add green onions and shake skillet 2 or 3 times. Carefully stir in vinegar, sugar, salt and pepper; boil 1 minute. Pour dressing over salad, toss quickly and serve at once. Makes 6 to 8 servings.

Southern Potato Salad with Boiled Dressing

In the days before vegetable oil, when even olive oil was a treat enjoyed only by the rich, Southern cooks created "boiled dressing"—an all-purpose dressing made without oil, used in every type of salad imaginable. Despite the name, boiled dressing is not boiled, nor is it actually a dressing; it is instead a variation on classic hollandaise sauce. It still shows up today in the rural South, most often in the good hearty potato salads or coleslaws served at church picnics and community suppers.

> **4 large russet potatoes (about 2-1/2 lbs. *total*), peeled**
> **2 medium onions, chopped**
> **3 celery stalks, chopped**
> **4 hard-cooked eggs, chopped**
> **5 green onions (including tops), chopped**
> **1-1/2 tablespoons minced fresh dill or 2 teaspoons dried dill weed**
> **Boiled Dressing, see below**
>
> *Boiled Dressing:*
> **1/4 cup sugar**
> **1-1/2 teaspoons dry mustard**
> **1/4 teaspoon celery seeds**
> **1/2 teaspoon salt**
> **1/2 teaspoon finely ground black pepper**
> **2 tablespoons all-purpose flour**
> **1/4 cup water**
> **1/4 cup apple cider vinegar**
> **2 egg yolks, beaten**
> **3 tablespoons unsalted butter, room temperature**
> **1/4 cup whipping cream**

❦ Place potatoes in a 5-quart pot and cover with cold water. Bring to a boil, then reduce heat, cover and simmer until potatoes are tender (about 25 minutes). Drain potatoes and refrigerate until well chilled. Cut chilled potatoes in half lengthwise; place halves cut side down and halve lengthwise again. Then cut each piece crosswise into slices of desired thickness. Place slices in a large bowl; add onions, celery, eggs, green onions and dill. Toss well. Cover and refrigerate while you prepare dressing. To serve, stir dressing into salad, blending well; transfer salad to a serving bowl. Makes 6 to 8 servings.

Boiled Dressing: Combine sugar, mustard, celery seeds, salt, pepper and flour in top of a double boiler. Whisk in water and continue whisking until mixture is smooth. Whisk in vinegar and egg yolks; set top of double boiler in place over simmering water. Cook, whisking, until mixture is thickened and light lemon-yellow in color (about 5 minutes). Remove from heat and whisk in butter, then slowly whisk in cream. Transfer to a small bowl and refrigerate until chilled before using.

Eggplant Salad

I was shocked to learn that people in foreign (non-Southern) areas of the country don't have eggplant on the dinner table at least twice a week. African slaves introduced eggplant into Southern cuisine, and for many years it was seen mainly in the wealthy areas of the South where slaves were held. (In Charleston, eggplant is often still called "Guinea squash," after its origin.) It would have been hard to keep something as good as eggplant a secret forever, though, and today it is a staple vegetable throughout the South: used in salads, fried, tucked into vegetable casseroles, combined with meat or seafood, stuffed or pureed into sauces. This salad is an excellent addition to the buffet table or picnic basket.

> **2 large eggplants (about 1-1/4 lbs. *each*)**
> **2 medium tomatoes, chopped**
> **6 green onions (including tops), chopped**
> **1 cup minced parsley, preferably flat-leaf**
> **2 large garlic cloves, minced**
> **2 celery stalks, finely chopped**
> **1/4 cup minced fresh basil or 1 tablespoon dried leaf basil**
> **1/2 cup red wine vinegar**
> **1/2 teaspoon Tabasco sauce**
> **1 teaspoon ground cumin**
> **1/2 teaspoon freshly ground black pepper**
> **1-1/2 teaspoons sugar**
> **1 teaspoon salt**
> **3/4 cup good-quality olive oil**

✿ Preheat oven to 400F (205C). Prick eggplants all over with a fork and place in a baking dish. Bake in preheated oven until skin is blistered and flesh is very tender (about 45 minutes). Remove eggplants from oven; set aside until cool enough to handle, then slice in half and scoop out pulp. Chop pulp; discard skins. In a medium bowl, combine chopped pulp, tomatoes, green onions, parsley, garlic, celery and basil. Toss to blend and refrigerate until chilled. When ready to assemble salad, combine vinegar, Tabasco sauce, cumin, pepper, sugar and salt in another medium bowl; whisk until blended. Whisking constantly, add oil in a slow, steady stream. Pour dressing over eggplant mixture; toss to combine. Let mixture stand 30 minutes at room temperature before serving, stirring often. Makes 4 to 6 servings.

Basic Homemade Mayonnaise

Like hot dogs and mustard and ketchup, mayonnaise is part of the real heart of American food. And any recipe made with mayonnaise will taste much better if you use the home-made variety: the rich, "give me some more" flavor of the real stuff can't be equaled by even the best commercial brands.

Most homemakers today own either a blender or a food processor, and these wonderful appliances make the preparation of mayonnaise easy. Remember, though, that homemade mayo contains no preservatives and is made from uncooked eggs, so it must be refrig-erated and used within 3 or 4 days.

2 egg yolks
1/2 teaspoon dry mustard
1 teaspoon salt
2 teaspoons fresh lemon juice
Dash of red (cayenne) pepper
2/3 cup vegetable oil
1/3 cup good-quality olive oil

❦ In a food processor fitted with the steel blade, process egg yolks, mustard, salt, lemon juice and red pepper until mixture is thickened and turns lighter in color (about 1 minute). Combine vegetable oil and olive oil. With machine running, pour combined oils through feed tube in a slow, steady stream. When all oil has been added, process 15 seconds longer to form a thick emulsion. Transfer to a jar with a tight-fitting lid and refrigerate until ready to use or up to 4 days. Makes about 1-1/4 cups.

Basic Stocks

Southern cooking is often bold and robust, and the stocks used by Southern cooks are correspondingly full-bodied: dark, rich, flavorful and quite unlike the more delicate stocks to which you may be accustomed. (Southern seafood stock, for example, bears absolutely no resemblance to the dainty, wine-scented, faintly marine French *fumet*.) The three basic stocks given here are time-consuming to prepare, but well worth the trouble for the sublime flavor they contribute to any dish in which they're used.

Of course, everyone must resort to canned stocks at times. On those (I hope, rare) occasions, select those brands with the lowest possible salt content, and even then be very cautious in salting the dishes in which you use them. If you draw the line at seafood stock and simply will not prepare it under any amount of coercion, you may substitute bottled clam juice with moderately satisfactory results.

Stocks can be stored in the refrigerator up to 2 days; if you want to keep them longer, transfer them to the freezer to minimize any risk of bacterial growth. Stocks freeze well in 1-quart or smaller containers up to 6 months. After this length of time, meat and poultry stocks rapidly lose flavor and taste like the freezer; seafood stocks, on the other hand, become increasingly "assertive" and unusable.

Because the quality of stocks is so important, use care in their preparation.

- Always use the proper pot. Your best choice is a stock pot: a tall, narrow pot which minimizes evaporation of the stock as it cooks.
- Get double use from fresh herbs: save the stems of all kinds, including parsley, for use in stock. Stems are more flavorful than leaves, and perfect for stock.
- Never salt stock while it is cooking; salt only the product in which the stock is used. (Stocks are often used in reduction sauces, and reduction would greatly increase the saltiness of a salted stock.)
- Never use internal organs (livers, hearts, gizzards or kidneys) in stock. These "variety meats" contain a lot of blood and produce stock with a strong, unpleasant flavor.
- When you brown bones for stock, the rendered fat will spit and sputter in the oven and produce a good deal of smelly smoke. For this reason, it's best not to prepare stock the same day you plan to entertain guests!
- Bring stock to a full boil and skim the gray foam from the surface *before* adding your seasonings, so they won't be skimmed away. Boil the stock until the gray foam is no longer visible.
- Skim surface fat from stock often as it cooks. After the stock has been chilled, remove any remaining fat from the surface. Animal fat becomes rancid quickly and would give your stock an unpleasant taste.
- When straining stock for use or storage, press down on the bones and vegetables hard to extract every possible bit of intense flavor.
- It is extremely important to cool stock as quickly as possible *before* storing: *Never* cover hot stock, and never place hot stock in the refrigerator for storage. Covering a hot stock creates a perfect environment for bacterial growth; at the very least, the stock may acquire a sour flavor. To cool a large pot of stock, strain it first, then pour it into small containers. Set the containers in a sink of ice-cold water. Change the water several times until the stock has cooled; then cover and refrigerate or freeze the containers.

Brown Stock

Don't be tempted to omit the pork bones; they are necessary for an authentic Southern flavor.

    6 pounds veal bones and knuckles, split in half
    5 pounds veal shoulder meat and shanks
    4 pounds pork neck bones
    7 medium onions, unpeeled, chopped
    4 carrots, chopped
    4 celery stalks (including leafy tops), chopped
    8 fresh thyme sprigs or 2 teaspoons dried leaf tyme
    3 bay leaves
    5 parsley sprigs, preferably flat-leaf
    1 tablespoon whole black peppercorns
    1 (6-oz.) can tomato paste

❦ Preheat oven to 425F (220C). Place all meat and bones in large roasting pans and brown in preheated oven until very dark (about 1-1/2 hours). Turn several times to assure even browning; check often to prevent burning. Place browned meat and bones in a 20-quart stock pot; set aside. Place onions, carrots and celery in roasting pans and stir to coat with fat, then place in oven and bake until vegetables are browned (about 45 minutes), turning often. Add vegetables to stock pot and add enough cold water to cover by 2 inches. Bring to a boil over high heat and skim gray foam from surface. Continue to boil until no more foam is produced. Add thyme, bay leaves, parsley, peppercorns and tomato paste; stir to blend. Reduce heat so liquid barely simmers and cook, uncovered, at least 8 hours, frequently skimming fat from surface. Strain stock and cool; refrigerate up to 2 days or freeze for longer storage. Makes about 10 quarts.

Poultry Stock

Southern poultry stock should have a very complex flavor, achieved by using as many types of poultry bones as possible. If your choice is limited, be sure to include at least one cut-up duck along with the chicken bones.

    15 pounds mixed poultry bones and carcasses, such as chicken, turkey, game hen, duck and quail
    5 large onions, unpeeled, chopped
    4 carrots, chopped
    4 celery stalks (including leafy tops), chopped
    6 parsley sprigs, preferably flat-leaf
    5 fresh thyme sprigs or 1-1/2 teaspoons dried leaf thyme
    1 tablespoon whole black peppercorns
    2 bay leaves

❧ Preheat oven to 425F (220C). Place all bones and carcasses in large roasting pans and brown in preheated oven until very dark (about 1 hour). Turn several times to assure even browning; check often to prevent burning. Place browned bones in a 20-quart stock pot; set aside. Place onions, carrots and celery in roasting pans and stir to coat with fat, then place in oven and bake until vegetables are browned (about 45 minutes), turning often. Add vegetables to stock pot and add enough cold water to cover by 2 inches. Bring to a boil over high heat and skim gray foam from surface. Continue to boil until no more foam is produced. Stir in parsley, thyme, peppercorns and bay leaves; reduce heat so liquid barely simmers. Cook stock, uncovered, at least 8 hours, frequently skimming fat from surface. Strain stock and cool; refrigerate up to 2 days or freeze for longer storage. Makes about 10 quarts.

Seafood Stock

You can use any non-oily, white-fleshed fish for this stock, but avoid deep-sea fish and be sure to discard all fish heads and skin. Shellfish (including the shells) add excellent flavor; blue crabs, lobster shells and crawfish provide a wonderful flavor perk.

> 10 to 12 pounds mixed shellfish, shells and fish carcasses
> 5 large onions, unpeeled, chopped
> 4 celery stalks (including leafy tops), chopped
> 2 large lemons, sliced
> 5 garlic cloves, smashed
> 1 teaspoon whole cloves
> 1 (3-oz.) package crab and shrimp boil
> 1 tablespoon whole black peppercorns

❧ Remove heads from any whole fish carcasses; rinse bones under running water to remove all traces of blood. (Fish heads and blood will give stock a very fishy flavor.) In a 20-quart stock pot, combine shellfish and fish carcasses, onions, celery and lemons. Add enough cold water to cover by 2 inches and bring to a boil over high heat; skim gray foam from surface. Continue to boil until no more foam is produced. Add garlic, whole cloves, shrimp and crab boil and peppercorns. Reduce heat so liquid barely simmers. Cook, uncovered, 3 hours, then strain and cool. Refrigerate up to 2 days or freeze for longer storage. Makes about 10 quarts.

Florida Conch Chowder

Bright-colored conch (pronounced *conk*) is eaten primarily in South Florida, where it was introduced from the Caribbean islands in the early 1800s. Though delicious and delicate in flavor, the meat has a tough and chewy texture; it is typically pounded, minced or ground for use in cooking.

> **6 ounces salt pork, rind removed, diced**
> **1 large onion, chopped**
> **1 medium green bell pepper, chopped**
> **1 (7-oz.) jar pimentos, drained, chopped**
> **3 large tomatoes (about 1-1/2 lbs. *total*), peeled, seeded, chopped**
> **3 medium garlic cloves, minced**
> **2 celery stalks (including leafy tops), chopped**
> **2 large russet potatoes (about 1-1/2 lbs. *total*), peeled, diced**
> **2 tablespoons minced parsley, preferably flat-leaf**
> **2 pounds conch meat, ground**
> **1 cup dry white wine**
> **10 cups Seafood Stock, page 39, or bottled clam juice**
> **1 teaspoon finely ground black pepper**
> **1/4 teaspoon Tabasco sauce**
> **Salt to taste**
> **Chopped green onions (including tops)**

❦ Cook salt pork in a heavy 6-quart pot over medium heat until all fat is rendered (about 20 minutes); leave remaining crisp bits of meat ("cracklin's") in pot. Add onion, bell pepper, pimentos, tomatoes, garlic, celery, potatoes and parsley. Cook, stirring often, until vegetables are slightly wilted and onion is transparent (about 8 minutes). Add conch, wine, stock, black pepper, Tabasco sauce and salt. Bring to a boil; then reduce heat, cover and simmer until potatoes have disintegrated and thickened soup (about 1-1/2 hours). Serve hot, garnished with a sprinkling of green onions. Makes 8 to 10 servings.

Charleston She-Crab Soup

The origin of this delicate soup is often hotly debated, with both Savannah, Georgia and Charleston, South Carolina taking credit for its creation in the early 1800s. Authentic she-crab soup gets its tangy, delectable taste from the meat and fertilized roe of mature female crabs, but because most states now prohibit the taking of female crabs with roe, a garnish of sieved hard-cooked egg yolk is generally used as a substitute for roe.

> **1-1/2 pounds backfin lump crabmeat, with roe, if available**
> **1/2 cup unsalted butter or margarine**
> **1 medium onion, chopped**
> **1 celery stalk, chopped**
> **1/4 cup all-purpose flour**
> **3 cups milk, heated slightly**
> **3 cups Seafood Stock, page 39, or bottled clam juice**
> **1 teaspoon Worcestershire sauce**
> **1/4 teaspoon red (cayenne) pepper**
> **1/4 teaspoon freshly grated nutmeg**
> **Salt to taste**
> **1/2 pint (1 cup) whipping cream**
> **4 green onions (including tops), finely chopped**
> **1/4 cup dry sherry**
> **Sieved yolks from 4 hard-cooked eggs**

❦ Carefully pick through crabmeat and remove any bits of shell and cartilage. Set aside. Melt butter or margarine in a heavy 6-quart pot over medium heat. Add onion and celery; cook, stirring often, until lightly browned (about 10 minutes). Add flour all at once; stir until blended. Cook, stirring, 3 to 4 minutes. Slowly stir in milk until blended. Add stock and bring to a boil. Reduce heat so soup barely simmers; add crabmeat and roe, Worcestershire sauce, red pepper, nutmeg and salt. Cover and cook 30 minutes. Stir in cream, green onions and sherry; cook 15 minutes longer. Serve hot, garnished with egg yolks. Makes 4 to 6 servings.

New Orleans Seafood Okra Gumbo

This rich and unique gumbo is made with one of the Southern bayou country's finest delicacies—frog legs. Frog legs are generally available frozen, in seafood specialty markets.

Seasoning Mix, see below
2 pounds head-on uncooked shrimp
1 pound plain white crabmeat
6 pairs small frog legs
1 cup lard or vegetable oil
1 cup all-purpose flour
2 medium onions, chopped
1 medium green bell pepper, chopped
1/2 cup chopped celery
4 medium garlic cloves, minced
4 quarts Seafood Stock, page 39, or bottled clam juice
1/2 medium lemon
2 bay leaves
1 tablespoon minced parsley, preferably flat-leaf
1 teaspoon dried leaf thyme
1 teaspoon freshly ground black pepper
1/2 teaspoon red (cayenne) pepper
Salt to taste
1 pound skinned redfish fillets or other mild-flavored, white-fleshed fish, cut into bite-size pieces
2 cups sliced fresh okra or 1 (10-oz.) package frozen sliced okra
5 cups hot cooked white rice
Chopped green onions and minced parsley, preferably flat-leaf

Seasoning Mix:
1/2 teaspoon *each* salt, freshly ground black pepper, red (cayenne) pepper, paprika, onion powder and garlic powder

❦ Prepare Seasoning Mix; set aside. Shell and devein shrimp; reserve heads and shells. Carefully pick through crabmeat and remove any bits of shell and cartilage. Refrigerate shrimp and crabmeat until ready to use. Using your fingers, pull meat from frog legs and spread on a baking sheet; discard bones. Sprinkle Seasoning Mix over meat; set aside at room temperature while you prepare roux. To make roux, heat lard or oil in a heavy (preferably cast-iron) 12-inch skillet over medium heat. Add flour all at once and whisk until smooth, then whisk constantly until a mahogany-colored roux forms (about 45 minutes). Add frog leg meat to hot roux and cook, stirring, until lightly browned (about 5 minutes). Add onions, bell pepper, celery and garlic; cook until onions are wilted and transparent (about 5 minutes). Meanwhile, bring stock to a boil in a 6-quart pot. Place reserved shrimp heads and shells, lemon half and bay leaves in a cheesecloth bag; tie securely with kitchen twine. Add bag to boiling stock. When stock has returned to a full boil, remove roux mixture from heat and stir it into stock, a large spoonful at a time. Add parsley, thyme, black pepper, red pepper and salt. Reduce heat so liquid barely simmers; cook, uncovered, 1 hour. Remove cheesecloth bag from pot and place in a fine strainer.

Hold strainer over pot and press down on bag with a large spoon to extract all possible liquid; discard bag. Add shrimp, crabmeat, redfish and okra to stock mixture. Cook until shrimp and redfish are opaque (about 20 minutes). Taste and adjust seasonings. To serve, place about 1/2 cup rice in each individual soup plate and ladle hot gumbo over rice. Sprinkle each serving with green onions and parsley. Makes 8 to 10 servings.

Seasoning Mix: Mix all ingredients in a small bowl until blended.

Oyster & Mushroom Cream Stew

This truly ethereal soup is often eaten as a meal in the South, accompanied with hot French bread and green salad. The taste will have your friends begging for more! This modern version calls for delicate oyster mushrooms, generally available at specialty produce stores; if you cannot find them, substitute large fresh button mushrooms.

36 small to medium oysters (about 3 pints), drained, liquor reserved
2 quarts (8 cups) whipping cream
6 tablespoons unsalted butter or margarine
1/2 cup finely chopped shallots
6 ounces oyster mushrooms, sliced
1/4 cup all-purpose flour
2 tablespoons fresh lemon juice
1/4 teaspoon Tabasco sauce
1/8 teaspoon freshly ground white pepper
Salt to taste
Snipped fresh chives

❦ Combine oyster liquor and cream in a 5- to 6-quart saucepan; cook over medium-high heat until reduced by 1/3 (about 20 minutes). Set aside. Melt butter or margarine in a heavy 6-quart saucepan over medium heat; add shallots and mushrooms. Cook until shallots are wilted and transparent (about 8 minutes). Add flour all at once; stir until blended. Cook, stirring, 3 to 4 minutes. Slowly stir in reduced cream mixture. Stir in lemon juice, Tabasco sauce, white pepper and salt. Cook until thickened, stirring. Reduce heat so soup barely simmers; cook 15 minutes. Stir in oysters. Taste and adjust seasonings. Cook, stirring often, just until edges of oysters curl (about 10 minutes). Serve hot in soup plates, topped with a light sprinkling of chives. Makes 4 to 6 servings.

Chicken & Oyster Filé Gumbo

Gumbo. The word conjures up thoughts of a dark and mysterious brew, a savory concoction made famous by the Cajuns and Creoles of South Louisiana. Early French settlers probably created the first gumbo as a New World version of their beloved *bouillabaisse,* but through the years, other ethnic groups in the territory added their own touches to the simmering pot. The Choctaw Indians (among Louisiana's original residents) added filé powder; Africans included okra; the Spanish contributed tomatoes and fiery chilies—and gumbo just got better and better as the years passed!

Gumbo can be prepared from whatever ingredients one has on hand, but all good gumbos feature a dark, slow-cooked roux made from animal fat and a rich, long-simmered stock.

> About 1 cup lard or solid vegetable shortening
> 6 chicken breast halves, skinned, boned
> Salt and freshly ground black pepper to taste
> 1 cup all-purpose flour
> 1 medium onion, chopped
> 3 celery stalks, chopped
> 1 medium green bell pepper, chopped
> 2 medium garlic cloves, chopped
> 2 bay leaves
> 1/2 teaspoon dried leaf thyme
> 2 tablespoons minced parsley, preferably flat-leaf
> 4 quarts Poultry Stock, page 38, or canned chicken broth
> 1 teaspoon freshly ground black pepper
> Red (cayenne) pepper to taste
> 24 oysters and their liquor (about 2 pints)
> 1 tablespoon filé powder
> Hot cooked white rice
> Chopped green onions (including tops)

❦ Melt 1 cup lard or shortening in a heavy 12-inch skillet over medium-high heat. Sprinkle both sides of chicken breasts with salt and black pepper, then add to hot fat and quickly brown on both sides. Remove from skillet, cut into bite-size pieces and set aside. Strain lard or shortening to remove all browned bits; measure. Return strained fat to clean skillet over medium heat and add enough additional fat to make 1 cup. Add flour all at once and whisk until smooth, then whisk constantly until a mahogany-colored roux forms (about 45 minutes). Add onion, celery, bell pepper, garlic, bay leaves, thyme and parsley. Cook, stirring often, until vegetables are wilted and onion is transparent (about 8 minutes). Meanwhile, pour stock into an 8-quart pot and bring to a boil. Add roux-vegetable mixture to boiling stock, a spoonful at a time. Reduce heat so liquid barely simmers; add chicken pieces, 1 teaspoon black pepper and salt and red pepper to taste. Cover and simmer 45 minutes. Add oysters and their liquor; cook 10 minutes longer. Remove from heat; stir in filé powder. Discard bay leaves. Serve over rice in soup plates; top with a sprinkling of green onions. Makes 6 to 8 servings.

TIP Once you have added filé powder to a gumbo, do not boil the brew or the filé will form thick, viscous "ropes," giving the broth an unpleasant texture.

Oysters Rockefeller Bisque

This heavenly soup is a thoroughly modern Southern dish—and where else could it have been concocted but New Orleans, the city responsible for Oysters Rockefeller? I first tasted it at a delightful tiny restaurant in Covington, Louisiana called Café Rani, then owned by Gary Darling. Other versions soon followed. My own rendition, to which I'm also rather partial, combines watercress, parsley and celery with the spinach, as in the original version of Oysters Rockefeller.

> 1 (10-oz.) package fresh spinach
> 1 bunch watercress
> 6 tablespoons unsalted butter
> 6 green onions (including tops), thinly sliced
> 2 medium celery stalks, chopped
> 1/4 cup minced parsley, preferably flat-leaf
> 1 medium garlic clove, minced
> 1/4 teaspoon dried leaf marjoram
> 1/4 teaspoon red (cayenne) pepper
> 1/2 teaspoon freshly ground black pepper
> 1/4 cup all-purpose flour
> 36 medium oysters, (about 3 pints), drained, liquor reserved
> 1 tablespoon Herbsaint or Pernod
> 3 cups Seafood Stock, page 39, or bottled clam juice
> 1-1/2 cups whipping cream
> Salt to taste

❦ Remove fibrous stems and midribs from spinach and watercress; finely chop leaves and set aside. Melt butter in a heavy 6-quart pot over medium heat. Add green onions, celery, parsley, garlic, marjoram, red pepper, black pepper and chopped spinach and watercress. Cook, stirring often, until vegetables are thoroughly wilted (about 10 minutes). Add flour all at once; stir until combined. Cook, stirring, 3 to 4 minutes. Slowly stir in reserved oyster liquor, Herbsaint and stock, stirring constantly. Boil until thickened. Add oysters; reduce heat so liquid barely simmers and cook 30 minutes, stirring occasionally. Remove soup from heat and puree in batches in a blender or a food processor fitted with the steel blade until very smooth. Return soup to pot over medium heat; stir in cream and salt. Heat through (about 15 minutes). Makes 6 to 8 servings.

Pendennis Turtle Soup

Created at Louisville's legendary Pendennis Club, this delicious version of the classic turtle soup was once billed as "the soup that made Kentucky famous." The claim may have been a bit exaggerated, but the soup is certainly worthy of fame! To prepare it, you will need to make a sort of twice-cooked stock. Don't be tempted to try shortcuts; the quality of the soup depends upon this rich broth with the "double whammy" flavor.

1/2 cup vegetable oil
2 pounds meaty veal shanks, cut into 1/2-inch slices
2 carrots, chopped
2 medium onions, chopped
2 medium garlic cloves, minced
6 tablespoons all-purpose flour
3 quarts Brown Stock, page 38, or canned beef broth
1 (16-oz.) can stewed tomatoes
1/2 cup tomato puree
10 whole cloves
2 teaspoons whole black peppercorns
2 pounds boned turtle meat, trimmed of fat and tendons, diced
Salt to taste
1/2 teaspoon Tabasco sauce
1 large lemon, thinly sliced
1/2 cup dry sherry
2 hard-cooked eggs, finely chopped

❦ Preheat oven to 375F (190C). Heat oil in a 10-quart roasting pan and add veal shank slices, carrots, onions and garlic; stir to coat well with oil. Cover pan; roast in preheated oven 1 hour, turning meat and vegetables 3 or 4 times. Remove from oven, add flour all at once and stir until combined. Slowly stir in stock. Drain tomatoes, reserving liquid; chop tomatoes and add to pan along with reserved liquid, tomato puree, cloves and peppercorns. Return to oven and bake, covered, 1 hour longer. Strain through a fine strainer, pressing down hard on vegetables and meat to extract all liquid. Pour strained stock into a heavy 6-quart pot; add turtle meat, salt, Tabasco sauce and lemon. Bring to a boil, then reduce heat so liquid barely simmers. Cover and simmer until turtle meat is very tender (about 2 hours). Remove lemon slices; add sherry. Serve hot, garnished with chopped eggs. Makes 8 to 10 servings.

Black Bean Soup

The black or "turtle" bean, a gift from the Spanish *conquistadors,* is popular throughout the South. Louisiana's early Cajuns combined rice and black beans seasoned with tasso (a spicy smoked meat) to make a dish called *congri,* still served today; in Florida, Cuban immigrants introduced a now-famous black bean soup. To sample the authentic soup and get a taste of Cuban-style revelry at the same time, travel to Tampa in winter for the annual Gasparilla Festival.

   2 pounds dried black beans
   1/3 cup bacon drippings or lard
   2 large onions, chopped
   3 large garlic cloves, minced
   2 teaspoons ground cumin
   2 bay leaves
   4 quarts Brown Stock, page 38, or canned beef broth
   1-1/2 pounds smoked ham, cut into 1-inch cubes
   1/4 pound salt pork, rind removed, finely chopped
   1/4 cup fresh lemon juice
   1/2 cup red wine vinegar
   2 teaspoons dried leaf oregano
   1 teaspoon freshly ground black pepper
   1 teaspoon Tabasco sauce
   Salt to taste
   2/3 cup dry sherry
   1 lemon, sliced
   2 hard-cooked eggs, finely chopped

❦ Place beans in a large bowl, cover with water and let soak overnight. Drain beans in a colander and set aside. Melt bacon drippings or lard in an 8-quart pot over medium heat. Add onions, garlic, cumin and bay leaves; cook, stirring often, until onions have turned to mush (about 30 minutes; Cuban cooks refer to this step as "cooking the sofrito"). Add drained beans, stock, ham, salt pork, lemon juice, vinegar, oregano, pepper, Tabasco sauce and salt. Stir to blend. Bring to a boil, then reduce heat, cover and simmer until beans are very tender (about 3 hours). Remove from heat; discard bay leaves. Puree in batches until smooth in a food processor fitted with the steel blade or in a blender. Return soup to pot over medium heat; taste and adjust seasonings. Stir in sherry; cook 15 minutes. Serve hot. To garnish, lightly squeeze a lemon slice into each bowl, then float slice on soup. Top each bowl with a sprinkling of chopped eggs. Makes 8 to 10 servings.

Georgia Peanut Soup

That favorite American cocktail munchie, the peanut, came to the American South in the early colonial days, brought by Africans who arrived as slaves. Peanuts grew prolifically in the colonies, where they were used chiefly in sweet desserts such as cookies, cakes and candies—but they also went into savory dishes like this one. The original peanut soup was probably based on African stews which contained peanuts. The ingredients are fairly constant among the many peanut soup recipes I have consulted, though tomatoes seem to have been optional, depending on the cook's taste. I have included them here; I think they complement the other flavors in the soup.

5 ounces salt pork, rind removed, diced
1 medium onion, chopped
2 celery stalks, chopped
1 large garlic clove, minced
3 tablespoons all-purpose flour
4 cups Poultry Stock, page 38, or canned chicken broth
2 large tomatoes (about 1 lb. *total*), peeled, chopped
1/4 teaspoon freshly ground black pepper
Salt to taste
1/4 teaspoon ground ginger
1/4 teaspoon paprika
Dash of freshly grated nutmeg
1/2 pint (1 cup) whipping cream
1/2 cup finely ground roasted peanuts

❦ Cook salt pork in a heavy 4-quart saucepan over medium heat until all fat is rendered (about 20 minutes); leave remaining crisp bits of meat ("cracklin's") in pan. Add onion, celery and garlic; cook, stirring often, until onion is wilted and lightly browned (12 to 15 minutes). Add flour all at once and stir to blend. Cook, stirring, 3 to 4 minutes. Slowly stir in stock, bring to a boil and boil until slightly thickened. Reduce heat and add tomatoes, pepper, salt, ginger, paprika and nutmeg. Cover and simmer 15 minutes. Add cream and peanuts; stir well and simmer 15 minutes longer. Serve hot. Makes 4 to 6 servings.

MEATS & POULTRY

Throughout most of its history, the South has relied mainly on pork, poultry and seasonal game as the dietary mainstay. Even today in the Deep South, pork and poultry are the front-runners by a wide margin. Beef was not widely eaten until fairly recently; it is only during the past 20 years that steak has enjoyed a surge in popularity. As is true for all foods, Southerners take their steak very seriously. The favorite Southern steak is the rib-eye, the most naturally tender and desirable portion of the rib, cut into caveman-style slabs 1-1/2 to 2 inches thick and grilled or pan-broiled. This is *serious* eating, definitely not for the delicate-of-appetite Southern belle trying to maintain a 17-inch waistline!

Given all the available land in the South, many people find it difficult to understand why beef has never been an important part of the South-ern diet. The reason lies in the fact that agriculture was the backbone of the Southern economy from the very beginning. As the plantations grew and prospered from plantings of tobacco, indigo, rice, sugar cane and later, cotton, increasingly greater acreage was needed in the pursuit of greater economic returns. Cattle were brought to colonial America at various times and most plantations did keep a few dairy cows for milk, but large herds could not be maintained: there simply was no available pasturage of any appreciable size, nor was there land available for hay crops to feed cattle.

Pigs and chickens, on the other hand, did not require grazing acreage or special feed. They existed mainly on table scraps and corn, which was grown as a staple food crop. (Having eaten pork from slop-fed hogs in my childhood, I can't help feeling that we have lost something great each time I recall that juicy, succulent, "falling-off-the-bone tender" taste!) Both pigs and chickens also reproduced prolifically, ensuring a steady supply of meat year after year. And chickens provided income to many a family from their eggs.

After pigs were slaughtered in the fall, the meat was preserved by various methods. Hams were cured and smoked in the smokehouse, then hung to age; they required no refrigeration and could be enjoyed until slaughtering time the next year. Breast meat was cured and aged for bacon. The legs were cut into sections called "hocks" and smoked for use as seasoning meat; the feet (hooves removed) were pickled in a brine made from their own natural jelly. Scrap meats were pickled in some parts of the South, made into "salt meat" in others. Some of the meat was ground and seasoned, then stuffed into the intestines to make sausages of many varieties. In rural Georgia, meaty strips of cured belly fat—called "streak-o-lean"—made a delicious seasoning meat for vegetable dishes. In the Deep South, the meaty, fat jowls were smoked for use as both meat and seasoning. In South Louisiana, the tough cuts of pork were coated with a mixture of incendiary seasonings and slow-smoked to make a kind of pork jerky called "tasso"—the ultimate seasoning meat. Even the hog's head was boiled to make headcheese, which was molded in its own jelly and eaten in thick slices. And the fat was rendered into lard in huge iron kettles over outdoor fires and stored for use in cooking.

Game meats have always been a staple in Southern cooking. In rural areas, many families still count heavily on hunting and fishing season to fill the freezer for the coming year. Deer, squirrel, rabbit, opossum, raccoon, alligator, nutria (a beaverlike aquatic animal also trapped for its fur) and armadillo are all served up at Southern tables. Legions of birds are roasted, fried, stewed, "gumboed" and otherwise cooked throughout the South: wild turkey, ducks in myriad variety, geese, quail, dove, grouse, coot, jacksnipe, woodcock, blackbird (which really was made into pie!), crow and probably many more.

Many people object to the somewhat "wild" taste of game, which varies in intensity from animal to animal. The gamy flavor is largely concentrated in the fat, though, so much of the objectionable taste can be eliminated simply by removing as much of the fat as possible. Most game should also be marinated before cooking, both to mellow the flavor and tenderize the meat. Long, slow cooking is best—usually in a liquid. When cooking duck or geese, be sure to remove the oil gland just above the tail. The oil the birds use for preening and waterproofing their feathers is stored here, and the taste is downright terrible.

Liver à la Madame Begue

Madame Begue was the proprietress of one of the most famous old Creole restaurants in New Orleans. She gained a lasting reputation; many dishes still prepared by today's New Orleanians are *à la Madame Begue* ("in the style of Madame Begue").

> **1-1/2 pounds calf's liver, cut into bite-size cubes**
> **Salt and freshly ground black pepper**
> **5 parsley sprigs, preferable flat-leaf**
> **1 large onion, halved lengthwise, thinly sliced**
> **3/4 cup all-purpose flour seasoned with 1/2 teaspoon curry powder**
> **Vegetable oil for deep-frying**
> **Hot cooked white rice**
> **Minced parsley, preferably flat-leaf**

❦ Place liver cubes in a large bowl; season with salt and pepper. Place parsley sprigs on top of liver and cover with onion slices. Cover with plastic wrap and refrigerate 4 hours. In a heavy Dutch oven, heat 3 inches of oil to 400F (205C) or until a 1-inch bread cube turns golden brown in 20 seconds. Remove onion from liver and set aside. Discard parsley sprigs. Toss liver cubes with seasoned flour to coat well; shake in a medium strainer to remove excess flour. Combine liver and onions and place in hot oil. Deep-fry just until meat is lightly seared (only about 2 minutes). Empty liver and onions into a metal colander; drain 1 to 2 minutes. Serve over rice; sprinkle with parsley. Makes 4 to 6 servings.

Chicken Country Captain

It is, upon reflection, rather odd to find a decidedly curried dish like Country Captain with such a deeply rooted place in Southern cuisine. There's an interesting legend to explain its origin, though. The story goes something like this: The tall ships of the 1700s and 1800s regularly sailed between the East Indies and American ports in Virginia, South Carolina and Georgia, trading cargoes of rich spices for loads of rice and tobacco. During one long voyage, an inventive ship's cook tired of the monotonous and plainly seasoned rations; to vary the fare, he dipped into the ship's store of fragrant spices and used them to flavor chicken (live birds were regularly carried aboard, to provide eggs and meat). The result of this culinary experiment so pleased the captain that he prepared the recipe for his host when the ship made port in Savannah, Georgia. Country Captain is still served in the South today, much unchanged by modern trends. If you share Sunday dinner with a South Carolina family, it could well be on the menu.

1 cup all-purpose flour seasoned with 2 teaspoons *each* salt, freshly ground
 black pepper and paprika
1 (about 3-lb.) fryer-broiler chicken, cut into 10 pieces (including wishbone)
2 cups bacon drippings or lard
1 large onion, chopped
1 large green bell pepper, chopped
2 medium garlic cloves, minced
1-1/2 teaspoons curry powder
1/2 teaspoon dried leaf thyme
1/2 teaspoon freshly ground black pepper
Salt to taste
2 tablespoons minced parsley, preferably flat-leaf
1 (16-oz.) can stewed tomatoes
1/2 cup dried currants
6 cups hot cooked white rice
1/2 cup toasted sliced almonds

❦ Place seasoned flour in a paper bag. Add chicken pieces and shake to coat well; shake off excess flour and set chicken aside. Heat bacon drippings in a heavy Dutch oven over medium-high heat; add chicken and cook, turning once, until golden brown on both sides (about 15 minutes). Remove from pan and set aside. Pour off and discard all but 1/2 cup of fat from pan. Add onion, bell pepper, garlic, curry powder, thyme, black pepper and salt; cook until onion is slightly wilted and transparent (about 5 minutes). Drain tomatoes, reserving liquid; chop tomatoes and add to pan along with reserved liquid and currants. Stir to blend. Reduce heat so liquid barely simmers. Return chicken to pan. Cover and cook until chicken is tender and a rich sauce has formed in pan (about 45 minutes). To serve, arrange rice on a platter and arrange chicken pieces on it. Pour sauce over top and sprinkle with almonds. Serve hot. Makes 4 to 6 servings.

Poulet à la Bonne Femme

"The good woman's chicken" is indeed good chicken. In South Louisiana, many Cajun and Creole dishes bear the designation *à la bonne femme*, a compliment to the housewife who "has it all together." She is a good manager of the household, a good mother, a superlative wife and hostess; and she has a limitless repertoire of delicious, economical one-pot meals like this one. Serve with rice.

1 (about 3-lb.) fryer-broiler chicken, cut up
4 large russet potatoes (about 2-1/2 lbs. *total*), unpeeled, cut lengthwise into 1/2-inch-thick slices
Salt, freshly ground black pepper and red (cayenne) pepper
1 cup bacon drippings or lard
3/4 cup all-purpose flour
1 teaspoon dried leaf thyme
1 teaspoon ground sage
1/4 teaspoon dried leaf marjoram
1/2 teaspoon dried leaf rosemary, minced
1/4 teaspoon freshly grated nutmeg
1/2 teaspoon salt
1/2 teaspoon freshly ground black pepper
1/2 teaspoon red (cayenne) pepper
4 cups Poultry Stock, page 38, or canned chicken broth
4 medium onions, halved lengthwise, thinly sliced
2 medium green bell peppers, chopped
6 green onions (including tops), chopped
1/4 cup minced parsley, preferably flat-leaf

❦ Sprinkle both sides of chicken pieces and potato slices with salt, black pepper and red pepper; set aside. Heat bacon drippings or lard in a heavy 12-inch skillet over medium heat. Add chicken and brown quickly on all sides, turning once. Remove from skillet and drain on paper towels. In same fat, cook potato slices, turning once, until quite brown on both sides (about 12 minutes). Then remove potatoes and drain on paper towels, taking care not to break slices. Preheat oven to 350F (175C). Add flour to skillet all at once and whisk until smooth, then whisk constantly until a light peanut butter-colored roux forms (15 to 20 minutes). Add thyme, sage, marjoram, rosemary, nutmeg and 1/2 teaspoon *each* salt, black pepper, and red pepper, then slowly add stock, whisking to blend. Boil until thickened; remove from heat. Arrange a single layer of potato slices in bottom of an 8- to 10-quart roasting pan. Lay browned chicken pieces on top. Scatter onions and bell peppers over chicken, then sprinkle with green onions and parsley. Place remaining potato slices on top and pour sauce over them. Cover and bake in preheated oven 1 hour. Uncover and continue to bake until lightly browned (about 15 minutes longer). Serve hot. Makes 4 to 6 servings.

Southern Fried Chicken

No other Southern food—not even biscuits or barbecue—arouses as much controversy as fried chicken. Southern cooks can get just plain ornery about the merits of one frying method over another! Do you use peanut oil, vegetable oil, lard or solid shortening? Should you use a batter or just a light coating of flour—and if you use a batter, how should it be made? Do you use lots of oil and actually deep-fry the chicken, or do you shallow-fry it? How long do you cook it? Must it be cooked in cast iron? The questions go on—and I'm certain the arguments will, too, as long as two Southerners are left frying chicken!

Despite all the controversy surrounding the subject, two things are generally agreed upon. First, if your market sells fresh (as in unfrozen) chickens or better yet, free-range chickens (chickens allowed to run free rather than being locked up in cages), your fried chicken will have a definite edge over all contenders.

Second, you should always purchase whole fryers and do the cutting yourself. For authentic Southern fried chicken, you must end up with ten pieces, the tenth being the wishbone (or "pulley-bone," as it's known in the South). Southern children would never make it through Sunday dinner without the promise of tugging on the pulley-bone afterward to see who gets the big half and wins the right to make a wish! The upper portion of the back (the ribs) contains virtually no meat and is normally reserved for stock.

The recipes on pages 54 and 55 represent the two most popular ways of frying chicken in the South. Both are good, and perhaps one will become your favorite. For a totally Southern meal, serve either one with rice, your favorite green vegetable and biscuits.

Southern Fried Chicken with Cream Gravy

This is the chicken-frying method used by Southern fried chicken purists. They want only the taste of the chicken and no fancy seasonings. The cream gravy is a must; it's never served over the chicken, but rather over the accompanying rice or mashed potatoes.

> 1 (about 3-lb.) fryer-broiler chicken, cut into 10 pieces (including wishbone);
>   upper back (ribs) may be used
> 2 cups buttermilk
> About 1-1/2 pounds lard or solid vegetable shortening
> 2 cups all-purpose flour
> 1-1/2 teaspoons salt
> 2 teaspoons finely ground black pepper
> Cream Gravy, see below

> *Cream Gravy:*
> 1/3 cup pan drippings from frying chicken, with crisp browned bits from
>   skillet bottom remaining
> 1/3 cup all-purpose flour
> 2 cups milk
> Salt and finely ground black pepper to taste
> Tabasco sauce to taste

❦ Place chicken pieces in a 13" x 9" baking dish and pour buttermilk over them. Cover with plastic wrap and refrigerate overnight, turning pieces occasionally. Melt lard in a heavy (preferably cast-iron) 12-inch skillet over medium heat. It should melt to a depth of about 1/2 inch; if depth falls short of 1/2 inch, add additional lard or shortening. Meanwhile, in a brown paper bag, combine flour, salt and pepper. Drain chicken pieces and place them in bag with seasoned flour. Holding top of bag closed, shake to coat all chicken pieces with flour. Remove pieces and shake off excess flour. Using meat tongs, place dark-meat pieces in hot fat, skin side down, then add light-meat pieces, skin side down. Cover skillet and cook exactly 15 minutes. Remove cover, turn pieces with meat tongs and cook, uncovered, 15 minutes longer. Remove chicken from skillet and drain on paper towels while preparing Cream Gravy. Serve hot; pass gravy separately. Makes 4 to 6 servings.

Cream Gravy: Pour off all but 1/3 cup of the fat from skillet, leaving any crisp browned bits in bottom of skillet. Return skillet to medium heat. Add flour all at once; stir to blend. Cook, stirring, 4 to 5 minutes. Slowly add milk, stirring constantly; boil until gravy thickens. Season with salt, pepper and Tabasco sauce; cook 5 minutes longer. Serve hot.

Southern Batter-Fried Chicken

Southerners who like a very thick, crispy crust on their chicken often prefer this deep-fried version of fried chicken. The batter has a hint of spiciness, a feature much appreciated in South Louisiana and Mississippi.

        2-1/2 pounds lard or solid vegetable shortening
        1 (about 3-lb.) fryer-broiler chicken, cut into 10 pieces (including wishbone);
            upper back (ribs) may be used
        3 cups all-purpose flour
        2 teaspoons salt
        2 teaspoons finely ground black pepper
        2 teaspoons red (cayenne) pepper
        2 teaspoons paprika
        3 eggs beaten with 2 cups milk

❦ Melt lard or shortening in a heavy (preferably cast-iron) 12-inch Dutch oven or chicken fryer over medium heat. Heat fat to 365F (185C) or until a 1-inch bread cube turns golden brown in 60 seconds. In a medium bowl, combine flour, salt, black pepper, red pepper and paprika. Dredge chicken pieces in seasoned flour and shake off excess; next, dip pieces in egg-milk mixture. Then dredge again in flour; shake off excess. Using meat tongs, place dark-meat pieces in hot fat, skin side down, then add light-meat pieces, skin side down. Cover skillet and cook 15 minutes. Remove cover, turn chicken with meat tongs and cook, uncovered, 15 minutes longer. Remove chicken from skillet and drain on paper towels. Serve hot. If desired, you may prepare Cream Gravy from the pan drippings according to the recipe opposite. Makes 4 to 6 servings.

Stuffed Roast Turkey with Giblet Gravy

In the South, turkey is traditional for Christmas and Thanksgiving—but it's by no means limited to those occasions. Many Southern dishes made from turkey are served year round. Turkey Hash, page 179, is a favorite at Virginia hunt breakfasts and Derby Day brunches; turkey and sausage gumbo is staple fare in Cajun Louisiana. And in the South, turkey parts go into the economical stews and soups that help make ends meet.

A few words of caution are in order regarding the stuffing of birds. Any stuffing must be well chilled before it's placed in the body or neck cavity, and the stuffed bird must either be refrigerated briefly or baked at once. To prevent the growth of possibly harmful bacteria, never allow a stuffed bird to stand at room temperature, either before or after cooking.

8 cups Southern Corn Bread Dressing, opposite, well chilled
1 (12- to 13-lb.) turkey, giblets, neck and fat reserved
1/2 cup unsalted butter, melted
Salt and freshly ground black pepper
2 cups Poultry Stock, page 38, or canned chicken broth
Giblet Gravy, see below

Giblet Gravy:
Reserved giblets and neck from turkey
4 cups Poultry Stock, page 38, or canned chicken broth
Reserved turkey fat, rendered and mixed with enough melted unsalted butter
    to make 1/4 cup
1/4 cup all-purpose flour
1/2 teaspoon freshly ground black pepper
2/3 cup degreased drippings from roasting pan
Salt to taste
2 hard-cooked eggs, finely chopped

❦ Prepare dressing and refrigerate. Remove turkey neck and giblets and reserve for gravy; also pull off any large lumps of fat to render for gravy. Preheat oven to 325F (175C). Stuff some dressing into neck cavity of turkey; pull neck skin over back and secure with a poultry pin. Stuff body cavity and insert poultry pins across opening to draw the 2 sides together. Using heavy kitchen twine, lace pins together as though you were lacing a boot; secure with a knot. Fasten wing tips to body with poultry pins and tie legs together securely with kitchen twine. Place turkey, breast up, on a lifting rack in a roasting pan and brush with some of the melted butter. Sprinkle with salt and pepper. Pour stock into pan, cover and place in preheated oven. Cover. Roast until a meat thermometer inserted in thickest part of thigh (not touching bone) registers 185F (85C), about 4-1/2 hours. Baste turkey every 20 minutes during cooking, first with some of the melted butter, then with pan drippings. Uncover for last 45 minutes of roasting to let turkey brown. When bird is done, leg joints should move freely and meat on fleshy part of thighs should feel very tender. While turkey is roasting, cook giblets for gravy as directed opposite. Turkey is done, remove to a carving board (with the aid of the lifting rack) and rest for 15 minutes before carving. Degrease pan drippings and reserve. Meanwhile, prepare gravy. Remove trussing twine and poultry pins and carve. Serve with gravy. Makes 12 servings.
Giblet Gravy: Remove tough outer skin from gizzard. Place giblets and neck in a heavy saucepan with stock. Bring to a boil; reduce heat, cover and simmer until giblets are very

tender when pierced (about 2 hours). Remove giblets from stock and chop fine. Pull meat from neck and chop fine; combine with chopped giblets and set aside. Reserve stock. Cook rendered turkey fat-butter combination in deep-sided 12-inch skillet over medium heat until hot. Add flour all at once and cook, stirring constantly, 3 to 4 minutes. Slowly stir in stock; boil until thickened. Add pepper and drippings from roasting pan; season with salt. Add chopped giblets, neck meat and eggs. Heat through. Serve hot. Makes 3 cups.

Southern Corn Bread Dressing

When Thanksgiving and Christmas roll around each year with visions of juicy turkey and savory dressing, any Southerner will make the same unequivocal statement: there is only one kind of dressing fit for the holiday table, and that is corn bread dressing. It is true that many useful ideas have filtered down from the northern tier of states, but Southerners have steadfastly refused to allow any type of Yankee dressing across the Mason-Dixon Line—and corn bread dressing has remained unchanged over the years. To stuff a 12-pound turkey, double the recipe; you'll have a bit leftover to bake as a side dish.

> 1/2 cup bacon drippings or vegetable oil
> 1 large onion, chopped
> 1 medium green bell pepper, chopped
> 3 green onions (including tops), chopped
> 2 celery stalks, chopped
> 3 ounces streak-o-lean, see page 50, or fatty bacon, finely chopped
> 3 ounces smoked ham, ground
> 1/4 teaspoon dried leaf marjoram
> 1/2 teaspoon dried leaf oregano
> 3/4 teaspoon dried rubbed sage
> 1/2 teaspoon dried leaf thyme
> 3/4 teaspoon dried leaf basil
> 1/4 teaspoon red (cayenne) pepper
> 1/2 teaspoon freshly ground black pepper
> 3 cups lightly packed crumbled corn bread (about 3 oz.)
> 2 cups lightly packed torn French bread (about 2 oz.)
> 2 eggs, beaten until frothy
> 1 to 1-1/2 cups Poultry Stock, page 38, or canned chicken broth
> Salt to taste

❦ Preheat oven to 350F (175C). Heat bacon drippings or oil in a heavy 12-inch skillet over medium heat. Add onion, bell pepper, green onions, celery, streak-o-lean or bacon, ham, marjoram, oregano, sage, thyme, basil, red pepper and black pepper. Cook, stirring often, until vegetables are very wilted and onion is transparent (about 15 minutes). Meanwhile, combine corn bread and French bread in a large bowl and stir in beaten eggs. Pour vegetable mixture over bread mixture and stir to blend. Add enough stock to form a moist dressing. Season with salt. Turn mixture into a 3-quart baking dish and bake in preheated oven until lightly browned on top (about 1 hour), adding more stock as necessary to keep dressing moist. Makes 6 to 8 servings (about 6 cups).

Smothered Duck with Turnips

Yes, turnips! They may have slipped from the list of this year's trendiest foods, but they have always held a position of eminence in the South. The Southern cooking method of "smothering" really brings out their zesty yet delicate flavor. You'll find the combination of duck and turnips irresistible!

> **6 wild ducks, or 2 domestic mature ducks, quartered**
> **Worcestershire sauce**
> **8 medium garlic cloves, pureed**
> **Salt, freshly ground black pepper and red (cayenne) pepper**
> **2 tablespoons unsalted butter or margarine**
> **1/3 cup vegetable oil**
> **1/2 cup brandy**
> **2 medium onions, chopped**
> **1 medium green bell pepper, chopped**
> **4 medium turnips (about 14 oz. *total*), peeled, halved lengthwise, sliced**
> **4 cups Poultry Stock, page 38, or canned chicken broth**
> **6 green onions (including tops), chopped**
> **1/4 cup minced parsley, preferably flat-leaf**

❧ Remove and discard tail section with oil gland from ducks. Sprinkle duck pieces thoroughly with Worcestershire sauce. Rub garlic over skin of duck pieces and season well with salt, black pepper and red pepper. Place in a large bowl, cover with plastic wrap and refrigerate overnight. Melt butter or margarine in a heavy 10-quart Dutch oven over medium heat; add oil. When fat is hot, add duck pieces and brown on both sides, turning once. Add brandy to pan and immediately ignite (not beneath a vent or near flammable items); baste duck constantly until flame dies. Add onions, bell pepper and turnips. Add stock and cover pan. Reduce heat so liquid barely simmers. Cook, stirring occasionally until drumsticks move loosely at joints (about 1-1/4 hours). Stir in green onions and parsley; cook 5 minutes. Serve meat with vegetables and pan juices, skimming off any accumulated fat. Makes 4 to 6 servings.

Roast Quail with Sherried Honey Sauce

Quail is cooked by a variety of methods in the South and even eaten for breakfast at elegant weekend brunches. In a Southern hunter's home, there's almost always a good supply of these fat and tasty little birds in the freezer—unless it's nearly hunting season again! You needn't be a hunter to enjoy quail, though; farms in several areas of the South now ship dressed birds to supermarkets and specialty food stores all over the country.

> **8 whole dressed quail**
> **Brandy**
> **Salt and freshly ground black pepper**
> **16 bacon slices**
> **16 whole brine-packed grape leaves, rinsed**
> **2 cups Poultry Stock, page 38, or canned chicken broth**
> **2/3 cup honey**
> **1/2 cup dry sherry**
> **6 green onions (including tops), chopped**
> **6 ounces mushrooms, sliced**
> **1-1/2 cups whipping cream**
> **Hot cooked white rice**

❦ Preheat oven to 400F (205C). Sprinkle each bird inside and out with brandy. Sprinkle generously with salt and pepper, then wrap 2 bacon slices around each bird. Lay 8 grape leaves on a work surface and place 1 quail, breast side down, on each leaf. Cover each bird with a second grape leaf. Using kitchen twine, tie leaves securely around birds. Place wrapped birds in a metal 13" x 9" baking pan, breast side down; add 1 cup stock. Bake in preheated oven 30 minutes. Remove from oven and snip twine, then remove and discard grape leaves. Set baking pan aside. Place birds in a second baking pan, breast side up, and return to oven. Continue to bake until golden brown (about 20 minutes longer). While birds are roasting, skim any accumulated fat from juice in baking pan, then place pan on burner over medium-high heat. Add remaining 1 cup stock and cook, stirring to scrape up all browned bits from bottom of pan, until mixture is reduced to a thick glaze (8 to 10 minutes) Stir in honey, sherry, green onions, mushrooms and cream. Cook until sauce is thickened (about 10 minutes). Season with salt and pepper. To serve, remove quail from oven. Place a mound of rice on each of 4 individual plates and nest 2 quail into rice on each plate. Drizzle some of sauce over each serving and serve at once. Makes 4 servings.

Squirrel or Rabbit Sauce Piquant

Sauce piquant (*pee-KAWNT*)—similar to the famous Creole sauce of New Orleans, but a bit spicier—is a "category" of Cajun food from South Louisiana. The dish is roux-based and generally contains tomatoes; red wine is an optional ingredient. Any meat, fish or shellfish may be used, but local game, alligator and turtle are particularly popular. Here I've called for squirrel, commonly eaten in the rural South. Though tasty, the meat has a slightly gamy flavor and tends to be rather tough—but if marinated and then braised in a dish like this one, it's a real delicacy. (Store-bought domestic rabbit may substitute for the squirrel.) Sauce piquant is traditionally served over rice, but if you want to be trendy, spoon it over your favorite pasta!

> 4 squirrels or 2 rabbits, dressed
> Marinade, see below
> 2 cups all-purpose flour seasoned with 2 teaspoons *each* salt, freshly ground
>   black pepper and red (cayenne) pepper
> 1-2/3 cups lard or vegetable oil
> 1 cup all-purpose flour
> 2 medium onions, chopped
> 1 large green bell pepper, chopped
> 2 celery stalks, chopped
> 3 medium garlic cloves, minced
> 2 medium tomatoes, peeled, chopped
> 1 teaspoon dried leaf oregano
> 1 tablespoon sugar
> 1/2 teaspoon red (cayenne) pepper
> 1/2 teaspoon freshly ground black pepper
> 1/4 cup tomato paste
> 1/4 cup bottled picante sauce, preferably Tabasco brand
> 2 cups Brown Stock, page 38, or canned beef broth
> Salt to taste
> Hot cooked white rice or hot boiled pasta, cooked *al dente*
> 6 green onions (including tops), chopped
>
> *Marinade:*
> 1 cup red wine vinegar
> 1/2 cup vegetable oil
> 2 bay leaves
> 4 medium garlic cloves, smashed
> 1 medium lemon, sliced
> 2 teaspoons whole black peppercorns
> 1 tablespoon Worcestershire sauce

❧ Wash squirrel or rabbit under running water and pat dry on paper towels. Cut into serving-size pieces: first remove forelegs from body at shoulder joint, then cut and remove hind legs at hip. Finally, separate rib section from loin. Place pieces in a non-metal 13" x 9" baking dish. Prepare Marinade and pour over meat. Cover with plastic wrap and refrigerate overnight, turning pieces over several times. To brown meat, place 2 cups seasoned flour in a medium bowl. Heat 2/3 cup lard in a heavy 12-inch skillet over medium heat.

Meanwhile, remove meat from Marinade and pat dry on paper towels. Strain Marinade and reserve 1/2 cup; set aside. When fat is hot, dredge meat in seasoned flour, turning to coat well. Shake off excess flour; place meat in hot fat and cook, turning as needed, until browned on both sides. Remove from skillet and set aside. Heat remaining 1 cup lard in a heavy Dutch oven over medium heat. Add 1 cup flour all at once and whisk until smooth, then whisk constantly until a mahogany-colored roux forms (about 45 minutes). Add onions, bell pepper, celery, garlic and tomatoes. Cook until vegetables are slightly wilted and onions are transparent (about 5 minutes). Add oregano, sugar, red pepper, black pepper and tomato paste. Stir to blend, then add picante sauce and reserved 1/2 cup Marinade. Slowly stir in stock. Season with salt. Add meat and reduce heat so liquid barely simmers. Cover and cook until meat is very tender (about 1-1/2 hours). To serve, place a portion of rice on each plate and top with 2 or 3 pieces of meat. Stir green onions into sauce in pan and spoon a liberal amount of sauce over each serving. Makes 4 to 6 servings. **Marinade:** In a small bowl, combine all ingredients.

Fried Rabbit with Pan Gravy

Rabbit has been a favorite at Southern tables since the early colonial days. Until fairly recently, the cook had to depend upon the hunter's luck for a supply of fresh rabbit, but today, commercially prepared, cut-up, farm-raised rabbit is widely available in supermarkets, and it's enjoying a nationwide surge in popularity. If you haven't tried cooking rabbit, you're sure to be won over by dishes like this one—so delicious, yet so simple to prepare. Serve with rice.

> 1 (about 3-lb.) rabbit, cut into serving-size pieces (see instructions for cutting
>   up rabbit in Squirrel or Rabbit Sauce Piquant, opposite)
> 1/3 cup lard or vegetable oil
> 1 cup all-purpose flour seasoned with 1 teaspoon *each* salt, freshly ground
>   black pepper and red (cayenne) pepper
> 1 medium onion, chopped
> 1 cup Brown Stock, page 38, or canned beef broth
> 1 tablespoon apple cider vinegar
> 2/3 cup whipping cream
> Salt and freshly ground black pepper to taste

❦ Wash rabbit pieces under running water; pat dry on paper towels. Heat lard in a heavy 12-inch skillet over medium-high heat. When fat is hot, dredge rabbit pieces in seasoned flour; shake off excess. Place pieces in hot fat, skin side down; cook, turning once, until browned on both sides (12 to 15 minutes). Carefully pour off and discard all fat from skillet, then return skillet to heat. Add onion, stock and vinegar. Cover skillet and simmer until rabbit is very tender (about 1 hour). Remove rabbit from skillet and set aside to keep warm. Add cream to skillet and cook, stirring often, until slightly thickened (about 8 minutes). Season with salt and pepper. Pass hot gravy in a separate bowl to spoon over rabbit. Makes 4 to 6 servings.

Sausage-Stuffed Roast Pork Loin

A juicy boneless pork roast is one of the Southern cook's favorite meats to stuff, and this version of stuffed pork is packed with flavor: the meat is filled with an herb-seasoned sausage mixture, coated with a spicy seasoning blend before roasting, and served with a tasty gravy made from the pan drippings. Red currant jelly and Tabasco sauce add to the gravy's complex, sweet-spicy flavor.

> 1 (3-1/2- to 4-lb.) boneless center-cut pork loin roast
> Sausage Stuffing, see below
> Seasoning Mix, see below
> 1-1/2 cups Brown Stock, page 38, or canned beef broth
> 1/2 cup red currant jelly
> 1/2 teaspoon Tabasco sauce
> Salt and freshly ground black pepper to taste
> Curly-leaf parsley sprigs
>
> *Sausage Stuffing:*
> 10 ounces lean ground pork
> 1/2 small onion, finely chopped
> 3 green onions (including tops), finely chopped
> 1/2 teaspoon salt
> 1/2 teaspoon freshly ground black pepper
> 3/4 teaspoon red (cayenne) pepper
> 1 teaspoon ground sage
> 1/4 teaspoon dried leaf thyme
> 1 tablespoon minced parsley, preferably flat-leaf
> 1 egg, lightly beaten
>
> *Seasoning Mix:*
> 1 teaspoon *each* salt, paprika, freshly ground black pepper, red (cayenne)
>   pepper and garlic powder

❦ Lay meat on a cutting board, fat side up. Using a large chef's knife or slicing knife, butterfly meat: cut meat along entire length from middle of thick side about 3/4 of the way through to other side, then open meat out to resemble butterfly wings. Set aside. Prepare stuffing and set aside. Preheat oven to 350F (175C). Lay stuffing along crease of butterflied meat, packing it together tightly. Fold roast back together, keeping all stuffing tucked inside. Tie securely with kitchen twine. Prepare Seasoning Mix and pat onto fat side and ends of the meat. Place meat in a metal 13″ x 9″ roasting pan and bake in preheated oven until a meat thermometer inserted in center of meat registers 160F (70C) (about 1 hour and 20 minutes). Remove meat from pan; set on a carving board while preparing gravy. To make gravy, pour off fat from roasting pan and place pan on a burner over medium-high heat. Add stock and stir to scrape up all browned bits from bottom of pan. Add jelly and Tabasco sauce; cook rapidly until reduced by half (about 10 minutes). Season with salt and pepper. Pour gravy into a gravy boat. Remove twine from roast; cut into 1/2-inch slices. Arrange on a platter; garnish with parsley. Serve hot; pass gravy. Makes 8 servings.
Sausage Stuffing: In a medium bowl, combine all ingredients.
Seasoning Mix: In a small bowl, combine all ingredients.

Roast Pork Tenderloin with Henry Bain Sauce

The tenderloin is by far the most tender cut of meat on the hog. Unfortunately, it is also the most expensive—hence the old adage "living high on the hog." The higher the cut of meat on the hog, the finer the quality of the meat, so only the wealthy could afford the upper cuts of pork such as the loin and tenderloin!

Henry Bain Sauce, a staple on every table at the famed Pendennis Club in Louisville, Kentucky, is excellent on all types of meat. It is a rich and unusual sauce prepared with one of Kentucky's finest products, good bourbon whiskey, as an essential ingredient.

> **Henry Bain Sauce, see below**
> **2 whole pork tenderloins (about 1 lb. *each*)**
> **Salt and freshly ground black pepper**
> **1/2 pound bacon slices**
>
> *Henry Bain Sauce:*
> **2 cups Major Grey's chutney**
> **2/3 cup coarsely chopped pickled walnuts**
> **1-3/4 cups ketchup**
> **1-1/4 cups A-1 Brand steak sauce**
> **1-1/4 cups Worcestershire sauce**
> **1-1/2 cups bottled chili sauce**
> **2/3 cup good-quality Kentucky bourbon whiskey**
> **2 teaspoons Tabasco sauce**

❦ Prepare Henry Bain Sauce. Preheat oven to 375F (190C). Sprinkle pork with salt and pepper. Wrap each tenderloin in bacon slices and place in an open roasting pan. Bake in preheated oven 1 hour or until no longer pink in center. Remove from oven and cut into 1/2-inch-thick slices (do not remove bacon). Serve hot, topped with Henry Bain Sauce. Makes 4 to 6 servings.

Henry Bain Sauce: Sterilize four 1-pint canning jars and one 1/2-pint canning jar; set aside. Place chutney and pickled walnuts in a food processor fitted with the steel blade and process until smooth. Add ketchup, steak sauce, Worcestershire sauce, chili sauce, bourbon and Tabasco sauce. Process until blended. Pour sauce into sterilized jars, leaving 1/2 inch head space. Seal jars according to manufacturer's directions and process 10 minutes in a boiling water bath that covers jars by 2 inches. Cool jars completely before storing. Makes 4-1/2 pints.

Baked Ham Loaf with Mustard Sauce

Virginia, Kentucky, North Carolina and Tennessee are Southern ham country. The finest hams in the nation are produced in these states (particularly in Virginia), using time-honored methods. Southern cooks don't waste a scrap of their superb hams; this loaf puts the leftover tidbits to a delicious use.

> 1 pound smoked ham, ground
> 1/2 pound lean ground pork
> 1 tablespoon minced parsley, preferably flat-leaf
> 1 small onion, chopped
> 1 cup sauerkraut, well drained, chopped
> 1/2 teaspoon dry mustard
> 1/2 teaspoon salt
> 1/2 teaspoon freshly ground black pepper
> 2 eggs, beaten
> 1/3 cup tomato sauce
> 1 tablespoon firmly packed light brown sugar
> 1 cup fresh bread crumbs
> Mustard Sauce, see below
>
> *Mustard Sauce:*
> 1 cup sugar
> 2 tablespoons dry mustard
> 2-1/2 teaspoons cornstarch
> 1/4 teaspoon salt
> 2 egg yolks, beaten
> 1/2 pint (1 cup) whipping cream, heated slightly
> 1-1/2 tablespoons apple cider vinegar

❦ Preheat oven to 350F (175C). Lightly grease a 9″ x 5″ loaf pan; set aside. In a large bowl, combine all ingredients except Mustard Sauce and mix well, using your hands or a large wooden spoon. Pack mixture into greased loaf pan and bake in preheated oven until loaf is set (about 1 hour). Remove from oven and turn out onto a platter. Prepare Mustard Sauce. Slice loaf and serve hot with hot Sauce. Makes 4 to 6 servings.

Mustard Sauce: Combine sugar, mustard, cornstarch and salt in a medium saucepan. Stir in egg yolks until blended. Slowly add cream, whisking constantly. Cook over medium-low heat until sauce begins to thicken (5 to 6 minutes), whisking often; do not allow to boil. Add vinegar and whisk to blend. Remove from heat and serve.

Baked Smithfield Ham

Smithfield, Virginia is a tiny town in the eastern part of the state, in the heart of peanut-growing country. The town is best known for what many people, myself included, believe to be the finest country hams produced *anywhere*. Made from hogs that forage in the peanut fields after the crop is harvested, Smithfield hams have a flavor that's quite unlike any other pork. The meat is cured by a special and very secret process, then aged for a minimum of one year. The final product is a delectable ham which has earned a worldwide reputation as one of the South's finest foods.

> **1 (12- to 13-lb.) Smithfield ham, rind on**
> **Whole cloves**
> **Freshly ground black pepper to taste**
> **1-1/2 cups dry sherry**
> **1-1/2 cups firmly packed brown sugar**
> **2 teaspoons dry mustard**
> **1/2 cup apple cider vinegar**

❦ Place the ham in a heavy 15- to 20-quart stock pot and add cold water to barely cover. Soak ham 12 hours at room temperature. Then bring to a boil over medium-high heat, skimming gray foam from surface. Reduce heat so liquid barely simmers, cover and cook ham 5 hours, adding water to maintain original level. Cool ham in cooking broth; when ham is completely cool, remove it from broth. (Broth may be saved for use as a soup stock.) Remove rind from ham, then place ham in a roasting pan with a lid. Score top diagonally, making a diamond pattern. Insert a whole clove in each "diamond." Sprinkle surface of ham liberally with pepper and drizzle sherry over top. Preheat oven to 450F (230C). Combine brown sugar, mustard and vinegar in a small bowl and stir to form a smooth paste. Spread paste over surface of ham; place ham in preheated oven, cover and bake until glaze is browned and bubbly (about 30 minutes). Remove ham to a cutting board, cover to keep warm and let rest 15 minutes. Slice and serve. Makes 15 to 18 servings.

Baked Fresh Ham Steak with Raisin Sauce

In the South, a "fresh" ham is one that has not been heavily smoked or cured by the processes used to make "country" ham. This simple dish is a popular family meal; serve it with Hoppin' John, page 114, and Kale with Kohlrabi & Smoked Hog Jowl, page 112.

> 1-1/2 pounds fresh ham, cut about 2 inches thick
> Freshly ground black pepper
> Raisin Sauce, see below
>
> *Raisin Sauce:*
> 1/3 cup unsalted butter or margarine
> 2/3 cup firmly packed brown sugar
> 1/3 cup all-purpose flour
> 1/2 teaspoon salt
> 1/2 teaspoon finely ground black pepper
> 1 cup Brown Stock, page 38, or canned beef broth
> 1/3 cup apple cider vinegar
> 1/2 cup unsweetened pineapple juice
> 2/3 cup golden raisins

❧ Preheat oven to 325F (165C). Score fat on edges of ham steak; place steak in a heavy shallow baking pan. Sprinkle with pepper. Bake in preheated oven until lightly browned and tender (about 45 minutes). Meanwhile, prepare Raisin Sauce. Slice ham and serve with sauce. Makes 4 or 5 servings.

Raisin Sauce: Melt butter in a medium saucepan over medium heat; blend in brown sugar, flour, salt and pepper. Cook, stirring often, 3 to 4 minutes. Whisk in stock, vinegar and pineapple juice. Boil over medium-high heat, whisking constantly, until thickened (about 3 minutes). Stir in raisins and cook just until heated through. Serve hot. Makes about 2-1/2 cups.

North Carolina Barbecued Pork

Among connoisseurs, North Carolina is known as the "Barbecue Capital of the World," and I will certainly not argue the point. Because they make the best, North Carolinians are adamant about barbecuing procedures—and most of all about the meat. They will tell you that there was only one meat created for barbecuing, and that is *pork*.

A large trench (about 3 feet deep and 4 feet wide) is dug early in the morning. A roaring fire (hickory wood, please) is built in the bottom and allowed to burn down to a layer of brightly glowing coals. Young pigs around 6 weeks old are dressed, split down the back, strung up in chicken wire frames and laid across the fire, then cooked very slowly (12 or 13 hours) and constantly basted with a spicy, vinegary, yellowish sauce which is generally applied with mops. None of that sweet, ketchup-based stuff most Americans know as "barbecue sauce"! The meat is pulled from the bones, coarsely chopped, mixed with just enough sauce to make it mushy and served with such Southern staples as potato salad, coleslaw, baked beans and hush puppies.

For home barbecuing, pork shoulder is generally substituted for whole pigs. I have found that the best implement for basting is a 2-inch-wide paintbrush, which should be purchased new, hidden away in a secret place and used only for barbecue, other uses by family members at the risk of bodily harm.

Barbecue Sauce, see below
1 (3-lb.) boneless pork shoulder

Barbecue Sauce:
2 cups apple cider vinegar
1 cup firmly packed brown sugar
1 cup ballpark-style mustard
1/2 teaspoon red (cayenne) pepper
1-1/2 teaspoons finely ground black pepper
1/2 teaspoon salt
1 tablespoon Worcestershire sauce
1 teaspoon Tabasco sauce

Soak hickory wood chips in water 1 hour. Prepare Barbecue Sauce; set aside. Prepare a charcoal fire in a barbecue kettle or smoker and place grill about 8 inches above coals. When coals are evenly red and glowing, with a slight white haze, drain hickory chips and lay them on top of coals. Glaze pork all over with sauce, then place pork on grill. Cover and cook until meat is very tender and has a brown, crisp crust (3 to 3-1/2 hours); baste often with sauce and turn several times during cooking. Remove meat from fire and pull it apart into shreds, then roughly chop meat and stir in just enough of the leftover sauce to make a slightly mushy mixture. Serve hot. Makes 8 to 10 servings.
Barbecue Sauce: Combine all ingredients in a medium saucepan and simmer slowly 30 minutes. Sauce may be stored in refrigerator almost indefinitely. Makes about 3-1/2 cups.

Kentucky Burgoo

Burgoo is a thick, hearty stew that originated in Western Kentucky. Mutton, an essential ingredient in the dish, is consumed widely only in this particular region of the country; Owensboro, Kentucky is the home of the annual Mutton Festival, where thousands of visitors each year sample barbecued mutton and burgoo. Over the years, burgoo has become traditional Derby Day fare in Louisville. It's often prepared for large crowds, cooked in huge iron pots over outdoor fires and stirred with long wooden paddles or boat oars.

1 (about 4-lb.) stewing hen
2 bay leaves
1 tablespoon whole black peppercorns
1 teaspoon dried leaf thyme
1 teaspoon dried leaf sage
3 small dried or fresh hot red (cayenne) chiles
7 quarts water
2 pounds mutton breast or lamb breast, cut into chunks
1 pound boneless pork shoulder, cut into chunks
1 pound lean boneless beef chuck, cut into chunks
2 pounds meaty veal shanks
2 large russet potatoes (about 1-1/4 lbs. *total*), peeled, cut into bite-size pieces
2 large onions, chopped
4 carrots, chopped
5 celery stalks (including leafy tops), chopped
2 medium green bell peppers, chopped
1 small head green cabbage (about 1-1/2 lbs.), cored, chopped
1 (16-oz.) can stewed tomatoes
1 (10-oz.) package frozen lima beans
1 (17-1/2-oz.) can whole-kernel corn, drained
2 cups sliced fresh okra or 1 (10-oz.) package frozen sliced okra
1-1/2 tablespoons Worcestershire sauce
1 tablespoon apple cider vinegar
1-1/2 teaspoons freshly ground black pepper
Salt to taste
3 tablespoons minced parsley, preferably flat-leaf

❦ In a 15- to 20-quart stockpot, combine hen, bay leaves, peppercorns, thyme, sage, chiles and water. Bring to a boil over high heat; skim gray foam from surface. Reduce heat so liquid barely simmers and cook, uncovered, 1-1/2 hours. Remove and discard chiles. Add mutton, pork, beef and veal shanks. Cover and continue to cook until all meats are tender enough to pull away from bones (about 1-1/2 hours longer). Strain and reserve stock; set meats aside to cool. When meats are cooled, pull from bones (discard chicken skin) and coarsely chop. Skim fat from reserved stock, then pour into a heavy 12-quart pot and return meat to stock. Add potatoes, onions, carrots, celery, bell peppers, cabbage and tomatoes and their liquid. Stir to combine; bring to boil. Then cover, reduce heat and simmer 30 minutes. Add lima beans and corn; cook 1 hour longer. Add okra, Worcestershire sauce, vinegar, black pepper, salt and parsley. Stir to combine; continue to cook until stew is very thick (30 minutes longer). Serve hot in large soup plates. Makes 12 to 15 servings.

FISH & SHELLFISH

ishing is a way of life in most areas of the South. The region has a lot of water, and no matter where you are, you don't have to drive a "fer piece" to get to it. In Louisiana, fishing can be as simple as netting crawfish out of ditches or trapping crabs off a boat dock. In Florida, it can mean hooking a swordfish on a deep-sea fishing boat. It can be cane-pole fishing for catfish anywhere, or going after shad on North Carolina's Outer Banks. In many areas of the South, families even retain second homes in areas where dad can fish. But whatever the method, wherever the location, all Southerners know that *nothing* beats the taste of fish just a few hours out of the water!

I have always been surprised to learn that many people do not associate fish and shellfish dishes with Southern cooking. I am quick to point out that the food of the South is indeed much more complex than eternal bowls of red beans and rice on Mondays and pan-fried chicken on Sundays with some greens, chittlins and black-eyed peas cooked up in between! Some of the best-loved, best-known classic seafood dishes were born in the South. Who has not heard of shrimp Creole or pompano en papillote or oysters Rockefeller or she-crab soup? Who has not savored the crisp cornmeal crust and slightly musky flesh of fried catfish? The list goes on and on, with enticing specialties for all the myriad fish and shellfish native to Southern waters.

The South boasts double bounty in the fish department, culling treasures from both its extensive inland lakes, rivers and bayous and from the Gulf of Mexico on the southern coast, the Atlantic Ocean on the southeastern seaboard. From fresh waters come catfish, pan-sized perch for frying, sturgeon, bass, bluegill, river shrimp, crawfish and Louisiana's beloved *sac-a-lait* (crappie), to name only a few. Salt-water favorites include clams, scallops, shrimp, blue crabs, oysters, eels, lobsters, rock shrimp, stone crabs, langoustines, conch, redfish, red snapper, mullet, grouper, sheephead, speckled trout and pompano, as well as large deep-sea fish like tuna, swordfish, cobia and dozens more.

"Calabash-Style" Flounder

The "calabash-style" of cooking seafood originated in North Carolina, where the term refers simply to batter-fried seafood. Now, there are batters and there are batters—and some are decidedly better batters than others! The best calabash-style seafood I have come across is prepared at Tego Bay, a great restaurant outside of Charleston, South Carolina on the highway to Savannah. The batter may be used to fry any type of fish or shellfish.

> 8 (4- to 6-oz.) flounder fillets, skinned
> Whole milk
> 1 cup commercial pancake mix
> 1 cup white cornmeal, preferably stone-ground
> Vegetable oil for deep-frying
> Lemon wedges and curly-leaf parsley sprigs

❦ Place flounder fillets in a shallow baking dish; pour in enough milk to cover. Set aside 15 minutes. In a large bowl, combine pancake mix and cornmeal, tossing with a fork to blend. In a heavy 12-inch skillet, heat 2 inches of oil to 365F (185C) or until a 1-inch bread cube turns golden brown in 60 seconds. Drain fish and dredge each fillet in cornmeal mixture, coating well on both sides. Shake off excess. Add fillets to hot oil and deep-fry, turning once, until golden brown and crisp on both sides (about 4 minutes); take care to maintain correct oil temperature. Drain on paper towels and serve hot, garnished with lemon wedges and parsley sprigs. Makes 4 to 6 servings.

Broiled Trout au Gratin

The sweet speckled trout, or "spec" as it's called by fishermen in the South, may well be one of the most delicious pieces of fish you have ever put in your mouth. Prepared with a simple tomato sauce and topped with cheese, it's moist and juicy, piquant and just plain GOOD!

> 6 (6- to 8-oz.) Gulf speckled trout fillets
> Salt and freshly ground black pepper to taste
> 1/2 cup unsalted butter
> 1 small onion, chopped
> 2 medium garlic cloves, minced
> 2 medium tomatoes, peeled, chopped
> 1/2 cup picante sauce, preferably Tabasco brand
> 1/4 pound Monterey jack cheese, shredded
> 6 green onions (including green tops), chopped
> 1 tablespoon minced parsley, preferably flat-leaf
> Lemon wedges

❦ Position oven rack 4 inches below heat source; preheat broiler. Lightly grease a large baking pan; set aside. Pat fish dry on paper towels; sprinkle salt and pepper on both sides of each fillet. Place on greased baking sheet; set aside. Melt butter in a heavy 12-inch skillet over medium heat. Add onion and garlic; cook until onion is slightly wilted and transparent (about 5 minutes). Remove from heat and stir in tomatoes and picante sauce. Pour mixture over fish and place under preheated broiler 5 minutes; remove from oven. Combine cheese, green onions and parsley, tossing well. Sprinkle cheese mixture evenly over fish and return to broiler until cheese is melted and bubbly (2 to 3 minutes longer). Serve hot, garnished with lemon wedges. Makes 4 to 6 servings.

Trout Meunière

This classic dish, served throughout the Southern coastal region, proves that the simplest foods are sometimes the tastiest. This dish is a snap to prepare, but your guests will be so impressed by the flavor they'll never suspect it.

> **6 (6- to 8-oz.) Gulf speckled trout fillets, skinned**
> **3 cups all-purpose flour seasoned with 2 teaspoons *each* salt, freshly ground black pepper and red (cayenne) pepper**
> **1/2 cup vegetable oil**
> **3 eggs beaten with 1 cup milk**
> **1 cup unsalted butter, melted**
> **1 teaspoon freshly ground black pepper**
> **Salt to taste**
> **2 tablespoons all-purpose flour**
> **1/4 cup fresh lemon juice**
> **1/2 teaspoon Tabasco sauce**
> **1/2 cup Seafood Stock, page 39, or bottled clam juice**
> **Lemon wedges and curly-leaf parsley sprigs**

❦ Pat fish dry on paper towels and set aside. Place seasoned flour in a medium bowl; set aside. Heat oil in a heavy 12-inch skillet over medium heat. When oil is hot, dredge fish fillets in seasoned flour; shake to remove excess. Then place fish in egg-milk mixture and turn to coat both sides; finally dredge again in seasoned flour, coating well. Shake off excess. Gently lower fillets into hot oil and cook, turning once, until light golden brown on both sides (about 4 minutes). Remove to individual plates and set aside to keep warm. Pour off oil from skillet, leaving browned bits in bottom. Return skillet to medium heat, add butter and stir until melted, scraping up all browned bits from skillet bottom. Add pepper, salt and 2 tablespoons flour, stirring to blend. Cook until mixture is a light golden brown (7 to 8 minutes). Add lemon juice, Tabasco sauce and stock; stir to blend, then cook until slightly thickened (about 5 minutes). Remove butter sauce from heat and drizzle a portion over each fillet. Serve hot, garnished with lemon wedges and parsley sprigs. Makes 4 to 6 servings.

Shark Nuggets in Beer Batter

Fearsome though they may be, some species of shark have tender, delicious white flesh that adapts especially well to deep-frying. Serve these crisp little morsels as a main dish or as a party finger food.

 2-1/2 pounds trimmed shark meat, cut into 1-1/2-inch cubes
 Vegetable oil for deep-frying
 3-1/2 cups all-purpose flour
 4 eggs
 2 teaspoons salt
 1 tablespoon baking powder
 1/4 cup vegetable oil
 1 (12-oz.) can (1-1/2 cups) beer
 2 teaspoons red (cayenne) pepper
 3 tablespoons tomato ketchup
 1/4 cup prepared horseradish
 1 tablespoon fresh lemon juice
 4 teaspoons Worcestershire sauce
 1/3 cup minced green onions (including green tops)
 Lemon wedges and curly-leaf parsley sprigs

❦ Pat shark very dry on paper towels; set aside. In a deep-sided 12-inch skillet, heat 1 inch of oil to 360F (180C) or until a 1-inch bread cube turns golden brown in 60 seconds. Meanwhile, in a large bowl, combine flour, eggs, salt, baking powder, 1/4 cup oil, beer, red pepper, ketchup, horseradish, lemon juice, Worcestershire sauce and green onions. Whisk to form a smooth batter, free of lumps. Place shark in batter and turn to coat well. Add shark cubes to hot oil, 4 or 5 at a time, being careful not to crowd pan. Deep-fry until golden brown (about 4 minutes); take care to maintain correct oil temperature. Drain on paper towels and serve hot, garnished with lemon wedges and parsley sprigs. Makes 4 to 6 servings.

Fried Catfish with Dill Sauce

The first person to eat a catfish was brave indeed. Left to their own resources in Southern rivers and lakes these flat-headed, bewhiskered and gaff-equipped denizens of the deep often reach weights of 50 pounds or more. They must be skinned before eating, and the flesh is very bony. Despite these characteristics, catfish are the most popular fish in the South—and one taste of the tender, ever-so-slightly musky flesh and you'll know why. Now being farmed throughout the South, fresh, grain-fed catfish, both filleted and whole, are available at supermarkets throughout the country. Serve with a "mess of greens" and steaming hot corn bread or hush puppies.

> Dill Sauce, see below
> 4 (10- to 12-oz.) whole catfish, cleaned, skinned, heads removed
> 1 cup corn flour or all-purpose flour
> 1 cup yellow cornmeal, preferably stone-ground
> 2 teaspoons salt
> 2 teaspoons finely ground black pepper
> 2 teaspoons red (cayenne) pepper
> 2 teaspoons paprika
> Lard or vegetable oil for deep-frying
>
> *Dill Sauce:*
> 1-1/2 cups rich mayonnaise, preferably homemade, page 36
> 1/3 cup fresh lemon juice
> 1/4 cup sugar
> 1/2 cup dairy sour cream
> 1 teaspoon Tabasco sauce
> 1/4 cup minced fresh dill or 2 tablespoons dried dill weed
> 1/2 teaspoon salt
> 1/2 teaspoon freshly ground black pepper
> 1/4 cup minced green onions (including green tops)
> 2 tablespoons minced pimento-stuffed green olives

✤ Prepare Dill Sauce and refrigerate. Pat catfish very dry on paper towels. In a 13" x 9" baking dish, combine corn flour, cornmeal, salt, black pepper, red pepper and paprika. Toss with a fork to blend. In a heavy 12-inch skillet, heat 1 inch of melted lard or oil to 350F (175C) or until a 1-inch bread cube turns golden brown in 65 seconds. Dredge fish in cornmeal mixture to coat both sides well; shake off excess. Place fish in hot oil, 2 fish at a time, and fry, turning once, until crisp and golden brown on both sides (about 7 minutes per side). Take care to maintain correct oil temperature. Drain fish on paper towels and serve hot with Dill Sauce. Makes 4 servings.
Dill Sauce: In a bowl, combine all ingredients and whisk to blend. Cover and refrigerate until ready to serve.

Biloxi Bacon

The mullet is a somewhat bony fish caught in the Gulf coastal waters and along the Eastern seaboard. It's often overlooked as "trash fish"—and that is unfortunate, because it's both very tasty (better than catfish, in my opinion) and very nutritious. Along the Gulf Coast, smoking is a favorite treatment for mullet; the smoked fish is called "Biloxi Bacon," after Biloxi, Mississippi, where it is especially popular. If you like, substitute catfish or your favorite local fresh- or salt-water fish for mullet in this recipe.

Brine, see below
8 whole mullet (about 1 lb. *each***), cleaned, scaled, heads removed; or substitute**
your favorite local fish of the same size
1 (1-liter) bottle "jug"-quality burgundy wine
1 large onion, unpeeled, coarsely chopped
1 tablespoon whole black peppercorns

Brine:
4 quarts water
1-1/2 cups salt
3/4 cup firmly packed light brown sugar
3 tablespoons finely ground black pepper
1-1/2 tablespoons dried leaf tarragon
8 bay leaves
1/4 cup Tabasco sauce

❧ Prepare Brine. Place fish in Brine, cover with plastic wrap and refrigerate 24 to 48 hours. (The longer the fish remain in the brine solution, the spicier the taste will be.) When ready to smoke fish, soak mesquite or hickory wood chips in water 1 hour, then prepare a charcoal fire in lower dish of home-type meat smoker. Drain wood chips and add to fire. In upper dish of smoker, combine wine, onion and peppercorns. Cover smoker and allow fire to burn down 30 minutes. Remove fish from Brine and pat very dry inside and out, using paper towels. Place fish on grill above wine mixture and cook, covered, until skin is dry and somewhat crisp and shriveled (about 1-1/4 hours), turning once. Remove from fire and serve, or refrigerate and serve chilled, if desired. Makes 6 to 8 servings.
Brine: Combine all ingredients in a bowl or pan large enough to hold fish. Stir to dissolve salt and brown sugar.

Redfish with Saffron Sauce

Salads made of flaked, chilled cooked fish have always been popular in the South. Use redfish or any favorite local fish in this tasty luncheon or light supper dish.

About 4 pounds cleaned, scaled whole redfish
1-1/2 tablespoons salt
2 teaspoons whole black peppercorns
1 teaspoon dried dill weed
1 bay leaf
3 parsley sprigs, preferably flat-leaf
1 medium onion, thinly sliced
2 celery stalks, coarsely chopped
2 carrots, coarsely chopped
3 cups water
3 cups dry white wine
Saffron Sauce, see below
Red-leaf lettuce leaves
Lemon and tomato wedges

Saffron Sauce:
1/8 teaspoon saffron threads, crumbled
1 tablespoon hot strained fish-cooking liquid
1 cup rich mayonnaise, preferably homemade, page 36
2 tablespoons fresh lime juice
2 tablespoons fresh lemon juice
1/2 teaspoon salt
1/4 teaspoon freshly ground white pepper
1/2 teaspoon Tabasco sauce
1 teaspoon Creole mustard or other whole-grain mustard
1 tablespoon pureed onion
3 tablespoons strained fish-cooking liquid

❦ Wrap fish in cheesecloth, tying cloth at both ends and leaving long free ends for ease in handling. In a fish poacher or roasting pan large enough to hold fish, combine salt, peppercorns, dill weed, bay leaf, parsley, onion, celery, carrots, water and wine. Add fish, bring liquid to a boil and boil 5 minutes. Reduce heat so liquid barely simmers, cover and cook 40 minutes, turning fish once after 20 minutes. Remove fish to a platter. Strain cooking liquid and reserve 1/4 cup to use in sauce. Unwrap fish and remove all skin; gently pull flesh from bones, place in a bowl, cover and refrigerate. Prepare Saffron Sauce and refrigerate. When ready to serve, gently separate fish into flakes, taking care to remove any stray bones. Serve on lettuce leaves and top with Saffron Sauce; garnish with lemon and tomato wedges. Makes 4 to 6 servings.
Saffron Sauce: Steep saffron in 1 tablespoon hot fish cooking liquid until dissolved. Combine with remaining ingredients; whisk. Cover and refrigerate until ready to serve.

Caribbean Creole-Style Red Snapper

The classic tomato-laden Creole sauces for which New Orleans is famous are presumed to have been markedly influenced by the Caribbean style of cooking. But Creole-style fish prepared in true Caribbean fashion is first marinated in citrus juice, then fried and finally simmered only briefly in the Creole sauce. This version is served throughout the coastal South.

4 (6- to 8-oz.) fillets of red snapper or any mild-flavored, white-fleshed fish
Marinade, see below
1/2 pound salt pork, rind removed, diced
1/2 cup all-purpose flour
1 medium onion, chopped
1 medium green bell pepper, chopped
2 medium garlic cloves, minced
1/2 cup chopped celery
2 tablespoons minced parsley, preferably flat-leaf
4 large tomatoes (about 2 lbs. *total*), peeled, chopped
1/2 teaspoon Tabasco sauce
1 teaspoon freshly ground black pepper
Salt to taste
5 green onions (including green tops), chopped

Marinade:
2/3 cup fresh lime juice (about 4 large limes)
5 green onions (including green tops), chopped
2 medium garlic cloves, minced
1 teaspoon freshly ground black pepper
Salt to taste

❦ Place fish in a non-metal 13″ x 9″ baking dish. Prepare Marinade and pour over fish; cover with plastic wrap and refrigerate 2 hours. Drain fish and discard Marinade, then pat fish very dry on paper towels. Set aside. Cook salt pork in a heavy 12-inch skillet over medium heat until all fat is rendered (about 20 minutes). Remove remaining crispy bits of meat ("cracklin's") and set aside. Dredge fish in flour and shake to remove excess. Add fish to hot fat and cook, turning once, until golden brown on both sides and opaque in center (about 10 minutes). Remove fish and set aside, reserving drippings. To prepare Creole sauce, add onion, bell pepper, garlic, celery and parsley to drippings and cook until onion is wilted and transparent (about 10 minutes). Add reserved salt pork cracklin's, tomatoes, Tabasco sauce, black pepper and salt; cover and cook until sauce is thickened and vegetables are very soft (about 45 minutes). Add green onions and stir to blend. Place fish in sauce and cook just until heated through (about 5 minutes). Serve fish covered by a portion of sauce. Makes 4 servings.
Marinade: In a small bowl, combine all ingredients.

Marinated, Fried & Baked Sheephead

Pretty it's not—with large, bulging eyes, a rather fearsome-looking set of teeth and a serious overbite. But what the sheephead lacks in looks, it makes up for in taste. The meat, which flakes into large lumps when cooked, is so sweet and delicious that Southern cooks sometimes substitute it for crabmeat. If you can't get sheephead, just use your favorite local "trash fish." To cook a whole fish you'll need a very large (14- to 16-inch) skillet.

Marinade, see below
1 (4- to 6-lb.) whole sheephead, gutted, scaled
1 cup yellow cornmeal, preferably stone-ground
1 cup corn flour
2 teaspoons salt
2 teaspoons red (cayenne) pepper
2 teaspoons freshly ground black pepper
2 teaspoons dried leaf basil
2 teaspoons dried leaf thyme
2 cups vegetable oil for deep-frying
2 cups all-purpose flour
3 eggs beaten with 2 cups milk
14 lemon slices
Paprika

Marinade:
1 cup herb-flavored vinegar
1 cup fruit-flavored vinegar
1 cup vegetable oil
3 cups water
1 tablespoon Tabasco sauce
3 large garlic cloves, minced
6 green onions (including green tops), chopped
2 parsley sprigs, preferably flat-leaf, coarsely chopped
1 tablespoon sugar
2 teaspoons freshly ground black pepper

❦ Prepare Marinade; set aside. Score fish 3 or 4 times on each side, using a sharp knife and cutting all the way to the bone. Place fish in a 14″ x 10″ baking dish and pour Marinade over top. Cover with plastic wrap and refrigerate about 12 hours, turning often. Preheat oven to 375F (190C). Remove fish from Marinade and pat dry on paper towels; set aside. In a large bowl, combine cornmeal, corn flour, salt, red pepper, black pepper, basil and thyme, tossing with a fork to blend. Set aside. Heat oil in a heavy 14- to 16-inch skillet over medium heat. When oil is hot, dredge fish through all-purpose flour; shake to remove excess. Coat fish next with egg-milk mixture, then dredge through seasoned cornmeal mixture to coat well. Shake off excess and gently lower fish into hot oil. Cook fish, turning once, until a crisp, golden crust forms on the outside (about 5 minutes per side). Remove from skillet and place on a baking sheet. Overlap lemon slices in a row down middle of fish and dust with paprika. Bake in preheated oven 20 minutes. Makes 4 to 6 servings.
Marinade: In a large bowl, combine all ingredients, whisking to blend well.

Baked Grouper with Shrimp & Crabmeat

Grouper is a popular sport fish in Southern coastal regions. The fish can grow to 40 or 50 pounds or more, but the pure white flesh has a delicate taste. It's often substituted for redfish.

6 (6- to 8-oz.) grouper fillets
1/4 cup unsalted butter or margarine, melted
2/3 cup dry white wine
Salt and freshly ground black pepper to taste
Shrimp & Crab Topping, see below
1/2 cup grated Parmesan cheese (about 1-1/2 oz.)
Lemon wedges and curly-leaf parsley sprigs

Shrimp & Crab Topping:
1/2 pound backfin lump crabmeat
1/2 cup unsalted butter or margarine
1/2 cup minced green onions (including green tops)
2 medium garlic cloves, minced
1/2 teaspoon freshly ground black pepper
Salt to taste
1/4 teaspoon red (cayenne) pepper
1/2 cup all-purpose flour
1-1/2 cups whipping cream
1/2 cup reserved fish-cooking liquid
1/2 pound shelled, deveined cooked small shrimp

❦ Preheat oven to 375F (190C). Lightly butter a large shallow-rimmed baking pan, such as a jelly-roll pan. Lay fish fillets in pan. Drizzle melted butter or margarine over fillets, then pour wine into pan. Sprinkle fillets with salt and pepper. Bake in preheated oven until fillets are opaque throughout (about 8 minutes). Remove from oven and carefully drain off cooking liquid, reserving 1/2 cup. Set fish in pan aside while you prepare topping. Place oven rack 4 inches below heat source and preheat broiler. Spoon topping evenly over fish fillets, then sprinkle evenly with cheese. Place under preheated broiler until golden brown and bubbly on top (4 to 5 minutes). Arrange on plates; garnish with lemon wedges and parsley sprigs and serve. Makes 6 servings.

Shrimp & Crab Topping: Carefully pick through crabmeat and remove any bits of shell and cartilage; be careful not to break up lumps of meat. Set aside. Melt butter or margarine in a heavy 12-inch skillet over medium heat; add green onions, garlic, black pepper, salt and red pepper. Cook, stirring, until onions are slightly wilted (about 5 minutes). Add flour all at once and stir to blend. Cook, stirring, 3 to 4 minutes. Slowly add cream and reserved 1/2 cup fish cooking liquid. Bring to a boil; boil until thickened, stirring often. Reduce heat to a simmer and stir in crabmeat and shrimp, taking care not to break up lumps of crabmeat. Cook just until heated through.

Shrimp-Stuffed Mirlitons with Hollandaise Sauce

The mirliton—also known as chayote or vegetable pear—is a bright green tropical vegetable introduced to the South through early trade with the Caribbean. By whatever name, mirlitons are quite delicious; in this recipe, they're halved and filled with a mixture of shrimp and vegetables. This dish is traditional fare among country folk in South Louisiana and Mississippi.

> 2 large mirlitons
> 6 tablespoons unsalted butter or margarine
> 1 medium onion, chopped
> 4 green onions (including green tops), chopped
> 2 medium garlic cloves, minced
> 1 small green bell pepper, chopped
> 1-1/2 cups shelled, deveined, chopped uncooked shrimp
> 1/2 cup minced cooked ham
> 1 tablespoon minced celery leaves
> 1 tablespoon minced parsley, preferably flat-leaf
> 1/8 teaspoon dried leaf thyme
> 2/3 cup tightly packed French bread cubes soaked in 1/2 cup evaporated milk
> 2 eggs, beaten until frothy
> 1/2 teaspoon salt
> 1/2 teaspoon freshly ground black pepper
> 2/3 cup fine dry bread crumbs tossed with 2 tablespoons melted unsalted
>   butter
> Easy Hollandaise Sauce, page 192

❦ Place mirlitons in rapidly boiling water; parboil 15 minutes. Drain and set aside until cool enough to handle. Preheat oven to 375F (190C). Cut cooled mirlitons in half lengthwise, remove seeds and scoop out pulp, leaving a shell about 1/2 inch thick; finely chop pulp and set aside. Melt butter or margarine in a heavy skillet over medium heat. Add onion, green onions, garlic and bell pepper; cook until vegetables are slightly wilted and onion is transparent (about 5 minutes). Add shrimp, ham, celery leaves, parsley, thyme and reserved chopped mirliton pulp. Cook, stirring often, until all moisture has evaporated from pulp (about 20 minutes). Stir bread mixture into beaten eggs; mix into mirliton mixture, then season with salt and pepper. Spoon mixture into mirliton shells and top with buttered bread crumbs. Place stuffed mirlitons in a baking dish; bake in preheated oven until filling is bubbly and light golden brown (about 20 minutes). Meanwhile, prepare Easy Hollandaise Sauce. Serve stuffed mirlitons hot, topped with sauce. Makes 4 servings.

Creole Shrimp Jambalaya

Inspired by the spicy Spanish *paella*, the thrifty Cajuns of South Louisiana created this filling rice dish as a means of stretching small amounts of meat or fish. The name "jambalaya" is thought to derive from *jambon*, the French word for ham: ham is a traditional ingredient in the dish, no matter what other meats are included. Serve jambalaya with French bread.

3 pounds uncooked medium shrimp
1/2 cup bacon drippings or vegetable oil
1 medium onion, chopped
1 medium green bell pepper, chopped
2 medium garlic cloves, minced
1 celery stalk, minced
1/4 pound smoked ham, minced
1-1/2 cups uncooked long-grain white rice
1 bay leaf
1/8 teaspoon dried ieaf thyme
2 tablespoons minced parsley, preferably flat-leaf
1/4 teaspoon red (cayenne) pepper
1/2 teaspoon freshly ground black pepper
1 (16-oz.) can stewed tomatoes, drained, chopped
2 cups Brown Stock, page 38, or canned beef broth
Salt to taste
6 green onions (including green tops), finely chopped

❡ Shell, devein and coarsely chop shrimp; set aside. Heat bacon drippings or oil in a heavy Dutch oven over medium-high heat. Add onion, bell pepper, garlic, celery and ham. Cook, stirring often, until vegetables are slightly wilted and onion is transparent (about 5 minutes). Add rice, bay leaf, thyme, parsley, red pepper and black pepper. Cook, stirring, until rice is light golden (about 5 minutes). Add tomatoes and shrimp; stir to blend. Add stock and salt. Cover and cook until rice is tender and all liquid is absorbed (about 45 minutes). Discard bay leaf. Stir in green onions and cook 10 minutes longer. Serve hot. Makes 4 to 6 servings.

Shrimp Creole

Shrimp Creole is an all-time classic Creole dish that has gained the status of an American classic, as well. Subtly spicy and full of tomatoes, it's the archetypal example of New Orleans-style food.

6 tablespoons unsalted butter or margarine
1 large onion, chopped
1 medium green bell pepper, chopped
2 celery stalks, chopped
2 medium garlic cloves, minced
2 tablespoons minced parsley, preferably flat-leaf
Dash of dried leaf thyme
1/2 teaspoon freshly ground black pepper
1/2 teaspoon Tabasco sauce
3 tablespoons all-purpose flour
6 medium tomatoes (about 2-1/2 lbs. *total*), peeled, chopped
1 (8-oz.) can tomato sauce
1 teaspoon sugar
2 cups Seafood Stock, page 39, or bottled clam juice
Salt to taste
4 pounds uncooked medium shrimp, shelled, deveined
6 green onions (including green tops), chopped
Hot cooked white rice

❦ Melt butter or margarine in a heavy, deep-sided skillet over medium heat. Add onion, bell pepper, celery, garlic, parsley, thyme, black pepper and Tabasco sauce. Cook, stirring often, until vegetables are slightly wilted and onion is transparent (about 5 minutes). Add flour and stir to blend; cook, stirring, 3 to 4 minutes. Add tomatoes, tomato sauce, sugar and stock, stirring to combine well. Add salt. Bring to a boil, then reduce heat, cover and simmer 45 minutes. Stir in shrimp and green onions; cook until shrimp are a rich coral-pink color and firm to the touch (about 15 minutes longer). Serve over rice. Makes 6 servings.

Shrimp & Squash Casserole

Abundantly available in myriad variety, summer squash is a Southern favorite. In the hands of Southern home cooks, this humble vegetable is seemingly effortlessly transformed into memorable dishes. This tasty, one-dish family meal is a fine example.

6 tablespoons unsalted butter or margarine
1 large onion, chopped
1 medium green bell pepper, chopped
1 medium red bell pepper, chopped
3 large garlic cloves, minced
1-1/2 teaspoons dried leaf oregano
1 teaspoon dried leaf basil
1/2 teaspoon dried leaf savory
2 tablespoons minced parsley, preferably flat-leaf
2 medium yellow crookneck squash (about 1/2 lb. *total*), thinly sliced crosswise
2 medium zucchini (about 1/2 lb. *total*), thinly sliced crosswise
2 large tomatoes (about 1 lb. *total*), peeled, chopped
2 teaspoons sugar
1 teaspoon salt
1/2 teaspoon freshly ground black pepper
1/4 teaspoon red (cayenne) pepper
2 pounds uncooked medium shrimp, shelled, deveined
1/2 cup fine dry bread crumbs
6 green onions (including green tops), chopped
3 ounces mozzarella cheese, shredded
3/4 cup grated Parmesan cheese (about 2-1/4 oz.)

❦ Melt butter or margarine in a deep-sided 12-inch skillet over medium heat. Add onion, green and red bell peppers, garlic, oregano, basil, savory and parsley. Cook until onion is slightly wilted and transparent (about 5 minutes). Add crookneck squash and zucchini; stir to blend. Add tomatoes, sugar, salt, black pepper and red pepper, incorporating well. Cover and simmer until vegetables have formed a rich, buttery sauce (about 30 minutes). Preheat oven to 350F (175C). Remove skillet from heat and stir in shrimp, bread crumbs, green onions and cheeses. Turn mixture into a 4-quart casserole or 4 to 6 individual au gratin dishes and bake in preheated oven until lightly browned and bubbly (about 25 minutes). Serve hot. Makes 4 to 6 servings.

Pickled Shrimp

Pickling shrimp is an old custom in Southern coastal regions. Every housewife has her own version of the spicy marinade that can transform one night's leftover boiled shrimp into the next day's luncheon. Serve with Charleston Ice Cream Muffins, page 127.

> 2/3 cup red wine vinegar
> 1-1/2 teaspoons dry mustard
> 2 teaspoons Tabasco sauce
> 1 teaspoon freshly ground black pepper
> 1 teaspoon salt
> 1 teaspoon sugar
> 1 tablespoon Worcestershire sauce
> 1 teaspoon dried leaf basil
> 1/4 teaspoon dried leaf marjoram
> 1 tablespoon bottled chili sauce
> 1-1/2 cups vegetable oil
> 2-1/2 pounds shelled, deveined, boiled shrimp
> 1 bay leaf
> 1 medium onion, halved lengthwise, thinly sliced
> 2 tablespoons minced parsley, preferably flat-leaf
> 2 tablespoons capers
> 2/3 cup sliced ripe olives
> Red-leaf lettuce leaves
> Tomato wedges

❦ To make the marinade, in a medium bowl combine vinegar, mustard, Tabasco sauce, pepper, salt, sugar, Worcestershire sauce, basil, marjoram and chili sauce. Whisk until blended, then add oil in a slow, steady stream, whisking to incorporate. Spread shrimp in a non-metal 13" x 9" baking dish. Scatter bay leaf, onion, parsley, capers and olives evenly over shrimp and pour marinade on top. Cover with plastic wrap and refrigerate overnight or up to 3 days. Discard bay leaf. To serve, drain and arrange on lettuce leaves. Garnish with tomato wedges. Makes 4 to 6 servings.

New Orleans Shrimp Remoulade

One of the most popular first courses served in the Southern coastal region, this classic dish doubles as a luncheon entree when served with crusty French bread.

> 3 eggs
> 1/4 cup Creole mustard or other whole-grain mustard
> 1/4 cup ballpark-style mustard
> 1/2 cup ketchup
> 2 tablespoons red wine vinegar
> 1/4 cup prepared horseradish
> 2 tablespoons Worcestershire sauce
> 1 tablespoon paprika
> 2 celery stalks, coarsely chopped
> 3 large garlic cloves, minced
> 1/4 cup minced parsley, preferably flat-leaf
> 2 bay leaves, minced
> 1 teaspoon salt
> Juice of 1 medium lemon
> 1-1/2 teaspoons Tabasco sauce
> 1/2 cup good-quality olive oil
> 2-1/2 pounds shelled, deveined boiled medium shrimp, well chilled
> Boston lettuce leaves
> Curly-leaf parsley sprigs and lemon wedges

❦ In a food processor fitted with the steel blade, combine eggs, Creole mustard, ballpark-style mustard, ketchup, vinegar, horseradish, Worcestershire sauce, paprika, celery, garlic, parsley, bay leaves, salt, lemon juice and Tabasco sauce. Process until smooth. With machine running, pour oil through feed tube in a slow, steady stream, processing to form a smooth emulsion. To serve, arrange shrimp on lettuce leaves and top generously with sauce. Garnish plates with parsley sprigs and lemon wedges. Makes 4 to 6 servings.

Creole Shrimp Stew

When the Cajuns reinterpreted the classic New Orleans shrimp Creole, they added their beloved roux to create a completely different dish! This rich and hearty one-pot meal is fit for a king.

1/2 cup lard or bacon drippings
1/2 cup all-purpose flour
4 celery stalks, chopped
1 large onion, chopped
1 large green bell pepper, chopped
6 green onions (including green tops), chopped
1 cup tomato paste
2 cups Seafood Stock, page 39, or bottled clam juice
2-1/2 cups water
2 teaspoons minced fresh thyme or 1/2 teaspoon dried leaf thyme
2 tablespoons fresh lemon juice
1 tablespoon sugar
Salt to taste
1/2 teaspoon freshly ground black pepper
1/2 teaspoon red (cayenne) pepper
3 pounds uncooked medium shrimp, shelled, deveined, or 2 pounds shelled cooked crawfish tails with fat
6 green onions (including green tops), chopped
1/4 cup minced parsley, preferably flat-leaf
Hot cooked white rice

❡ Melt lard or bacon drippings in a heavy Dutch oven over medium heat. Add flour all at once and whisk until smooth, then whisk constantly until a peanut butter-colored roux forms (20 to 25 minutes). Add celery, onion, bell pepper and 6 green onions. Cook, stirring, until vegetables are wilted and onion is transparent (about 10 minutes). Add tomato paste, stock, water, thyme, lemon juice, sugar, salt, black pepper and red pepper. Stir to blend liquids into roux. Bring to a boil; reduce heat, cover and simmer, stirring often, until sauce is thick (about 30 minutes). Add shrimp or crawfish tails, 6 green onions and parsley. Stir gently to blend and simmer until shrimp turn a rich coral-pink color or crawfish are heated through (about 15 minutes). Taste and adjust seasonings. Remove from heat; serve over rice. Makes 4 to 6 servings.

Cajun Popcorn with Creole Mayonnaise Sauce

Frying is one of the most delicious ways to prepare crawfish tails. Louisiana and Mississippi folks have been eating fried crawfish for years, but with the recent rise in the popularity of Cajun-Creole foods, they're now on restaurant menus all over the country. Chef Paul Prudhomme, the "King of Cajun," coined the trendy name—and "Cajun popcorn" took off like wildfire.

Creole Mayonnaise Sauce, see below
4 eggs
3 cups milk
1-1/2 cups yellow cornmeal, preferably stone-ground
1-1/2 cups corn flour
1 tablespoon red (cayenne) pepper
1 tablespoon finely ground black pepper
1 tablespoon salt
3 cups all-purpose flour
Vegetable oil for deep-frying
3 pounds shelled cooked crawfish tails

Creole Mayonnaise Sauce:
2 medium garlic cloves, peeled
1 egg
1 tablespoon Creole mustard or other whole-grain mustard
l teaspoon salt
1 teaspoon Tabasco sauce
1/2 teaspoon paprika
2 tablespoons red wine vinegar
1/2 cup good-quality olive oil
1 cup vegetable oil

❦ Prepare sauce and refrigerate to allow flavors to meld. In a medium bowl, beat together eggs and milk. In a separate bowl, combine cornmeal, corn flour, red pepper, black pepper and salt, tossing with a fork to blend. Place all-purpose flour in a third bowl. To prepare Cajun popcorn, in a deep-sided 12-inch skillet, heat 1 inch of oil to 365F (185C) or until a 1-inch bread cube turns golden brown in 60 seconds. Dredge crawfish tails in all-purpose flour, coating well; shake off excess. Next, coat tails thoroughly with egg-milk mixture; finally, dredge in cornmeal mixture, coating well. The secret to the success of the dish hangs in the balance right here! Each tiny piece must be coated individually with the cornmeal mixture, and no 2 pieces should be stuck together. Place coated tails in a medium strainer and shake to remove excess coating. Place a portion of tails in a single layer in a fry basket; lower into hot oil. Do not crowd pan or tails will stick together in 1 giant glob! Deep-fry until golden brown and crisp (3 to 4 minutes); take care to maintain correct oil temperature. Remove tails from oil and drain on paper towels. Serve hot with Creole Mayonnaise Sauce. Makes 4 to 6 servings.

Creole Mayonnaise Sauce: In a food processor fitted with the steel blade, and with machine running, drop garlic through the feed tube. Stop machine and scrape down side of bowl. Add remaining ingredients except olive oil and vegetable oil; process until smooth. Combine olive oil and vegetable oil. With machine running, pour combined oils through feed tube in a slow, steady stream, processing to form a smooth emulsion. Place in a bowl, cover tightly and refrigerate until ready to use.

Shrimp Rabbit

This old North Carolina coastal dish probably evolved from the classic Welsh Rarebit. Serve it for an elegant luncheon with Charleston Green Salad with Benne Seeds, page 32, and your favorite Southern bread.

> 1/4 cup unsalted butter or margarine
> 1 pound American cheese, cut into 1-inch cubes
> 1-1/2 teaspoons Worcestershire sauce
> Salt to taste
> 1 teaspoon dry mustard
> 1/4 teaspoon red (cayenne) pepper
> 1/2 cup beer
> 6 green onions (including green tops), chopped
> 2 pound shelled, deveined cooked small to medium shrimp
> 2 eggs, beaten
> Holland rusks or toast points
> Curly-leaf parsley sprigs

❦ Melt butter or margarine in top of a double boiler over hot water. Add cheese and cook, stirring, until melted (about 15 minutes). Do not allow mixture to boil. Add Worcestershire sauce, salt, mustard, red pepper and beer. Whisk to blend; stir in green onions and shrimp. Cook just until heated through (about 5 minutes). Add eggs and cook, stirring vigorously, just until mixture is thickened (about 4 to 5 minutes). Remove from heat and serve at once over rusks or toast points. Garnish with parsley sprigs. Makes 4 to 6 servings.

Creole Barbecued Shrimp

"Barbecued" shrimp in New Orleans never saw a barbecue grill: they aren't barbecued at all, but rather boiled in a really spicy butter mixture. No one knows where this good and messy dish originated; the most well-known version today is served at Pascal's Manale Restaurant on Napoleon Avenue in uptown New Orleans. Every home cook in South Louisiana has her own version. After enjoying the dish a few times, you may well concoct your own variation. One word of caution: The sauce is very spicy so the shrimp must be cooked *in the shells* or the seasoning will sear your tastebuds. In New Orleans restaurants when you order this dish, you get a bib to wear while eating your deliciously drippy shrimp—and a nice hot towel to clean up afterwards. Serve with coleslaw and Louisiana French Bread, page 139.

1 cup unsalted butter
1 cup vegetable oil
1 (12-oz.) can (1-1/2 cups) beer
1 cup Seafood Stock, page 39, or bottled clam juice
3 tablespoons fresh lemon juice
1 tablespoon Worcestershire sauce
1 tablespoon tomato paste
1-1/2 teaspoons red (cayenne) pepper
1 tablespoon finely ground black pepper
1 teaspoon dried leaf basil
1 teaspoon dried leaf oregano
1 teaspoon paprika
2 teaspoons filé powder
6 green onions (including green tops), chopped
6 pounds uncooked medium shrimp in shells

✣ Combine all ingredients except shrimp in a heavy 6-quart roasting pan over medium heat. Stir to blend; bring to a simmer. Simmer 20 minutes to allow flavors to meld. Preheat oven to 375F (190C). Stir shrimp into sauce, coating well. Place pan in preheated oven and bake, stirring often, until shrimp turn a rich coral-pink color (15 to 20 minutes). To serve, spoon shrimp into soup plates and top each serving with a portion of sauce. Makes 4 to 6 servings.

Broiled Rock Shrimp

Although it has the texture of lobster meat, the rock shrimp actually does belong to the shrimp family. Native to Florida, it has a spiny, very hard shell (hence the name) and flesh that tastes more delicate than regular shrimp yet more assertive than lobster. Rock shrimp can be used in any shrimp recipe, with the possible exception of deep-fried dishes; broiled in a spicy butter sauce, they're hard to beat.

3 pounds uncooked rock shrimp
1 cup unsalted butter or margarine
4 large garlic cloves, minced
1-1/2 tablespoons fresh lemon juice
1-1/2 teaspoons Worcestershire sauce
1 teaspoon Tabasco sauce
2 tablespoons dry white wine
1/2 teaspoon salt
1/2 teaspoon freshly ground black pepper
Fine dry bread crumbs
Minced parsley, preferably flat-leaf

❦ Position oven rack 4 inches below heat source and preheat broiler. Using kitchen shears, cut hard shell of each shrimp lengthwise down middle, taking care not to cut into meat. Pull sides of shell apart; remove meat. Remove and discard sand vein which runs lengthwise down back. Divide shrimp among 4 to 6 individual au gratin dishes; set aside. In a saucepan, combine butter or margarine, garlic, lemon juice, Worcestershire sauce, Tabasco sauce, wine, salt and pepper. Cook over medium heat until butter or margarine is a light hazelnut brown (about 10 minutes). Drizzle seasoned butter over shrimp; top each serving with a light sprinkling of bread crumbs. Place under preheated broiler; broil just until meat is opaque and tails have curled (2 to 3 minutes). Sprinkle with parsley and serve at once. Makes 4 to 6 servings.

Low Country Boiled Seafood Dinner

This giant one-pot meal is typical of seafood boils throughout the Southern coastal region. The cooking usually takes place outdoors in huge pots placed over butane burners. The pots have heavy mesh lining baskets. When the seafood is ready to eat, the baskets are lifted out and dumped in the middle of the newspaper-covered tables, and the guests dig in and enjoy. The only accompaniments are seafood cocktail sauce, butter for the potatoes—and of course, a big roll of paper towels! Simple fare, but some of the best eating the South has to offer.

2 (3-oz.) packages crab and shrimp boil
1/2 cup salt
2 tablespoons whole black peppercorns
1/2 cup red (cayenne) pepper
7 lemons, quartered
30 medium new potatoes
30 small onions, unpeeled
24 live blue crabs
15 ears fresh corn, husked, halved crosswise
10 pounds uncooked large shrimp in shells

❦ Place a 40- to 50-quart stock pot over medium heat and fill 2/3 full with water. Place a heavy wire mesh draining basket in pot. Add crab and shrimp boil, salt, peppercorns, red pepper and lemons; bring to a rapid boil. Add potatoes and onions; cook 20 minutes. Add crabs and corn; cook 15 minutes. Add shrimp and cook 10 minutes longer. Remove draining basket; serve shellfish and vegetables hot. Makes 10 to 12 servings.

Fried Soft-Shell Crabs

Soft-shell crabs are one of the most delicious creatures on earth. Many of the small restaurants dotting the Gulf Coast have acquired great reputations based simply upon the quality of their fried soft-shell crabs! Surprising to some, soft-shell crabs and hard-shell crabs are the same animal—at different stages of their life. The blue point crab sheds its hard shell many times as it grows to maturity. Fishermen trap the crabs when they are ready to shed their old shells and hold them in tanks until the hard shell is completely sloughed, then rush them to market while the new shell is still soft.

> 8 soft-shell blue crabs
> 3 cups all-purpose flour seasoned with 1 tablespoon red (cayenne) pepper,
>   1 tablespoon finely ground black pepper and 2 teaspoons salt
> Vegetable oil for deep-frying
> 6 eggs, separated
> 1-1/2 cups milk

❧ To prepare each crab, use kitchen shears to snip off eyes and small antennae in front of eyes. Carefully lift shell by points on each side; remove the "dead man's fingers" (gills) just beneath shell on each side. Pat shell back into place. Lightly press crabs dry between paper towels. Set aside. Place seasoned flour in a large bowl; set aside. In a deep-sided 12-inch skillet, heat 2 inches of oil to 360F (180C), or until a 1-inch bread cube turns golden brown in 60 seconds. Meanwhile, in a separate large bowl, whisk together egg yolks and milk until frothy; set aside. In a separate bowl, beat egg whites until they hold medium-stiff peaks. Set aside. Batter crabs 1 at a time as you cook them: dip each crab first in seasoned flour and shake off excess, then dip in egg-milk mixture and turn to coat well. Dip again in seasoned flour, coating well; shake off excess. Finally, dredge crab in beaten egg whites, coating both sides. Don't worry if crabs look very messy at this point! As soon as crab is battered, lower it into hot oil and deep-fry, turning once, until golden brown on both sides (6 to 7 minutes). Do not crowd pan; take care to maintain correct oil temperature. Drain crabs on paper towels and serve at once. Makes 4 to 6 servings.

Crabmeat Ravigote

Crabmeat Ravigote is a very old dish which originated in New Orleans. It's rarely found on restaurant menus today, and that is sad, because it is wonderful. I have sampled many renditions of the dish, but the following is closest to the earliest versions, and I don't think it can really be improved upon! The combination of sweet crabmeat with a 19th-century-style herbed mayonnaise sauce is irresistible. Though generally served as a first course, the dish also makes a nice luncheon entree.

1 pound backfin lump crabmeat
Ravigote Sauce, see below
Boston lettuce leaves
Lemon wedges and curly-leaf parsley sprigs

Ravigote Sauce:
1-1/2 tablespoons minced parsley, preferably flat-leaf
1-1/2 tablespoons minced watercress
1-1/2 teaspoons minced fresh tarragon or 1/2 teaspoon dried leaf tarragon
1 teaspoon salt
1/4 teaspoon red (cayenne) pepper
2 egg yolks
2 heaping teaspoons Creole mustard or other whole-grain mustard
2 teaspoons fresh lemon juice
2 medium garlic cloves
1-1/4 cups good-quality olive oil

❦ Carefully pick through crabmeat and remove any bits of shell and cartilage. Take care not to break up lumps of meat. Set aside. Prepare Ravigote Sauce. Gently fold sauce into crabmeat, combining well. To serve, place lettuce leaves on individual plates and top with a portion of crabmeat mixture. Garnish with lemon wedges and parsley sprigs. Makes 4 to 6 servings.

Ravigote Sauce: In a food processor fitted with the steel blade, combine parsley, watercress, tarragon, salt, red pepper, egg yolks, mustard and lemon juice. Process until smooth. With machine running, drop garlic through feed tube. Stop machine and scrape down side of bowl; then, with machine running, pour oil through feed tube in a slow, steady stream, processing to form a smooth emulsion.

Baked Crab Imperial

Throughout the South there are hundreds of versions of this dish. I have eaten it in restaurants from Louisiana to Florida and up the Southeastern coast in versions ranging from inedible to barely edible to mediocre to excellent to sublime. However, it's easy to achieve consistent success with Crab Imperial in your own kitchen: First and foremost the crabmeat must be backfin lump and it must be fresh. Elderly crabmeat with an ammonia-like scent will not improve with cooking. Second the succulent lumps of crabmeat must not be stirred, beaten or otherwise tortured into a stringy mass of mush homogenized into an over-thickened, tasteless white sauce!

In this recipe, a variation from Raleigh, North Carolina, the crab is lightly mixed with vegetables and seasonings, then topped with a flavorful sauce.

> 2 pounds backfin lump crabmeat
> 1/2 cup unsalted butter or margarine
> 1 large green bell pepper, halved, cut lengthwise into thin slices
> 1 large red bell pepper, halved, cut lengthwise into thin slices
> 6 green onions (including green tops), chopped
> 5 eggs
> 1-1/2 tablespoons herb-flavored vinegar
> 1 tablespoon Dijon-style mustard
> 2 teaspoons fresh lemon juice
> 2/3 cup bottled chili sauce
> 2 teaspoons Worcestershire sauce
> 1 teaspoon Tabasco sauce
> 2-1/4 cups good-quality olive oil
> Minced parsley, preferably flat-leaf

❦ Carefully pick through crabmeat and remove any bits of shell and cartilage, being careful not to break up lumps of meat. Set aside. Melt butter or margarine in a heavy 12-inch skillet over medium heat; add green and red bell peppers and green onions. Cook, stirring often, until vegetables are slightly wilted (5 to 6 minutes). Add crabmeat and stir just to blend, again taking care not to break up large lumps. Remove from heat and spoon into 4 to 6 individual au gratin dishes. Set aside. Position oven rack 6 inches below heat source and preheat broiler. Meanwhile, prepare topping: in a food processor fitted with a steel blade, combine eggs, vinegar, mustard, lemon juice, chili sauce, Worcestershire sauce and Tabasco sauce. Process until smooth, then process 60 seconds longer. With machine running pour oil through feed tube in a slow, steady stream, processing to form a smooth emulsion. Spoon an equal portion of topping over each serving of crab and place under preheated broiler. Broil until lightly browned and bubbly (about 5 minutes). Sprinkle parsley over each serving; serve hot. Makes 4 to 6 servings.

Savannah Crab Cakes

Fried crab cakes are an excellent way to make a filling meal of the less expensive claw meat from blue crabs. Traditional for family suppers, the cakes are often served in restaurants on the Southeastern coast. The cakes may be prepared ahead of time and refrigerated, tightly covered. Batter and fry when ready to serve. Try them with Creole Mayonnaise Sauce, page 86.

> 1 pound claw crabmeat
> 2 (1-inch-thick) French bread slices
> 1 egg, beaten
> 1/2 cup whipping cream
> 1 hard-cooked egg, minced
> 4 green onions (including green tops), minced
> 2 teaspoons fresh lemon juice
> 2 teaspoons Worcestershire sauce
> 1 teaspoon Tabasco sauce
> 2 tablespoons unsalted butter or margarine, melted
> 1/2 teaspoon salt
> 1/2 teaspoon freshly ground black pepper
> Vegetable oil for frying
> 2 eggs beaten with 3/4 cup milk
> 2 cups fine dry bread crumbs

❦ Carefully pick through crabmeat and remove any bits of shell and cartilage; set aside. Tear bread slices into small pieces and place in a medium bowl. Add beaten egg and cream; stir to blend. Add hard-cooked egg, green onions, lemon juice, Worcestershire sauce, Tabasco sauce, melted butter or margarine, salt, black pepper and crabmeat. Mix well with your hands and form into 9 to 12 cakes, each about 3 inches in diameter. (At this point, you may cover and refrigerate cakes 4 to 5 hours.) Pour enough oil into a heavy 12-inch skillet to coat bottom of skillet. Heat oil over medium heat. Then dredge crab cakes in egg-milk mixture, coating both sides well; next, dredge in bread crumbs, coating both sides well. Shake off excess. Add cakes to hot oil, 5 or 6 at a time; cook, turning once, until golden brown on both sides (7 to 8 minutes). Serve hot. Makes 4 to 6 servings.

Crawfish-Stuffed Bell Peppers

Southerners love to stuff green bell peppers with various mixtures of meat, rice, bread and what-have-you. This spicy crawfish filling is a favorite in Louisiana. For a satisfying meal, serve the peppers with Butter Beans in Roux, page 105, and your favorite bread.

6 large green bell peppers
1/2 cup lard or vegetable oil
1/2 cup all-purpose flour
1 medium onion, finely chopped
1 small green bell pepper, finely chopped
2 medium garlic cloves, minced
6 green onions (including green tops), finely chopped
1/4 cup minced parsley, preferably flat-leaf
1/2 teaspoon dried leaf oregano
1/2 teaspoon dried leaf basil
1/2 teaspoon red (cayenne) pepper
1/2 teaspoon freshly ground black pepper
1/2 teaspoon salt
1 large tomato, peeled, minced
1 pound shelled cooked crawfish tails with fat, minced
1 cup Seafood Stock, page 39, or bottled clam juice
1-1/2 cups cooked white rice

❦ Cut off and discard tops of 6 large bell peppers. Carefully scoop out seeds and large veins. Plunge trimmed peppers into rapidly boiling water and parboil 3 minutes. Remove from water and drain in a colander; set aside. Preheat oven to 350F (175C). Heat lard or oil in a heavy 12-inch skillet over medium heat. When fat is hot, add flour all at once and whisk until smooth, then whisk constantly until a peanut butter-colored roux forms (20 to 25 minutes). Add onion, chopped bell pepper, garlic, green onions, parsley, oregano, basil, red pepper, black pepper and salt. Cook, stirring, until vegetables are slightly wilted and onion is transparent (about 5 minutes). Add tomato and crawfish; stir to incorporate, then cook 5 minutes. Add stock slowly, stirring to blend; cook 15 minutes. Remove skillet from heat and stir in rice, blending well. Trim bottoms of parboiled bell peppers, if necessary, so that they will sit flat without tipping over; then stuff peppers with crawfish mixture and set in a 13" x 9" baking dish. Bake in preheated oven 20 minutes. Serve hot. Makes 4 to 6 servings.

Florida-Style Broiled Stuffed Lobster Tails

Along the coast of the Florida panhandle and extending west to Mobile and the Biloxi-Gulfport area, it is the custom to split open the shells of small "chicken lobster" tails and spoon in a crabmeat dressing. The stuffed tails make a truly regal and filling meal that offers a wonderful taste experience; your taste buds are awakened by the sweet and spicy crabmeat dressing, then soothed by the buttery taste and firm, chewy texture of the lobster beneath.

> 4 (6- to 7-oz.) lobster tails
> 1/2 pound plain white crabmeat
> 2 eggs, beaten
> 1/2 cup evaporated milk
> 3 (1-inch-thick) French bread slices
> 1/4 cup unsalted butter or margarine
> 1 small onion, finely chopped
> 1 medium celery stalk, finely chopped
> 1/3 cup finely chopped green bell pepper
> 1 medium garlic clove, minced
> 1 teaspoon Worcestershire sauce
> 2 tablespoons dry sherry
> 1/2 teaspoon freshly ground black pepper
> 1/4 teaspoon red (cayenne) pepper
> Salt to taste
> 3 green onions (including green tops), minced
> 2 tablespoons minced parsley, preferably flat-leaf
> 3 tablespoons unsalted butter or margarine, melted
> 1/4 cup fine dry bread crumbs

❦ Using kitchen shears, split top shell of each lobster tail down the middle, from top of tail to the point where it joins end fins. Do not cut into lobster meat. Spread shell apart slightly. Set lobster tails aside. To prepare dressing, carefully pick through crabmeat and remove any bits of shell and cartilage. Set aside. In a medium bowl, whisk together eggs and evaporated milk, then add bread slices, pushing them down into liquid. Set aside. Melt 1/4 cup butter or margarine in a heavy 10-inch skillet over medium heat. Add onion, celery, bell pepper and garlic. Cook, stirring often, until onion is wilted and transparent (about 8 minutes). Add Worcestershire sauce, sherry, black pepper, red pepper, salt, green onions and parsley. Stir to blend. Add crabmeat and stir to blend. Using a large spoon, break up bread in egg mixture; then add to skillet, stirring to blend. Cook, stirring, until thickened (6 to 7 minutes). Remove from heat and set aside. Drizzle 3 tablespoons melted butter or margarine over split lobster tails. Place in a steamer and steam over boiling water 8 minutes. Meanwhile, position oven rack 6 inches below heat source and preheat broiler. Remove lobster tails from steamer and place on a baking sheet. Spoon 1/4 of crabmeat dressing into each shell, packing it down tightly and mounding it up toward the center, above level of shell. Sprinkle stuffed lobster tails evenly with bread crumbs. Place under preheated broiler; broil until lightly browned and bubbly (6 to 8 minutes). Serve hot. Makes 4 servings.

Conch Ceviche

Conch is a tasty shellfish eaten primarily in South Florida. Because the flesh is quite tough, it is usually minced or ground before cooking. Serve this spicy dish as a first course or luncheon entree.

> **1 pound conch meat, minced**
> **1-1/2 cups fresh lime juice (about 9 large limes)**
> **1 teaspoon Worcestershire sauce**
> **1 bay leaf**
> **1 teaspoon dried leaf oregano**
> **1 pickled jalapeño chile, seeded, minced**
> **1/2 teaspoon salt**
> **1 teaspoon celery salt**
> **1/2 teaspoon freshly ground black pepper**
> **1 teaspoon Tabasco sauce**
> **1 tablespoon minced parsley, preferably flat-leaf**
> **1 small onion, diced**
> **1 large ripe tomato, seeded, diced**
> **1/3 cup minced pitted unstuffed green olives**
> **1 large garlic clove, minced**
> **1 tablespoon minced capers**
> **1 large celery stalk, diced**
> **1/3 cup diced pimentos**
> **Red-leaf lettuce leaves**
> **Curly-leaf parsley sprigs and cucumber rounds**

❡ Spread conch in bottom of a non-metal 8-inch-square baking dish. In a medium bowl, combine lime juice, Worcestershire sauce, bay leaf, oregano, chile, salt, celery salt, pepper, Tabasco sauce, minced parsley, onion, tomato, olives, garlic, capers, celery and pimentos. Blend well. Pour mixture over conch; stir to combine. Cover with plastic wrap and refrigerate 48 hours before serving. Discard bay leaf. To serve, drain liquid from dish and spoon ceviche onto lettuce leaves. Garnish with parsley sprigs and cucumber rounds. Makes 4 to 6 servings.

Artichokes Rockefeller

Deemed so very rich it could only be named Rockefeller, Oysters Rockefeller originated at New Orleans's famed Antoine's Restaurant around the turn of the century. This interesting variation on the original may become a classic in your culinary repertoire.

24 medium canned artichoke bottoms, drained
24 medium shucked oysters
1 (10-oz.) package frozen chopped spinach, thawed
6 tablespoons unsalted butter or margarine
1 bunch watercress, finely chopped
1/4 cup minced parsley, preferably flat-leaf
6 green onions (including green tops), minced
1 tablespoon minced green bell pepper
2 tablespoons minced celery
1/2 teaspoon freshly ground black pepper
1/2 teaspoon dried leaf marjoram
1/2 teaspoon dried leaf basil
Salt to taste
1/2 teaspoon Tabasco sauce
1 tablespoon Herbsaint or Pernod
2/3 cup whipping cream
5 bacon slices, crisp-cooked, minced
Topping, see below

Topping:
1/3 cup grated Parmesan cheese (about 1 oz.)
1/4 cup fine dry bread crumbs
1/2 teaspoon paprika
1/4 teaspoon salt

❦ Place artichoke bottoms on a baking sheet. Pat oysters dry and place one in each artichoke bottom. Preheat oven to 400F (205C). Meanwhile, prepare filling: place spinach in a strainer and press firmly to squeeze out all moisture; set aside. Melt butter or margarine in a heavy 12-inch skillet over medium heat. Add drained spinach, watercress, parsley, green onions, bell pepper and celery; cook, stirring, until vegetables are slightly wilted (about 5 minutes). Stir in black pepper, marjoram, basil, salt, Tabasco sauce, Herbsaint or Pernod, cream and bacon. Cook, stirring often, until mixture is thick and creamy (about 10 minutes). Divide mixture equally among artichoke bottoms, placing an even layer over each oyster. Prepare topping; spoon over filled artichoke bottoms. Bake in preheated oven until lightly browned and bubbly on top (about 15 minutes). Makes 24 appetizers.
Topping: In a small bowl, toss all ingredients together until blended.

Oysters Evangeline

Fresh herbs and oysters got together a long time ago in the Deep South, and they have been very happy over the years. The harmony of flavors is truly outstanding—as exemplified in this dish by the subtle taste of fresh sage and oysters in a cream sauce.

24 medium oysters in shells
1/4 cup sausage drippings (preferably) or bacon drippings
1/2 cup finely chopped green onions (including green tops)
6 tablespoons all-purpose flour
1/2 cup whipping cream
1/2 teaspoon salt
1/4 teaspoon freshly ground black pepper
1/2 teaspoon red (cayenne) pepper
2 tablespoons minced parsley, preferably flat-leaf
1 heaping tablespoon minced fresh sage or 1 teaspoon dried rubbed sage
1/2 pint (1 cup) dairy sour cream
2 teaspoons Worcestershire sauce
1/4 cup dry white wine
Rock salt
3/4 cup fresh bread crumbs
1/4 cup grated Parmesan cheese (about 3/4 oz.)

❦ Shuck oysters; drain well, reserving 1/2 cup liquor. Scrub and reserve 24 half shells. Melt sausage or bacon drippings in a heavy 10-inch skillet over medium heat; add green onions and cook just until slightly transparent (3 to 4 minutes). Add flour all at once and blend, then cook, stirring, 3 to 4 minutes. Slowly stir in whipping cream, blending to make a smooth paste. Add salt, black pepper, red pepper, parsley, sage and reserved oyster liquor, stirring to blend. Cook 5 minutes longer, whisking constantly. Stir in sour cream, Worcestershire sauce and wine; cook just until heated through. Taste and adjust seasonings. Preheat oven to 400F (205C). Line a 15" x 10" baking sheet with rock salt. Place oyster shells on rock salt, nesting each into salt to prevent tipping. Pat oysters very dry on paper towels and place 1 in each shell. Spoon some of sauce over top of each oyster. Combine bread crumbs and cheese; sprinkle over tops of oysters. Bake in preheated oven until a light golden crust forms on tops of oysters (10 to 15 minutes). Serve hot. Makes 24 servings.

Lennox's Ginger-Fried Oysters

This is one of the best-tasting, most innovative oyster dishes I have ever encountered, and I am delighted to share it. There's a story behind the recipe: When I taught a week-long cooking class on Cajun-Creole food at a large cooking school in Atlanta, Billy McKinnon and Lennox Gavin, owners of the city's two premier Cajun-Creole restaurants, were among the students. One day the class announced that they were going to cook dinner for me that night, with each person preparing his or her specialty. What a treat that meal was, with French wines and wonderful dishes ranging from Cuban to Chinese in origin! In view of the fact that I adore oysters, this splendid first course or entree was a particular favorite. Because the dish is so rich and filling, for an appetizer serve no more than two oysters per person.

1-1/2 cups dry sherry
1 cup good-quality soy sauce
1 heaping tablespoon grated gingerroot
Salt and freshly ground black pepper to taste
24 shucked oysters, drained well, patted dry
1-1/2 cups canned mixed party nuts, ground medium-fine
12 bacon slices
48 (2" x 2") pieces thinly sliced smoked ham
5 green onions (including green tops), cut into 2-inch lengths
Batter, see below
Vegetable oil for deep-frying
1/4 cup honey

Batter:
1 cup all-purpose flour
2 eggs
1-1/2 cups whipping cream

❦ In a bowl, combine sherry, soy sauce, gingerroot, salt and pepper; whisk to blend. Place oysters in a single layer in a shallow baking dish and pour sherry mixture over them. Refrigerate 1 hour; then drain oysters, reserving liquid. Dredge each oyster in ground mixed nuts, coating well. Cut each bacon slice in half and place a nut-coated oyster on each half-slice. Place 2 pieces of ham and a green onion piece on top of each oyster. Wrap bacon completely around oyster, ham and onion; secure with wooden picks. Refrigerate oysters while you prepare Batter. In a deep-sided 12-inch skillet, heat 2 inches of oil to 350F (175C) or until a 1-inch bread cube turns golden brown in 65 seconds. Dredge each bacon-wrapped oyster in Batter to coat lightly. Add oysters to hot oil about 3 at a time, being careful not to crowd pan. Deep-fry, turning once, until golden brown (about 5 minutes); take care to maintain correct oil temperature. Drain on paper towels. Add honey to reserved liquid to make a dipping sauce; whisk to blend. Place sauce in individual bowls and serve with oysters. Makes 4 to 6 servings.
Batter: In a medium bowl, combine flour, eggs and cream; whisk well to form a thin batter about the consistency of crepe batter.

Cornmeal-Fried Oysters with Tartar Sauce

In the Gulf South, fried oysters are an all-time favorite, typical of the region's "down-home" style of eating. The secret is a crunchy crispy outer crust, leaving a soft, almost liquid, oyster inside.

Tartar Sauce, see below
2 cups all-purpose flour
1 cup corn flour
1 cup yellow cornmeal, preferably stone-ground
2 teaspoons red (cayenne) pepper
2 teaspoons salt
2 teaspoons finely ground black pepper
2 teaspoons garlic powder
48 medium to large shucked oysters, drained well
Lard for deep-frying
4 eggs beaten with 3 cups milk

Tartar Sauce:
2 cups rich mayonnaise, preferably homemade, page 36
2/3 cup minced dill pickles
1/3 cup minced pimento-stuffed green olives
1 tablespoon minced capers
2 tablespoons minced green onion (including green tops)
1 teaspoon Tabasco sauce
1/2 teaspoon salt
1 teaspoon sugar
1 teaspoon finely ground black pepper
2 tablespoons fresh lemon juice

❖ Prepare Tartar Sauce and refrigerate. Place all-purpose flour in a medium bowl. In a separate bowl, combine corn flour, cornmeal, red pepper, salt, black pepper and garlic powder, tossing with a fork to blend. Pat oysters very dry on paper towels. In a heavy 12-inch skillet, heat 1-1/2 inches of melted lard to 365F (185C) or until a 1-inch bread cube turns golden brown in 60 seconds. Dredge each oyster in all-purpose flour, turning to coat well; shake off excess. Then dip in egg-milk mixture, covering well. Finally, coat each oyster with cornmeal mixture, coating well. Shake off excess. Add oysters to hot fat 8 to 10 at a time, depending on size; be careful not to crowd pan. Oysters should not touch each other while frying. Deep-fry, turning once, until golden brown on both sides (3 to 4 minutes); take care to maintain correct oil temperature. Drain fried oysters on paper towels. Serve hot, allowing 8 to 12 per serving. Pass Tartar Sauce separately. Makes 4 to 6 servings.
Tartar Sauce: In a medium bowl, combine all ingredients and whisk to blend. Cover and refrigerate until ready to serve.

Mesquite-Smoked Oysters

Grilling over mesquite is a popular trend in cooking, as suitable for seafood as it is for thick steaks or slabs of beef brisket. The rich, bold flavor of the smoke does subtle and wonderful things for oysters grilled "on the half-shell."

8 bacon slices
24 medium oysters in shells
24 well-scrubbed oyster shells
1/2 cup unsalted butter, melted
1/8 teaspoon liquid smoke
2 medium garlic cloves, minced
2 tablespoons minced green bell pepper
2 tablespoons minced peeled tomato
2 teaspoons fresh lemon juice
2 teaspoons Worcestershire sauce
1/2 teaspoon salt
1/2 teaspoon freshly ground black pepper

❦·Soak several mesquite wood chunks in water 1 hour. Prepare a charcoal fire in an outdoor cooker with a cover. When coals are evenly red and glowing, drain mesquite wood and add to fire. Position grill 6 inches above coals and cover. Position oven rack 4 inches below heat source and preheat broiler. Cut each bacon slice into 3 pieces and spread pieces on a baking sheet. Place baking sheet under preheated broiler and broil bacon slices until about 3/4 cooked (2 to 3 minutes). Remove and drain on paper towels; set aside. Shuck oysters; drain, reserving liquor. Pat oysters very dry on paper towels and place an oyster in each shell; set aside. In a heavy 2-quart saucepan, combine reserved oyster liquor with butter, liquid smoke, garlic, bell pepper, tomato, lemon juice, Worcestershire sauce, salt and black pepper. Stir to blend and cook over medium heat 10 minutes. Spoon about 1-1/2 tablespoons of butter sauce over each oyster and top with a piece of partially cooked bacon. Place oysters on grill, close cover and smoke until oysters curl at edges (about 10 minutes). Remove carefully, using tongs and taking care not to spill sauce. Serve hot. Makes 24 half-shell servings.

VEGETABLES & SIDE DISHES

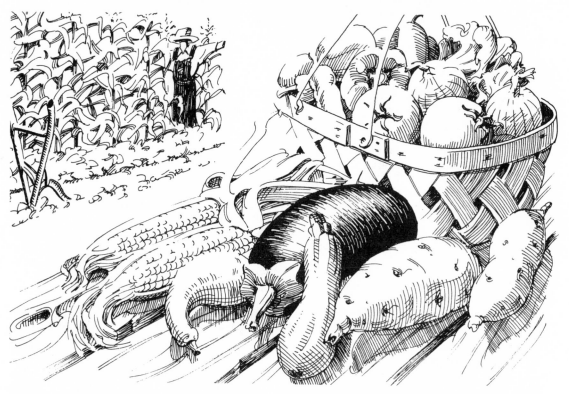

Even in today's nutrition-conscious world, any Southerner who is really telling the truth will admit that he or she prefers vegetables cooked the traditional way. Never mind bright color, crisp texture or maximum retention of vitamins and minerals—in the South, vegetables have always been cooked by methods which make them *taste* good. A Southern home cook's last consideration would be whether a finished dish is pleasing to the eye! Many vegetables go straight from the garden into a big pot of water or stock with a bit of seasoning meat, maybe an onion or other aromatic vegetable, salt, pepper and perhaps a little ground red pepper or a whole chili or two. Then the pot is placed on the back burner and left to bubble merrily away for hours. Admittedly, the vegetable has lost much of its color and eye appeal and certainly all of its crunch by the time it is declared to be done,

but ah, what it lacks in style is more than compensated for in taste. The rich and flavorful broth, known as "pot likker," now contains most of the nutrients and is an integral part of the dish. Plenty of pot likker is spooned over the vegetable in each individual serving bowl—and traditionally, drunk straight from the bowl once the vegetable has been eaten.

Southerners enjoy home gardening, and in many regions, the growing season lasts almost all year round. Most of us still favor the same vegetables that have been grown in the South for as long as 250 years, though many of them (kohlrabi and turnips, for example) are considered odd or out of vogue in the rest of the country. In the Old South, practical considerations dictated the choice of vegetables: the most frequently grown varieties were those which kept well or could be dried. Delicate vegetables such as summer squash were pickled or enjoyed fresh in season.

One major Southern root vegetable of great versatility is the sweet potato, first cultivated in this country in Virginia, perhaps as early as 1610. The sweet potato's skin ranges from orange-red to yellowish-white; its flesh is orange or yellow. The red-skinned, orange-fleshed type is often mistakenly referred to as a yam, but true yams have brown, barklike skin, white or very light yellow flesh and an impressive size—from 2 to 8 pounds each! These hefty tubers offer little more than calories and starch, while the sweet potato beloved of Southerners is an excellent source of vitamin A.

Along with other root vegetables—turnips, kohlrabi, russet potatoes, carrots, parsnips, rutabagas—sweet potatoes were stored in the ground in the Old South, in hay-lined pits dug about 4 feet deep (below the frost line). Once in the pit, the vegetables were topped with another layer of hay, then with dirt; finally, a layer of boards was fitted tightly into the lip of the pit as protection from rain and snow. In more affluent households, these vegetables were stored in more sophisticated "root cellars" beneath the house.

In the early South, vegetables were not canned as we know the process today, since the Mason-type jar and seal were not developed until the late 1800s. Instead, most soft and delicate vegetables were stored in a potent vinegar-sugar solution in tightly corked stoneware crocks. If the vegetables started to mold, the moldy portion was simply spooned off; the remainder was re-boiled in fresh vinegar solution and repacked. It's interesting to note that in those days, even the vinegar had to be made from scratch—usually from apple peels and cores, the flesh having been eaten fresh or dried for later use. The peels and cores were added to fresh rainwater collected in a wooden barrel, along with honey or molasses and a cup of last year's vinegar (the "mother") as a starter. The mixture was covered with a cloth and placed in the sun for several months to stew and bubble; eventually, the odoriferous ferment turned to vinegar.

Green pole beans were treated rather differently from other soft vegetables—they were dried, not pickled. The fresh beans were snapped into bite-size pieces, threaded onto lengths of cotton twine, hung in the sun until completely dry, and then stored in a dry place such as an attic (or perhaps hung from open kitchen rafters) and cooked as needed throughout the year. Pole beans thus treated are called "leather britches beans"; the taste is unique, and one receives a sort of pioneering thrill when tackling the drying process. If you wish to try it—and you won't be sorry if you do—be sure to bring the beans inside each evening (to protect them from dew) and whenever rains threaten. I have dried leather britches beans on screen wire racks rather than stringing them, but if you do this, take care to arrange the beans in a single layer with no overlap. It's also possible to dry the beans in a food dehydrator, but the sun really adds something to the flavor that no oven can replace.

When the beans are devoid of moisture and resemble little strips of very dark leather, then may be stored in jars with tight-fitting lids or in airtight plastic bags. To cook them, follow the recipe on page 106.

Notes on Cooking

Southerners use seasoning meats when cooking most green vegetables, peas and beans. The choice of meat is a regional option: in South Louisiana or Mississippi, it might be tasso or pickled pork; in the Deep South, salt pork, streak-o-lean or fatback; and in Virginia, Kentucky, Tennessee and parts of North Carolina, smoked ham hocks. The custom began in rural areas where vegetables were the dietary mainstay; cured or smoked meats were the only meat available, and even they could only be had in small amounts. Used as flavoring for a simmering pot of greens or beans, a little bit of meat could go a long way—and add body to an otherwise meager meal. Over the years, the complex flavor contributed by seasoning meats just became part of the way certain vegetables were supposed to taste, and modern Southerners will defend their methods to the last bean.

You will notice that many of the recipes in this chapter call for small amounts of sugar. Southern cooks discovered long ago that sugar is a natural flavor enhancer; it does something magical to the taste of vegetable dishes which makes them much more appealing to children (and to be honest, to grown-ups too).

Butter Beans with Roux

Practically everything in South Louisiana is cooked in a roux—often even vegetables. The Cajuns love the thick gravy that results when butter beans (lima beans) are cooked down in roux. In lean times or just when the mood strikes, this dish is served in large soup plates as the main course, accompanied by hot, crumbly corn bread.

1/2 cup lard or solid vegetable shortening
1/2 cup all-purpose flour
1 medium onion, chopped
2-1/2 cups Brown Stock, page 38, or canned beef broth
6 ounces smoked ham, cut into small dice
4 cups fresh butter beans or 1 (20-oz.) package frozen butter beans
Salt to taste
1 teaspoon freshly ground black pepper
1/2 teaspoon Tabasco sauce

❦ Melt lard or shortening in a heavy skillet over medium heat. Add flour all at once and whisk until smooth; then whisk constantly until a peanut butter-colored roux forms (20 to 25 minutes). Add onion and cook, stirring often, until slightly wilted and transparent (about 8 minutes). Meanwhile, bring stock to a full boil in a 6-quart pot. Add ham, beans, salt, pepper and Tabasco sauce to roux mixture and stir to blend. Stir onion-roux mixture into boiling stock, a heaping spoonful at a time. Reduce heat, cover and simmer until a thick gravy forms and beans are very soft (45 minutes). Stir often. Makes 4 to 6 servings.

Smothered Southern Green Beans

Green beans cooked down (smothered) in the old Southern manner are hard to beat for taste. When the beans are gone you have a *lagniappe*—a little something extra—the flavorful broth left at the bottom of the bowl. It is entirely permissible to drink the broth from your bowl—at least, in the South it is!

1-1/2 pounds fresh green pole beans, snapped into bite-size pieces
1/2 pound meaty smoked ham hocks
1 large onion, chopped
3 medium garlic cloves, minced
8 cups water
1 teaspoon finely ground black pepper
1 tablespoon sugar
Salt to taste

❦ Place all ingredients in a 6-quart saucepan. Bring to a boil, then reduce heat until water barely simmers. Cover and simmer about 2 hours; taste and adjust seasonings. Remove ham hocks from pan; chop meat and return to pan. Serve hot. Makes 4 to 6 servings.

Bell Pepper Casserole

Southern cooks manage to tuck bell peppers into just about everything—especially in Cajun-Creole regions where they belong to the culinary "holy trinity", which consists of celery, onions and bell peppers.

Red and green bell peppers are the same vegetable; if allowed to remain on the plant, green peppers will eventually turn red, acquiring their characteristically sweet taste in the process. This do-ahead dish uses the two colors together. Serve it with chicken or fish entrees.

> 6 tablespoons unsalted butter or margarine
> 2 large green bell peppers, halved lengthwise, sliced
> 2 large red bell peppers, halved lengthwise, sliced
> 2 medium onions, halved lengthwise, sliced
> 1 teaspoon salt
> 1/2 teaspoon freshly ground black pepper
> 1/2 teaspoon dried leaf basil
> 1/2 teaspoon dried leaf oregano
> 1 teaspoon sugar
> 1-1/2 cups Italian-seasoned fine dry bread crumbs
> 1/4 cup unsalted butter or margarine, melted
> 2 cups shredded sharp Cheddar cheese (8 oz.)
> 1-1/2 cups whipping cream

❧ Preheat oven to 350F (175C). Lightly butter a 13" x 9" baking dish and set aside. Melt 6 tablespoons butter or margarine in a heavy 12-inch skillet over medium heat. Add green and red bell peppers, onions, salt, black pepper, basil, oregano and sugar. Stir to blend, then cook until onions are slightly wilted and transparent (about 5 minutes). Remove from heat. Toss bread crumbs with 1/4 cup melted butter or margarine until well coated. Sprinkle half the buttered crumbs over bottom of buttered baking dish; spread bell pepper mixture evenly over crumbs. Sprinkle cheese over vegetables, then pour in cream. Top with remaining buttered bread crumbs, spreading evenly. Bake in preheated oven until golden brown and bubbly (about 35 minutes). Serve hot. Makes 6 to 8 servings.

Leather Britches Beans

Dried green pole beans, also known as "shuck beans," are still preferred over fresh beans in many rural mountain regions of the South. Before canning jars were readily available, sun-drying was the simplest way to preserve the crop for the winter. When simmered slowly with bacon and broth, the dried beans are quite delicious, and we may indeed have lost a unique taste when the Mason jar arrived on the scene. If you'ld like to experience the flavor, turn to page 104 for drying instructions.

2-1/2 cups dried green pole beans, see page 104
8 cups cold water
6 to 8 cups Brown Stock, page 38, or canned beef broth
1/4 pound smoked slab bacon, rind removed, diced
1 teaspoon freshly ground black pepper
1 teaspoon sugar
Salt

❧ Place beans in a large bowl, pour in cold water and let soak overnight. Drain beans and transfer to a heavy 6-quart pot. Add stock, bacon, pepper, sugar and salt; bring to a rapid boil. Reduce heat so liquid barely simmers, cover and cook 3 hours, adding more stock if necessary. Beans should be very soft. Taste and adjust seasonings, especially salt. Serve hot. Makes 6 to 8 servings.

Charleston Rice & Bell Pepper Casserole

A quick and simple vegetable dish to grace any meal, this is a variation of the classic "Spanish rice" of Charleston, South Carolina—though it bears no resemblance to the Spanish rice served in other areas of the South! That may be confusing, but the dish certainly is not; it's easily prepared ahead and can be baked just before serving.

1/3 cup vegetable oil
2 large green bell peppers, chopped
6 green onions (including tops), chopped
3 medium garlic cloves, minced
6 ounces smoked ham, minced
1/2 cup sliced almonds
1 (16-oz.) can stewed tomatoes
1/2 cup fine dry bread crumbs
2 tablespoons minced parsley, preferably flat-leaf
1 teaspoon salt
1/2 teaspoon freshly ground black pepper
1 teaspoon dried leaf basil
2 tablespoons picante sauce, preferably Tabasco brand
4 cups cooked white rice

❧ Preheat oven to 350F (175C). Lightly grease a 3-quart casserole and set aside. Heat oil in a heavy 12-inch skillet over medium heat. Add bell peppers, green onions, garlic and ham; cook until vegetables are slightly wilted and white part of onions is transparent (about 5 minutes). Add almonds and cook until lightly browned (about 5 minutes). Drain tomatoes, reserving liquid; chop tomatoes and stir into skillet along with reserved liquid. Remove from heat and fold in bread crumbs, parsley, salt, black pepper, basil and picante sauce. Stir in rice and blend. Turn mixture into greased casserole and bake in preheated oven 25 minutes. Serve hot. Makes 6 to 8 servings.

Fried & Braised Cabbage with Country Ham

Many varieties of cabbage grow prolifically in the South. Cabbage has long been popular, cooked or used raw in salads and slaws. This hearty country dish provides a filling, nutritious meal that is easy on the budget.

1/3 cup bacon drippings or lard
1 pound country ham steak, cut into bite-size pieces
2 medium russet potatoes (about 1 lb. *total*), unpeeled, diced
1 small head green cabbage (about 1-1/2 lbs.)
1/4 cup apple cider vinegar
1 cup Brown Stock, page 38, or canned beef broth
1 teaspoon Creole mustard or other whole-grain mustard
1 tablespoon firmly packed light brown sugar
1 teaspoon freshly ground black pepper
Salt to taste

❦ Melt bacon drippings in a deep-sided 12-inch skillet over medium heat. Add ham and potatoes and cook, stirring often, until lightly browned (about 10 minutes). Cut cabbage into quarters and remove core from each, then cut each quarter crosswise into 1/2-inch slices. Add cabbage to skillet and stir to combine well; cook, stirring often, until cabbage is wilted (about 10 minutes). Add vinegar, stock, mustard, brown sugar, pepper and salt. Stir to blend, cover skillet and cook, stirring occasionally, until cabbage is very soft and potatoes have broken apart (about 45 minutes). Serve hot. Makes 4 to 6 servings.

Eggplant Soufflé

In this recipe adapted from the innovative "concoction" of an old New Orleans family's beloved house cook, the lowly eggplant is fancified into a dish fit for the finest company dinner.

> 1 large eggplant (about 1-1/4 lbs.)
> 6 ounces ground smoked ham
> 1/2 cup unsalted butter or margarine
> 1 medium onion, finely chopped
> 1 small green bell pepper, finely chopped
> 2 large garlic cloves, minced
> 2 tablespoons minced parsley, preferably flat-leaf
> 1/2 teaspoon dried leaf oregano
> 1/2 teaspoon dried leaf basil
> 1/4 teaspoon red (cayenne) pepper
> 1/2 teaspoon freshly ground black pepper
> Salt to taste
> 1/2 cup all-purpose flour
> 1 pint (2 cups) half and half, heated slightly
> Fine dry bread crumbs
> 4 eggs, room temperature, separated
> 1 teaspoon baking powder

❦ Preheat oven to 400F (205C). Prick eggplant all over with a fork and place in a small baking dish. Bake in preheated oven until skin is blistered and flesh is very tender (about 45 minutes). Remove from oven and set aside until cool enough to handle; then scoop all pulp out of the skin. Discard skin; press pulp through a strainer or puree in a food processor fitted with the steel blade. Reduce oven temperature to 375F (190C) and place oven rack in lowest position. In a large bowl, combine ham and eggplant puree; set aside. Melt 1/2 cup butter or margarine in a heavy 12-inch skillet over medium heat. Add onion, bell pepper, garlic, parsley, oregano, basil, red pepper, black pepper and salt; stir to blend and cook until vegetables are very wilted and onion is transparent (about 10 minutes). Add flour all at once and stir to blend; cook, stirring, 2 to 3 minutes. Slowly add half and half, stirring constantly, and cook until mixture is thickened (about 5 minutes). Remove from heat and set aside until slightly cooled. Meanwhile, thoroughly butter sides of a deep 2-quart soufflé dish or round casserole dish and sprinkle with bread crumbs; shake out excess crumbs. Make a parchment paper collar to fit around dish, allowing top of collar to extend at least 6 inches above rim of dish. Thoroughly butter inside portion of collar that will extend above dish; sprinkle with bread crumbs and shake off excess. Tie prepared collar around dish with twine and set aside. Combine onion mixture with eggplant mixture, stirring to blend. Beat in egg yolks. In a large, very clean (grease-free) bowl, beat egg whites until frothy. Add baking powder and continue to beat at medium speed until whites hold medium-stiff peaks (3 to 4 minutes). Spoon a large dollop of beaten whites onto eggplant mixture and gently fold together. Then add eggplant mixture to remaining whites and fold together gently but thoroughly. Turn out mixture into prepared soufflé dish and immediately place in preheated oven. Bake until mixture has risen and is golden brown on top (about 45 minutes). Remove from oven and carefully peel away paper collar. Serve immediately. Makes 4 to 6 servings.

Mess o' Greens with Cornmeal Dodgers

It is customary to serve greens, with small bits of the seasoning meat, in large soup plates with plenty of their cooking liquid, known as "pot likker," spooned over the top. The dodgers—heavy cornmeal dumplings—are spooned into the likker to make a complete meal. When dumplings and greens have been eaten, just pick up the bowl and drink the pot likker, a flavorful treasure too precious to waste!

1 bunch turnip greens, thoroughly washed
1 bunch collard greens, thoroughly washed
1 bunch mustard greens, thoroughly washed
1 large onion, halved lengthwise, sliced
1/2 pound smoked ham, cut into bite-size pieces
2 teaspoons freshly ground black pepper
2 teaspoons sugar
Salt and Tabasco sauce to taste
Cornmeal Dodgers, see below

Cornmeal Dodgers:
1/2 cup all-purpose flour
1-1/2 teaspoons baking powder
2 teaspoons sugar
1 teaspoon salt
1-1/2 cups white cornmeal, preferably stone-ground
3 tablespoons bacon drippings or vegetable oil
1 egg, beaten
1 cup pot likker from greens

❦ Make sure leaves of all greens are washed thoroughly; no grit should remain. Remove fibrous stems and midribs and tear leaves into a heavy 8-quart pot. Place onion, ham, pepper, sugar, salt and Tabasco sauce in pot, then add enough cold water to cover greens completely. Bring to a full boil over medium-high heat, stirring occasionally. Reduce heat so liquid barely simmers, cover and cook 2 hours. Prepare Cornmeal Dodgers; spoon batter by rounded tablespoons into simmering pot likker. Cover pot and simmer until dodgers are firm to the touch and cooked through (about 35 minutes longer). Taste greens and adjust seasonings, especially salt. Serve hot with Cornmeal Dodgers. Makes 6 to 8 servings.
Cornmeal Dodgers: Sift flour, baking powder, sugar and salt into a medium bowl. Add cornmeal and toss with a fork to blend. Add bacon drippings or oil, egg and pot likker; stir until all ingredients are moistened.

Baked Hominy Casserole

Hominy is generally regarded to be the first corn-based dish the colonists learned from the native Algonquin Indians. In the early days, preparing it was a time-consuming task. First the corn was shucked and the irksome silk removed, then the kernels were removed from the cobs and scalded with water and lye or wood ash to remove the outer hull. Next the kernels were sun-dried, then boiled again to produce a soft and puffy kernel.

> **About 1/4 cup unsalted butter or margarine**
> **1/3 cup chopped green bell pepper**
> **1/3 cup chopped red bell pepper**
> **4 green onions, chopped**
> **1 (15-oz.) can whole yellow or white hominy, drained**
> **1 (8-oz.) can cream-style corn**
> **1 tablespoon sugar**
> **1 teaspoon salt**
> **1/4 teaspoon Tabasco sauce**
> **1/2 teaspoon freshly ground black pepper**
> **5 eggs, beaten until frothy**
> **3/4 cup milk**
> **3/4 cup whipping cream**
> **1 tablespoon cornstarch mixed with 1 tablespoon cold water**

❦ Preheat oven to 350F (175C). Butter a 13″ x 9″ baking dish; set aside. Melt butter in a heavy 10-inch skillet over medium heat. Add green and red bell pepper and green onions. Cook until vegetables are slightly wilted (about 5 minutes). Set aside. In a medium-sized bowl, combine hominy, corn, sugar, salt, Tabasco sauce, black pepper, eggs, milk, cream and cornstarch mixture. Stir to blend. Add bell pepper mixture; stir well. Pour mixture into buttered baking dish and bake in preheated oven until custard is firm and a knife inserted in center comes out clean (about 1 hour). Serve hot. Makes 6 to 8 servings.

Kale with Kohlrabi & Smoked Hog Jowl

Whether curly or smooth-leafed, kale is a popular winter vegetable in the South. It is usually boiled with some sort of seasoning meat—smoked hog jowl, in this popular example of soul food. Serve with Skillet Corn Bread, page 132, and butter for some "good eatin'." Kohlrabi, pronounced *kahl-uh-RA-bee* in the South, is a turniplike root vegetable with a more delicate flavor than the turnip. Though generally boiled, the firm bulb is sometimes grated into slaw-type salads.

> 1 large bunch kale (about 14 oz.), thoroughly washed
> 2 medium kohlrabi (about 3/4 lb. *total*), trimmed, peeled, diced
> 6 green onions (including tops), chopped
> 6 ounces smoked hog jowl, rind removed, diced
> 2 teaspoons sugar
> 1 teaspoon freshly ground black pepper
> Salt to taste

❦ Discard fibrous stems and midribs from kale; tear leaves into a heavy 6-quart pot. Add kohlrabi, green onions, hog jowl, sugar, pepper and salt. Then add enough cold water to cover greens by 2 inches. Bring to a full boil over medium heat, stirring occasionally. Reduce heat so liquid barely simmers; cover and simmer until greens are thoroughly cooked and kohlrabi is very tender (about 2-1/2 hours). Taste and adjust seasonings, especially salt. Serve in soup plates, taking care to add some of the meat and kohlrabi to each serving. Makes 6 to 8 servings.

Fried Apples with Onions

This quick and tasty side dish is a great accompaniment to roast pork or ham.

> 3 medium Granny Smith apples (about 1-1/4 lbs. *total*), peeled, cored, halved
> 2 tablespoons unsalted butter or margarine
> 1/3 cup vegetable oil
> 1 large onion, halved lengthwise, thinly sliced

❦ Cut apple halves into 1/4-inch-thick slices and set aside. Melt butter or margarine in a heavy 12-inch skillet over medium heat, then add oil. When butter-oil mixture is hot, add onion and cook, stirring often, until wilted and transparent (about 10 minutes). Add apples and stir to blend. Cook until apples are lightly browned and tender (about 10 minutes). Serve hot. Makes 4 to 6 servings.

Glazed Onions

Southerners eat onions raw, cooked into soups and stews, grated on the tops of casseroles and in any other way they can think of. These small onions coated with a rich, mahogany-colored glaze go well with simple meat entrees.

1-1/2 pounds small white boiling onions, each no more than 1 inch in diameter
2 tablespoons unsalted butter or margarine
1/2 cup vegetable oil
1/2 teaspoon salt
1/2 teaspoon freshly ground black pepper
2 tablespoons firmly packed light brown sugar
2/3 cup Brown Stock, page 38, or canned beef broth

❦ Using a sharp knife, cut root end from each unpeeled onion; set onions aside. Half-fill a 4- to 6-quart saucepan with water and bring to a rapid boil over medium-high heat. Add onions and parboil 1 minute. Drain in a colander; place under cold running water to cool quickly. When onions are cool enough to handle, peel them: grasp each at the stem and between your thumb and forefinger and squeeze lightly. The outer peel should slip off easily. Discard peels. Melt butter or margarine in a heavy 12-inch skillet over medium heat; add oil. When butter-oil mixture is hot, add onions, salt and pepper. Cook gently, shaking the skillet back and forth often, until onions are tender and evenly browned (about 15 minutes). Meanwhile bring stock to a boil in a medium saucepan. Reduce heat to low and sprinkle brown sugar over onions; stir gently to blend. Cook, shaking skillet constantly, until sugar turns deep brown (3 to 4 minutes). Add boiling stock and stir to blend with sugar syrup. Increase heat to medium-high and cook, shaking skillet, until liquid is reduced to a thick glaze (6 to 7 minutes). Serve hot. Makes 4 to 6 servings.

Purple-Hull Peas with Pickled Pork

Two very Southern foods are combined in this very traditional Southern vegetable dish. The tasty purple-hull pea, named for its vivid purple pod, grows throughout the Deep South. Pickled pork is made from fatty cuts of the hog, which are marinated in a brine solution for about two weeks. It is widely used as a seasoning meat in Louisiana and Mississippi, where it's often called simply "pickled meat." This homey dish is typically served in small bowls with plenty of the cooking liquid. Like most pea and bean dishes in the South, it's usually accompanied with corn bread.

      4 cups shelled purple-hull, black-eyed or crowder peas
      6 ounces pickled pork, salt pork or smoked slab bacon (rind removed), diced
      1 large russet potato, peeled, cut into small dice
      1 medium bell pepper, chopped
      1 medium onion, chopped
      1 teaspoon Worcestershire sauce
      2 tablespoons picante sauce, preferably Tabasco brand
      2 tablespoons minced parsley, preferably flat-leaf
      1 teaspoon freshly ground black pepper
      2 cups Brown Stock, page 38, or canned beef broth
      5 cups water
      Salt to taste

❦ Combine all ingredients in a heavy 4-quart saucepan. Bring to a boil over medium-high heat; skim gray foam from surface. Reduce heat so liquid barely simmers, cover and cook until peas are tender and potato has broken down to thicken the cooking liquid (1-1/2 to 2 hours). Taste and adjust seasonings. Serve hot. Makes 6 to 8 servings.

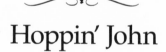

Hoppin' John

No one seems to know how this traditional Southern dish acquired its strange name, though we do know that it first appeared in the Gullah Low Country region of South Carolina. The black-eyed pea, one of its main ingredients, came to the American South with Nigerian slaves, who prepared a similar dish in their homeland. Southern tradition dictates that Hoppin' John must be served on New Year's Day to ensure good luck during the coming year.

2/3 cup bacon drippings or lard
1 large onion, chopped
1 medium green bell pepper, chopped
2 medium garlic cloves, minced
1/4 pound tasso, see page 50, or smoked ham, cut into bite-size pieces
1 (15-oz.) can black-eyed peas, drained well
2 cups uncooked long-grain white rice
1 large tomato, peeled, chopped
2 tablespoons minced parsley, preferably flat-leaf
2-3/4 cups Brown Stock, page 38, or canned beef broth
1 bay leaf
1 teaspoon freshly ground black pepper
1/4 teaspoon red (cayenne) pepper
Salt to taste
4 green onions (including tops), chopped

❦ Melt bacon drippings or lard in a heavy 6-quart saucepan over medium heat. Add onion, bell pepper and garlic. Cook until vegetables are slightly wilted and transparent (about 5 minutes). Add tasso or ham and cook until lightly browned (about 8 minutes). Stir in black-eyed peas. Add rice and cook, stirring gently, until rice is light golden brown (about 5 minutes). Add tomato and parsley and stir to blend; cook 5 minutes. Add stock, bay leaf, black pepper, red pepper and salt. Stir to blend, cover and cook until rice is tender and all liquid is absorbed (about 45 minutes). Add green onions and stir to blend. Cover and cook 5 minutes longer. Discard bay leaf. Serve hot. Makes 6 to 8 servings.

Boiled Poke

Poke, a delicate and delicious vegetable, comes from the pokeberry plant. Poke is grown in many areas of the rural South, where it is called "poke sallet." The thick, white roots and woody purple stalk of the mature pokeberry plant are poisonous, but the sprouts, best gathered when about 6 to 8 inches long, are a succulent treat. The tender green stalks resemble asparagus and are often referred to as "poke asparagus." The season runs from late March into April when it can be found in those fascinating back-road country markets, or gathered in fields. Poke is available canned in some regions of the South. Thicker sprouts are often rolled in cornmeal and fried; thin sprouts are boiled or steamed like asparagus.

1 pound young poke sprouts, 6 to 8 inches long
7 cups water
1/4 cup unsalted butter or margarine
1 teaspoon salt
1/4 teaspoon freshly ground black pepper

❦ Wash poke sprouts and cut them into equal lengths, leaving leaf cluster at top of each sprout. Bring 6 cups water to a full boil in a 3-quart saucepan. Add sprouts, reduce heat, cover and simmer 10 minutes. Drain poke and return to pan. Add remaining 1 cup water, butter, salt and pepper. Cover and cook at a bare simmer until sprouts are very tender and water has evaporated (about 25 minutes). Serve hot. Makes 4 to 6 servings.

Fried Plantain Patties

The plantain is yet another food introduced to the South from Africa and the Caribbean. Though related to the common dessert banana, it is larger, considerably lower in sugar and higher in starch, and unsuitable for eating raw. Cooked in a variety of ways, plantains are typically served as a vegetable side dish; these tasty patties are superb with roasted meats. Be sure to use very ripe plantains, because green ones are rock hard.

> **1 large very ripe plantain (about 14 oz.)**
> **Vegetable oil for deep-frying**
> **2 tablespoons powdered sugar**
> **1 teaspoon ground cinnamon**
> **1/4 cup unsalted butter**

❦ Peel plantain and cut it crosswise into 4 lengths, each about 2 inches long. In a deep-sided 12-inch skillet, heat 2 inches of oil to 365F (185C) or until a 1-inch bread cube turns golden brown in 60 seconds. Add plantain pieces and deep-fry until dark golden brown (3 to 4 minutes). Drain on paper towels and set aside until cool enough to handle. Combine powdered sugar and cinnamon, tossing with a fork to blend; set aside. Using a flat-surfaced meat mallet or the bottom of a drinking glass, smash each fried plantain piece into a round pattie. Melt butter in a heavy 10-inch skillet over medium heat. Add patties and cook, turning once, until golden brown on both sides (about 7 minutes). Remove and sprinkle with sugar-cinnamon mixture. Serve hot. Makes 4 servings.

Spinach & Artichoke Rice

When you are frantically searching your files for a delicious but quick side dish, look no further than this recipe. Guaranteed to win you compliments, it's made with two favorite Southern vegetables—spinach and marinated artichoke hearts—and it adds the perfect touch to any meal.

> **1/2 cup unsalted butter or margarine**
> **1 medium onion, chopped**
> **1 (10-oz.) package frozen chopped spinach, thawed, all moisture squeezed out**
> **1 (6-oz.) jar marinated artichoke hearts, drained, chopped**
> **4 green onions (including tops), chopped**
> **2 tablespoons minced parsley, preferably flat-leaf**
> **1/4 teaspoon red (cayenne) pepper**
> **1 teaspoon freshly ground black pepper**
> **1-1/2 teaspoons grated gingerroot**
> **Salt to taste**
> **3 cups cooked white rice**
> **1/3 cup dry sherry**

Melt butter or margarine in a deep-sided 12-inch skillet over medium heat. Add onion; cook until slightly wilted and transparent (about 5 minutes). Add spinach, artichoke hearts, green onions, parsley, red pepper, black pepper, gingerroot and salt. Cook, stirring, 5 minutes. Add rice and stir to blend. Stir in sherry and cook until bubbly and heated through (about 10 minutes). Remove from heat and spoon into a serving dish. Makes 4 to 6 servings.

The Best Sweet Potato Casserole

A dear woman by the name of Alama Smith shared this recipe with me. This lady's cooking has been described as the stuff of Southern legends, and I would be the first to agree with that assessment. When my husband's mother passed away, Mrs. Smith prepared copious amounts of food for the family. After the appropriate thank-you notes were written, the grandsons added a postscript to Alama's: it read simply, "Send more fudge!"

Mrs. Smith's wonderful casserole may be prepared ahead and baked just before serving; it tastes even better the next day.

> 4 large sweet potatoes (about 3 lbs. *total*), peeled, cooked, hot
> 1 cup unsalted butter or margarine, room temperature
> 1 cup sugar
> 4 eggs
> 2/3 cup evaporated milk
> 2 teaspoons vanilla extract
> Topping, see below
>
> *Topping:*
> 2 cups firmly packed light brown sugar
> 2/3 cup unsalted butter or margarine, room temperature
> 2/3 cup all-purpose flour
> 2 cups chopped pecans

❦ Preheat oven to 375F (190C). Lightly butter a deep-sided 13" x 9" baking dish; set aside. In a large bowl, mash hot potatoes thoroughly. Add butter or margarine, sugar, eggs, evaporated milk and vanilla. Beat with an electric mixer at medium speed until blended and smooth (3 to 4 minutes). Spoon mixture into buttered baking dish. Prepare Topping and spread over potato mixture. Bake in preheated oven until set and lightly browned on top (about 35 minutes). Makes 6 to 8 servings.
Topping: In a bowl, beat together brown sugar, butter or margarine and flour until smooth and fluffy. Fold in pecans.

Sautéed Sweet Potatoes with Apples

Sweet potatoes, a staple vegetable in the South, are extremely versatile. This is yet another delicious dish built around the humble tuber. Serve with pork chops or roast pork.

> 3 medium sweet potatoes (about 1-1/2 lbs. *total*), peeled, quartered
> 1/4 cup unsalted butter or margarine
> 3 medium apples (about 1-1/4 lbs. *total*), peeled, cored, cut into 1/4-inch cubes
> 1/2 teaspoon salt
> 4 teaspoons sugar
> 1 teaspoon ground cinnamon

❧ Place quartered sweet potatoes in a heavy 4-quart saucepan and add enough cold water to cover. Bring to a boil over medium-high heat. Reduce heat, cover and simmer until potatoes are tender (about 20 minutes). Drain potatoes and cool slightly, then cut each quarter crosswise into slices about 1/4 inch thick. Melt butter or margarine in a heavy 12-inch skillet over medium heat. Add potatoes and apples; cook, stirring often, until potatoes are browned (about 20 minutes). Sprinkle with salt, sugar and cinnamon; cook until potatoes and apples are lightly glazed (7 to 8 minutes longer), stirring often. Serve hot. Makes 4 to 6 servings.

Creamed Crookneck Squash

Summer squash of all kinds is highly favored in the South, and great quantities are grown to be served fresh. The delicate-flavored vegetable is pureed into soup, battered and deep-fried, lightly sautéed in butter, eaten raw in salad or as a crudité, stuffed and of course, baked in casseroles like this favorite dish. Even the squash blossoms are battered and fried, an old Southern trick that has recently come into fashion in modern American cuisine.

> 6 large yellow crookneck squash (about 2 lbs. *total*)
> 8 cups water
> 3 tablespoons unsalted butter or margarine
> 1 small onion, chopped
> 1/2 teaspoon pureed garlic
> 2/3 cup whipping cream
> 1/4 teaspoon Tabasco sauce
> 1/2 teaspoon dried leaf oregano
> 1 teaspoon salt
> 1/2 teaspoon freshly ground black pepper
> 2 eggs, beaten
> 1/2 cup fine dry bread crumbs
> 1/4 cup grated Parmesan cheese (about 3/4 oz.)

❦ Grease an 8-inch-square baking dish. Preheat oven to 350F (175C). Trim and discard stalk ends from squash. Bring water to a full boil in a heavy 6-quart pot. Add whole squash; reduce heat, cover and simmer until squash are very soft (20 to 25 minutes). Drain squash thoroughly and place in a large bowl. Using a potato masher, mash squash until thoroughly broken up but still lumpy. Add butter, onion and garlic; blend until butter or margarine is melted. In a separate bowl, combine cream, Tabasco sauce, oregano, salt, pepper and eggs, whisking to blend. Stir egg mixture into squash, combining well. Pour mixture into greased baking dish. Combine bread crumbs and cheese; sprinkle over squash mixture and bake in preheated oven until golden brown and bubbly on top (about 30 minutes). Serve hot. Makes 4 to 6 servings.

Charleston Red Rice

Red rice, known by a variety of names—pilau, perlo, perloo, purloo (all pronounced *PER-low*)—could perhaps be called the most traditional of all Charleston dishes. The recipe given here is an all-vegetable version, but there are dozens of variations featuring chicken or shrimp. Like many other Low Country dishes, red rice is similar to the famous jambalaya of Cajun South Louisiana. It also bears a remarkable resemblance to a traditional Trinidad dish called *pelau,* containing pigeon peas and chicken. Red rice is excellent with fried poultry and fish.

> **6 bacon slices, diced**
> **1 large onion, chopped**
> **1 medium green bell pepper, chopped**
> **4 green onions (including tops) chopped**
> **2 cups uncooked long-grain white rice**
> **3 medium tomatoes (about 1-1/4 lbs. *total*) peeled, chopped**
> **3 cups Poultry Stock, page 38, or canned chicken broth**
> **1/2 teaspoon dried leaf basil**
> **1/2 teaspoon dried leaf oregano**
> **1 small bay leaf**
> **1/4 teaspoon freshly ground black pepper**
> **Salt and Tabasco sauce to taste**

❦ Cook bacon in a heavy Dutch oven over medium heat until well browned. Remove and reserve bacon, leaving drippings in pan. Add onion, bell pepper and green onions to drippings. Cook until vegetables are slightly wilted and onion is transparent (about 5 minutes). Add rice and cook, stirring constantly to prevent sticking, 5 minutes. Stir in tomatoes. Simmer until tomato liquid has evaporated (about 8 minutes), stirring often. Add reserved bacon, stock, basil, oregano, bay leaf, black pepper, salt and Tabasco sauce. Stir to combine. Reduce heat to medium-low, cover and cook until rice is tender and all liquid is absorbed (about 45 minutes). Discard bay leaf. Serve hot. Makes 6 to 8 servings.

Southern Rice Dressing

Rice dressing, in one form or another, is found throughout the South. It is used as a stuffing for meats and poultry, stuffed into vegetables or served simply as a side dish. In South Mississippi and Louisiana the dish is called "dirty rice" and is traditionally made with gizzards and livers, but leaving out the sausage popular in other parts of the South.

> 1/2 cup sausage or bacon drippings
> 1/2 pound chicken or turkey gizzards, skins removed, ground
> 1/2 pound bulk-style pork sausage
> 1 medium onion, chopped
> 1 medium green bell pepper, chopped
> 2 medium garlic cloves, minced
> 4 green onions (including tops), chopped
> 2 tablespoons minced parsley, preferably flat-leaf
> 1 large bay leaf
> 1/2 teaspoon freshly ground black pepper
> 1/4 teaspoon Tabasco sauce
> Salt to taste
> 1-1/2 cups Brown Stock, page 38, or canned beef broth
> 2 cups cooked white rice

❦ Melt drippings in a heavy 4-quart saucepan over medium heat. Add ground gizzards and sausage. Cook, stirring often, until meats are lightly browned (about 10 minutes). Add onion, bell pepper, garlic, green onions, parsley, bay leaf, black pepper, Tabasco sauce and salt; cook, stirring often, until vegetables are very wilted and onion is transparent (about 15 minutes). Add stock and stir to blend. Bring to a boil; then reduce heat so liquid barely simmers. Cover and cook until mixture is thick and vegetables are completely mushy (about 20 minutes). Stir in rice and combine well. Cook just until rice is heated through; discard bay leaf. Serve hot. Makes 6 servings (about 5 cups).

BREADS & PASTRIES

When I first began sorting through the dozens of categories of Southern food to decide which among their tempting array would fill the chapters in this book, breads and pastries ranked foremost in my mind from the start. The Southern biscuit, corn breads, cracklin' breads, spoonbreads, hush puppies and fritters—all have been extolled in every medium from classic literature to modern-day magazines to television. And who, in any region of the country, is not familiar with Aunt Jemima's benevolent face smiling out from her pancake mix box? Throughout America, Southern breads and pastries are synonymous with great taste.

The subject of Southern breads and pastries is so vast and varied that it's easily worth an entire book of its own. The diversity results in part, of course, from the diverse origins of today's Southerners. The British, the French Huguenots, the Moravians, German farmers and merchants, the French Acadians and Spanish Criollos of South Louisiana, Cubans, Africans and Caribbean islanders: all these ''big bread-eaters'' have contributed to the South's complex blend of bread and pastry styles. The variety comes from another source, too; in the early days, the South grew no wheat. The original colonists learned from the native Indians to cultivate corn, and to grind the dried kernels into a meal which produced a tasty, coarse-grained bread. Corn was soon the South's most important grain, and corn bread became synonymous with the South in general. A family of four required 2-1/2 acres of cultivated corn per year just for household consumption.

All cornmeal breads may be made from either white or yellow cornmeal, and though Southerners will hotly debate the merits of one over the other, in the final analysis the choice depends strictly upon personal preference. White meal gives a more uneven texture (which some Southerners prefer), a crisper outside crust and a generally softer interior. Breads made with yellow cornmeal tend to be more even-textured but somewhat drier, with a slightly granular consistency.

Most cornmeal sold in supermarkets today is ground by steel rollers, with the germ and hull sifted out. Stone-ground cornmeal, on the other hand, is milled between huge grinding stones, much in the original manner, and contains both germ and hull. It has a richer taste than the de-germinated type, but because it still contains all its natural oils, it tends to turn rancid more quickly. To prolong shelf life, always store stone-ground meals in the freezer or refrigerator.

When Southerners eventually began to cultivate wheat, the variety which flourished was red winter wheat, a so-called "soft" wheat that yields flour with a low gluten content. Gluten is a protein that determines the elasticity of a flour when mixed with liquid. High-gluten flours are ideal for yeast breads, since they produce a very elastic and springy dough; lower-gluten flours, in contrast, are better for pie pastry, which should be a "loose" dough that does not spring back as you roll it out. The truly wonderful texture (and legendary reputation) of authentic Southern biscuits and pastries comes from using Southern soft wheat flour; if you use a "harder" type, you cannot expect the same results. To put it simply, remember: low protein for non-yeast products, high protein for yeast products.

To determine the gluten content of a flour, check the nutritional information printed on the package for the grams of protein per cup. A typical Southern soft wheat flour contains 8 to 9 grams of protein per cup, while all-purpose flour contains 12. Bread flour, a high-protein flour designed especially for bread making, normally has around 14 grams per cup.

On the subject of yeast breads: *anybody* can make quality homemade breads. All that is necessary is, of course, the desire, and a little background information to demystify the process. Over the years that I've taught classes of first-time bread bakers, I have found that most students produce loaves I have come to call "cannonballs." A typical cannonball has an average weight of about 10 pounds and an interior texture as dense as that of pound cake! These leaden loaves typically result from too little kneading or too much flour (or both).

A note on using the food processor: this wonderful tool lets you make superb breads in a hurry, but you must use caution in kneading. Just 25 seconds of processing will replace 10 minutes of kneading by hand! Overprocessing will literally cut the gluten network to ribbons, and the dough will not rise properly. When you use the processor recipes in this book, follow the processing times exactly, and never process dough longer than about 45 seconds.

Sweet Potato Biscuits

This delightful variation on the buttermilk biscuit is yet another delight from folks who love sweet potatoes. Great for any meal, but especially nice with pork or poultry entrees.

> **1 cup hot mashed sweet potato (about 1 medium sweet potato)**
> **2 tablespoons unsalted butter or margarine**
> **1 teaspoon baking soda**
> **1 cup buttermilk**
> **1 tablespoon honey**
> **2 cups all-purpose flour**
> **1 tablespoon baking powder**
> **1 tablespoon firmly packed brown sugar**

✿ Preheat oven to 400F (205C). Place well-mashed sweet potato in a bowl; stir in butter or margarine until melted and thoroughly blended. Set aside. In a separate bowl, stir together baking soda and buttermilk; stir in honey. In a large bowl, combine flour, baking powder and brown sugar. Add sweet potato mixture; work into flour mixture with your fingertips until mixture resembles coarse meal. Add buttermilk mixture, 1/4 cup at a time, blending well after each addition. Turn out onto a floured work surface and knead 3 or 4 times until dough holds together. Dough will be slightly sticky. Generously flour work surface and roll out dough 3/4 inch thick. Cut into rounds with a floured 3-inch biscuit cutter; reroll and cut scraps. Repeat until all dough has been used. Place biscuits on a baking sheet and bake in preheated oven until light golden brown (about 15 minutes). Serve hot. Makes about 18 biscuits.

Buttermilk Biscuits

Next to corn bread, the buttermilk biscuit is doubtless the South's most beloved bread. Truly, what could be better than a homemade biscuit with its light, flaky layers and beckoning aroma? I know Southern families who eat biscuits with all three meals every single day. To throw away even a cold, hard biscuit would be unthinkable; the children eat them for after-school treats, slathered with creamy butter and homemade preserves.

The secret to Southern biscuits is, of course, the Southern soft wheat flour. The dough should be very moist, even a bit sticky, and you should never, never handle it more than is absolutely necessary.

> 4 cups Southern soft wheat flour, see page 122
> 1 teaspoon baking soda
> 1-1/2 teaspoons salt
> 1 tablespoon baking powder
> 2/3 cup lard or solid vegetable shortening
> 1 cup buttermilk

✿ Preheat oven to 425F (220C). Sift flour, baking soda, salt and baking powder into a large bowl. Add lard or shortening; work fat into flour mixture with your fingertips until mixture resembles coarse meal. Add buttermilk and stir just to blend and moisten all ingredients. Turn out onto a floured work surface and gently knead 3 or 4 times until dough holds together. Dough should be slightly sticky. Generously flour work surface and roll out dough 1/2 inch thick. Cut into rounds with a floured 3-inch biscuit cutter; reroll and cut scraps. Repeat until all dough has been used. Place biscuits on a baking sheet, making sure sides do not touch. Bake in preheated oven until biscuits are light golden brown (10 to 12 minutes). Serve hot. Makes about 24 biscuits.

Beaten Biscuits

The beaten biscuit is a uniquely Southern bread, developed back in the days before baking powder and baking soda. At that time, pearlash and later saleratus were used as leaveners, but both imparted a bitter taste to the dough—not a desirable characteristic in a biscuit. Southern cooks discovered that if they repeatedly pounded and folded unleavened biscuit dough, they could form tiny air pockets in the dough. When the biscuits were baked the air pockets expanded and caused the biscuits to rise—and without the bitter taste of saleratus!

Few cooks have the time to make beaten biscuits today, but these little breads are delightful—crisp outside, with a crust somewhat like that of a cracker, and a soft inside. Over the years, various implements have been used to beat the dough—hammers, wooden mallets, the flat of an axe, old axe handles, flatirons and heavy wooden dowels. Chances are you have just the right tool lying around the house somewhere.

> 4 cups all-purpose flour
> 1 teaspoon salt
> 1/4 cup lard or solid vegetable shortening
> 2 tablespoons unsalted butter, room temperature
> 1 cup cold milk

❦ In a large bowl, combine flour and salt, tossing with a fork to blend. Add lard or shortening and butter; work fat into flour mixture with your fingertips until mixture resembles coarse meal. Make a well in center of mixture and add milk; stir to combine well. Turn out onto a lightly floured work surface and knead 3 or 4 times until dough holds together. Preheat oven to 400F (205C). Grease baking sheet; set aside. Pat out dough about 1 inch thick and begin to beat it, using a wooden mallet or other implement. The pounding need not be rambunctious, but rather steady and rhythmic. When entire surface has been well beaten, fold dough in half and repeat the process. Continue to beat and fold until dough is well blistered (20 to 30 minutes). Roll out dough 1/2 inch thick and cut into rounds with a floured 2-inch biscuit cutter; reroll and cut scraps. Repeat until all dough has been used. Prick top of each biscuit 3 times with a fork. Place biscuits on greased baking sheet; bake in preheated oven until golden brown (20 to 25 minutes). Serve hot. Makes about 24 biscuits.

Strawberry Muffins

I first tasted these muffins at the annual **Strawberry** Festival in Ponchatoula, Louisiana, Strawberry Capital of the World. If **you're ever** in Southeastern Louisiana in late spring, treat yourself to a flat of Ponchatoula strawberries from a roadside vendor. Acclaimed French food authority **Madelaine Kamman** considers these berries better than the fabled French *fraises!*

> **2 cups all-purpose flour**
> **1/3 cup sugar**
> **3/4 teaspoon salt**
> **1 tablespoon baking powder**
> **1 cup milk**
> **3 tablespoons unsalted butter or margarine, melted**
> **1 egg**
> **1 cup fresh strawberries, cut into small chunks; or 1 cup thawed, thoroughly**
> **drained frozen strawberries, cut into small chunks**
> **Sugar**

❦ Preheat oven to 400F (205C). Grease 18 muffin cups and set aside. Sift flour, 1/3 cup sugar, salt and baking powder into a large bowl. Make a well in center of flour mixture and set aside. Blend together milk, melted butter and egg; pour into well in flour mixture. Stir together quickly with a fork just to moisten all dry ingredients; do not beat. Lightly stir berries into batter just until evenly distributed. Pour into greased muffin cups, filling cups slightly more than half-full; sprinkle top of each muffin with a little sugar. Bake on middle rack of preheated oven until a wooden pick inserted in center of muffins comes out clean (25 to 30 minutes). Remove from oven. Using a small metal spatula, loosen sides of muffins; turn out muffins onto wire rack. Serve warm. Makes 18 muffins.

Fig Muffins with Satsuma Glaze

These rich and tasty muffins show off two of the South's favorite fruits—figs and satsumas. Everybody knows about figs, but few people outside of South Louisiana know about satsumas. Satsumas— "Christmas oranges" to folks in South Louisiana—are delectably sweet little oranges that taste much like Mandarin oranges; they are in season from October through December. Each year during the first week of December, there's a satsuma festival at Fort Jackson in Boothville, Louisiana.

1/4 cup unsalted butter or margarine, room temperature
1/2 cup sugar
3 eggs
2 cups fig preserves, finely minced, syrup reserved
1 cup old-fashioned rolled oats
1-1/2 cups all-purpose flour
2 teaspoons baking powder
1/2 teaspoon baking soda
1/2 teaspoon salt
Satsuma Glaze, see below

Satsuma Glaze:
1 (3-oz.) package cream cheese, room temperature
1/4 cup sifted powdered sugar
2 tablespoons fresh satsuma juice, tangerine juice or orange juice
1 teaspoon finely grated satsuma, tangerine or orange zest

❦ Preheat oven to 375F (190C). Grease 24 muffin cups and set aside. In bowl of an electric mixer, cream butter or margarine and sugar at medium speed until light and fluffy (about 3 minutes). Beat in eggs, 1 at a time, scraping down side of bowl after each addition. Add fig preserves, reserved syrup and oats; beat to blend. Sift flour, baking powder, baking soda and salt into a separate bowl; add sifted dry ingredients to creamed mixture and beat just to moisten. Pour batter into greased muffin cups, filling cups half-full. Bake on middle rack of preheated oven until a wooden pick inserted in center of muffins comes out clean (25 to 30 minutes). Remove from oven. Using a small metal spatula, loosen sides of muffins; turn out muffins onto a wire rack. Cool muffins slightly; prepare Satsuma Glaze and spread on tops of muffins. Makes 24 muffins.

Satsuma Glaze: Beat cream cheese in bowl of an electric mixer until light and fluffy. Add powdered sugar, juice and zest; blend to form a smooth glaze.

Charleston Ice Cream Muffins

This unusual recipe, adapted from the version printed in Gloria Mann Maynard's *Caterin-to-Charleston*, produces a sweet, fluffy-textured muffin. Use rich, egg-based ice cream.

2-1/2 cups rich vanilla ice cream, softened
2 cups self-rising flour
2 eggs, beaten until frothy
1 tablespoon unsalted butter or margarine, melted

❧ Preheat oven to 400F (205C). Thoroughly grease and flour 18 muffin cups. In a large bowl, combine ice cream and flour, beat to blend. Stir in eggs and butter. Pour into muffins cups, filling cups half-full. Bake on middle rack of preheated oven until a wooden pick inserted in center of muffins comes out clean (20 to 25 minutes). Using a small metal spatula, loosen sides of muffins; turn out onto wire racks and serve hot. Makes 18 muffins.
Variations
Use other ice cream flavors, such as butter pecan or chocolate; add nuts; or add flavorings, such as ground cinnamon, orange zest or lemon zest.

Fresh Peach Fritters

Fresh fruit fritters have long been a Southern favorite. They can take the place of bread with game bird entrees or serve as dessert for just about any meal.

Vegetable oil for deep-frying
1 egg, beaten until frothy
1 cup milk
1 cup peeled, finely chopped fresh peaches
1/4 cup granulated sugar
1/4 teaspoon salt
1/4 teaspoon ground cinnamon
1/2 teaspoon vanilla extract
2 cups all-purpose flour
1 tablespoon baking powder
Powdered sugar

❧ In a deep-sided 12-inch skillet, heat 2 inches of oil to 350F (175C) or until a 1-inch bread cube turns golden brown in 65 seconds. While oil is heating, combine egg, milk, peaches, granulated sugar, salt, cinnamon and vanilla in a small bowl. In a separate bowl, combine flour and baking powder. Make a well in center of flour mixture and pour in egg mixture; stir until blended. Drop by rounded tablespoonfuls into hot oil, being careful not to crowd pan; deep-fry, turning once, until golden brown on both sides (3 to 4 minutes). Take care to maintain correct oil temperature. Remove fritters from oil with a slotted spoon and drain on paper towels. Sprinkle with powdered sugar and serve hot. Makes about 24 fritters.

Corn Fritters

Corn fritters are an old-time treat in the South, always a big hit at barbecues. They're good with pork dishes, or even all by themselves as a snack.

    1 egg, beaten until frothy
    1 cup milk
    1 cup fresh corn kernels or 1 cup canned whole-kernel corn, drained well
    3 tablespoons finely chopped onion
    2 cups all-purpose flour
    1/2 teaspoon salt
    1/4 teaspoon red (cayenne) pepper
    1/4 cup granulated sugar
    1 tablespoon baking powder
    Vegetable oil for deep-frying
    Powdered sugar

✿ In a deep-sided 12-inch skillet, heat 2 inches of oil to 350F (175C) or until a 1-inch bread cube turns golden brown in 65 seconds. Meanwhile, in a medium bowl, combine egg, milk, corn and onion; set aside. Sift flour, salt, red pepper, granulated sugar and baking powder into a separate bowl. Stir egg mixture into flour mixture to blend and moisten all ingredients. Drop batter by rounded tablespoonfuls into hot oil, being careful not to crowd pan. Deep-fry, turning once, until golden brown (3 to 4 minutes). Take care to maintain correct oil temperature. Remove fritters from oil with a slotted spoon and drain on paper towels. Sprinkle with powdered sugar and serve hot. Makes about 24 fritters.

Rice Fritters

Called calas in New Orleans, these tasty fritters are an old tradition in the French Quarter. At one time vendors in the French Quarter sold the hot fritters from straw baskets and residents would awake to their cries of "Calas, belles calas, toutes chaudes!" as they sold their treats to the sleepy city. The cala vendors are gone now, but a few French Quarter breakfast eateries still serve the fritters.

    Vegetable oil for deep-frying
    6 tablespoons all-purpose flour
    3 tablespoons granulated sugar
    2 teaspoons baking powder
    1/2 teaspoon salt
    1/4 teaspoon freshly grated nutmeg
    2 cups hot cooked white rice
    2 eggs, beaten until frothy
    1 teaspoon vanilla extract
    Powdered sugar

❦ In a deep-sided 12-inch skillet, heat 2 inches of oil to 350F (175C) or until a 1-inch bread cube turns golden brown in 65 seconds. While oil is heating, combine flour, granulated sugar, baking powder, salt and nutmeg in a medium bowl. In a separate bowl, beat together rice, eggs and vanilla. Add dry ingredients to rice mixture and stir to blend. Drop by rounded tablespoonfuls into hot oil, being careful not to crowd pan; deep-fry, turning once, until golden brown on both sides (3 to 4 minutes). Take care to maintain correct oil temperature. Remove calas from oil with a slotted spoon and drain on paper towels. Sprinkle with powdered sugar and serve hot. Makes about 20 calas.

Hush Puppies

Much controversy has raged in recent years over the true origin of the hush puppy, but I still maintain that the original story seems the most logical. During the hard times after the Civil War, people and animals were on lean rations. The cooks would roll up bits of corn bread batter and drop them into the pot of hot cooking fat. These fried morsels were tossed to the hungry dogs attracted by the smell of food with the admonishment "Hush, puppy!" Whatever story you tell about hush puppies, just be sure they're always around when you serve fried catfish to a Southerner!

> **Vegetable oil for deep-frying**
> **1-1/3 cups white cornmeal, preferably stone-ground**
> **1/3 cup sugar**
> **1 teaspoon salt**
> **2 teaspoons baking powder**
> **2 tablespoons minced onion**
> **2 cups water**
> **6 tablespoons unsalted butter or margarine**

❦ In a deep-sided 12-inch skillet, heat 2 inches of oil to 350F (175C) or until a 1-inch bread cube turns golden brown in 65 seconds. While oil is heating, combine cornmeal, sugar, salt, baking powder and onion in a medium bowl. Combine water and butter in a small saucepan and bring to a boil over high heat; pour over dry ingredients and stir rapidly to blend. Set mixture aside until cool enough to handle. Form into about 24 equal balls. Drop hush puppies into hot oil, being careful not to crowd pan; deep-fry, turning once, until golden brown on both sides (3 to 4 minutes). Take care to maintain correct oil temperature. Remove hush puppies from oil with a slotted spoon and drain on paper towels. Serve hot. Makes about 24 hush puppies.

Les Oreilles de Cochon

The name means "pig's ears"—and that's just what these crisp little pastries resemble. A favorite after-school snack of Cajun children in South Louisiana, they are equally delicious for breakfast or brunch.

2 cups all-purpose flour
1/2 teaspoon salt
1/4 cup frozen unsalted butter, cut into 1/2-inch cubes
2 eggs, lightly beaten
Vegetable oil for deep-frying

Syrup Topping:
1 cup dark corn syrup or ribbon cane syrup
3/4 cup finely chopped pecans
1 teaspoon vanilla extract

❦ In a food processor fitted with the steel blade, combine flour, salt and frozen butter cubes. Process just until butter is broken into pea-size bits. Stop machine and add eggs; process just until dough holds together. In a deep-sided 12-inch skillet, heat 1 inch of oil until a 1-inch bread cube turns golden brown in 60 seconds. While oil is heating, turn out dough onto a lightly floured work surface and gather together to form a smooth ball. Divide dough into 24 roughly equal portions and roll each into a rough circle 3 to 4 inches in diameter. To form each "ear," lift a circle in your hand and stick tines of a fork into center; twist a half turn. Drop pastry from fork into hot oil and deep-fry, turning once, until golden brown (about 3 minutes); you can cook 2 or 3 "ears" at a time, but be careful not to crowd pan. Take care to maintain correct oil temperature. Drain pastries on paper towels. Prepare Syrup Topping; pour hot topping over pastries, cool slightly and serve. Makes 24 pastries.

Syrup Topping: Combine corn or cane syrup and pecans in a heavy 2-quart saucepan and cook over medium heat until thickened (6 to 7 minutes). Remove from heat and stir in vanilla.

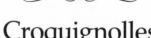

Croquignolles

Croquignolles *(CROAKS-n-yoles)* are tasty breakfast treats similar to the beignets made famous in the coffee houses of the French Quarter, though they do not contain yeast. The pastry probably came to the New World with the French settlers of the Louisiana Territory. Paul Prudhomme has fond memories of his mother preparing croquignolles for the family when he was a child. It's easy to keep a ready supply on hand for those "quickie" breakfasts: the dough rectangles can be frozen before cooking, then fried while still frozen.

2 cups all-purpose flour
1 teaspoon salt
1 tablespoon baking powder
2 tablespoons lard or solid vegetable shortening
1 egg, beaten until frothy
1/3 cup milk
Vegetable oil for deep-frying
1/4 cup sugar combined with 1 teaspoon ground cinnamon

❖ In a medium bowl, combine flour, salt and baking powder. With your fingertips, work lard or shortening into flour mixture until mixture resembles coarse meal. Add egg and milk and blend. Turn out onto a lightly floured work surface and knead 3 or 4 times until dough holds together. Roll out dough to a 12-inch square. Cut dough square into (4" x 3") rectangles; cut 2 slits, each 1-1/2 inches long, down each side of center of each rectangle. In a heavy 12-inch skillet, heat 1-1/2 inches of oil until 1-inch bread cube turns golden brown in 60 seconds. Add dough rectangles to hot oil, 4 or 5 at a time, being careful not to crowd skillet. Deep-fry, turning once, until golden brown on both sides (about 3 minutes); take care to maintain correct oil temperature. Remove pastries from oil with a slotted spoon and drain on paper towels. Sprinkle with sugar-cinnamon mixture and serve hot. Makes 12 pastries.

Hoe Cakes

The original hoe cakes were a native Indian dish called *appone* or corn pone. The Indians wrapped the small cakes in wet corn husks and baked them in the embers of a fire, but the settlers adopted a different technique, baking the cakes on the flat edge of a hoe held above the fire. In many areas of the South, the batter is baked as one large cake, as in the variation given below.

2 cups white cornmeal, preferably stone-ground
1 teaspoon salt
1 cup boiling water
1/4 cup bacon drippings or vegetable oil

❖ In a bowl, combine cornmeal and salt. Stirring constantly, add boiling water in a slow, steady stream. Stir to blend; cool. Divide cooled dough into 8 portions and pat each into a flat cake about 3 inches in diameter. Heat drippings or oil in a heavy 12-inch skillet, preferably cast iron; add hoe cakes and cook, turning once, until golden brown on both sides (about 10 minutes). Serve hot. Makes 8 hoe cakes.

Variation

Baked Hoe Cake: Preheat oven to 350F (175C). Place 3 tablespoons bacon drippings or vegetable oil in a 10-inch cast-iron skillet and swirl to coat bottom and sides of skillet. Place skillet in preheated oven until very hot. Meanwhile, combine 1 cup white cornmeal (preferably stone-ground), 1/2 teaspoon salt and 1 tablespoon bacon drippings or vegetable oil. Stir in 3/4 cup boiling water, blending until smooth. Pour batter into hot skillet and bake in preheated oven until a wooden pick inserted in center comes out clean (15 to 20 minutes). Cut into wedges and serve hot.

Skillet Corn Bread

The first colonists were unfamiliar with corn when they arrived in America, but the native Indians soon taught them to cultivate and use the prolific grain. Corn was ground into a coarse meal to produce breadlike products and a thick mush. Corn remained an important part of the Southern diet even after wheat became a successful crop. Traditionally, corn bread is baked in greased cast-iron skillets heated until blazing hot before the batter is added.

> 1 cup all-purpose flour
> 4 teaspoons baking powder
> 3 tablespoons sugar
> 1 teaspoon salt
> 1 cup white cornmeal, preferably stone-ground
> 2 eggs, beaten until frothy
> 1/4 cup melted bacon drippings or vegetable oil
> 1 cup milk

❧ Preheat oven to 425F (220C). Thoroughly grease bottom and sides of a 10-inch cast-iron skillet and place it in preheated oven while you prepare batter. Sift flour, baking powder, sugar and salt into a medium bowl. Add cornmeal and toss with a fork to blend. Add eggs, bacon drippings and milk; stir just to blend and moisten all ingredients. Remove sizzling-hot skillet from oven and pour in batter. Bake in preheated oven until golden brown and a wooden pick inserted in center of bread comes out clean (about 20 minutes). Cut into wedges and serve hot. Makes 8 to 10 wedges.

Macon Corn Bread

Macon is a charming city in Bibb County, Georgia, squarely in the middle of the state. Macon has produced legions of fine cooks whose food tastes so good it makes you profoundly happy just to be alive and enjoying such delicious things. I know, because my previous mother-in-law, the former Cecilia Plant Miller, was a Macon girl. To this great lady I owe the awakening of my interest in food and in learning to cook. This simple recipe is a Macon favorite—whole-kernel corn is added to the batter to produce a rich-tasting corn bread with an interesting texture.

3/4 cup all-purpose flour
1 tablespoon baking powder
1 tablespoon sugar
1 teaspoon finely ground black pepper
1/2 teaspoon salt
3/4 cup yellow cornmeal, preferably stone-ground
1 cup fresh corn kernels or 1 cup canned whole-kernel corn, drained well
3 eggs, beaten until frothy
2/3 cup half and half

❦ Preheat oven to 400F (205C). Thoroughly grease a 13″ x 9″ baking dish; set aside. Sift flour, baking powder, sugar, pepper and salt into a medium bowl. Add cornmeal and toss with a fork to blend. Add corn, eggs and half and half; stir just to blend and moisten all ingredients. Pour batter into greased baking dish and bake in preheated oven until golden brown (about 25 minutes). Cut into squares and serve hot. Makes 6 to 8 servings.

Cracklin' Bread

"Cracklin's," the crispy bits of meat left after rendering salt pork or fatback, have a variety of uses in the South. They're often seasoned with salt and red pepper and eaten as snacks; they're also a popular seasoning for bean and pea dishes. One of the tastiest ways to use them is in cracklin' bread, a homey bread with a coarse, crumbly texture and a wonderful, earthy taste that just says "country food"! Serve with a big bowl of Butter Beans with Roux, page 105, or Kale with Kohlrabi & Smoked Hog Jowl, page 112, for a down-home meal that would delight any king.

3/4 pound salt pork, rind removed, diced
2 cups yellow cornmeal, preferably stone-ground
1 teaspoon salt
1 cup boiling water
1/2 teaspoon baking soda
3/4 cup buttermilk

❦ Preheat oven to 450F (230C). Cook salt pork in a 10-inch cast-iron skillet over medium heat until all fat is rendered (about 20 minutes). The remaining crisp bits of meat—the "cracklin's"—should be golden brown. Remove cracklin's with a slotted spoon, drain on paper towels and cool until crisp. Pour off all rendered fat from skillet, swirling fat around skillet to coat bottom and sides well; reserve 3 tablespoons fat. Combine cornmeal, salt and reserved 3 tablespoons fat in a medium bowl; pour in boiling water all at once and stir to blend and moisten all ingredients. Stir baking soda into buttermilk and add to cornmeal mixture, stirring well. Stir in reserved cracklin's. Pour mixture into greased skillet and pat into an even layer. Bake in preheated oven until top is golden brown and crusty (about 25 minutes); entire bread should lift easily from skillet. Remove skillet from oven and invert bread onto plate. Cut into wedges and serve hot. Makes 8 to 10 wedges.

Old Southern Spoonbread

Spoonbread, so named because it is generally eaten with a spoon, is actually not a bread at all, but rather a soft, custardy cornmeal concoction. It is especially nice with baked ham but also makes a great accompaniment to any pork, poultry or game bird dish.

> 2 cups water
> 1 tablespoon sugar
> 1-1/2 teaspoons salt
> 1/4 cup unsalted butter or margarine
> 1-1/2 cups white cornmeal, preferably stone-ground
> 1-1/2 teaspoons baking powder
> 5 eggs, beaten until frothy
> 2 cups milk

❦ Preheat oven to 350F (175C). Thoroughly butter a 13″ x 9″ baking dish; set aside. In a heavy 2-quart saucepan, combine water, sugar, salt and butter. Bring to a rapid boil, then remove from heat. Quickly blend cornmeal with baking powder, then stir into water-butter mixture and set aside. Blend eggs and milk. Combine cornmeal mixture with egg mixture and stir just to blend. Pour batter into buttered baking dish. Bake in preheated oven until top is firm and a wooden pick inserted in center comes out clean (35 to 40 minutes). Remove from oven and serve hot, spooning from dish onto plates. Makes 6 to 8 servings.

Benne Seed Crisps

These crisp crackers originated in Charleston where the flavor of benne (sesame) seeds has long been much loved. The crackers are great with party dips or as the basis for canapés. Store them in airtight containers.

> 1 cup all-purpose flour
> 1/2 cup toasted wheat germ
> 1/3 cup toasted sesame seeds
> 1 teaspoon baking powder
> 1 teaspoon sugar
> 1/2 teaspoon salt
> 6 tablespoons frozen unsalted butter, cut into 1-inch cubes
> 1/4 cup ice water

✤ Preheat oven to 375F (190C). In a food processor fitted with the steel blade, combine flour, wheat germ, sesame seeds, baking powder, sugar and salt. Process to combine ingredients together; using 3 on-off pulses. Add butter; process just until butter is broken into pea-size bits. With machine running, pour ice water through feed tube and process just until dough begins to hold together. Turn out dough onto a floured work surface and gather together, lightly kneading once or twice. Roll out dough to 1/8 inch thick; cut dough into about 3" x 1-1/2" rectangles. Place crackers on ungreased baking sheets and bake in preheated oven until golden brown and crisp (12 to 14 minutes). Cool on wire racks. Makes about 30 crackers.

Barbara Brown's Colonial Apple Bread

Barbara Brown, from Atlanta, Georgia, is an expert on the subject of bread. When she wrote the recipe from which this one is adapted, she surely intended to create the epitome of Southern quick breads, and she certainly hit the mark. This dense, moist loaf is perfect for the holidays and is excellent as a breakfast or afternoon coffee bread.

>   3/4 cup apple cider
>   1 cup golden raisins
>   1-1/2 cups firmly packed dark brown sugar
>   1/4 cup unsalted butter or margarine
>   1/2 teaspoon salt
>   1/2 teaspoon ground cinnamon
>   1/2 teaspoon ground allspice
>   2-1/4 cups cake flour
>   1 teaspoon baking powder
>   1/2 teaspoon baking soda
>   2/3 cup chopped pecans
>   1 cup finely chopped unpeeled apple
>   Powdered sugar

✤ Preheat oven to 325F (165C). Thoroughly butter a 7-inch kugelhopf pan or bundt pan; set aside. In a heavy medium saucepan, combine cider, raisins, brown sugar, butter, salt, cinnamon and allspice. Boil 3 minutes, stirring often. Remove from heat and cool slightly. Sift flour, baking powder and baking soda into a large bowl. Stir pecans and apple into cider mixture, then pour into flour mixture. Stir to blend and moisten all ingredients. Turn batter into buttered pan and bake in preheated oven until a wooden pick inserted in center of loaf comes out clean (about 1 hour). Cool in pan 10 minutes, then invert onto a wire rack. Cool completely before serving; sprinkle with powdered sugar before slicing. Makes 12 to 15 slices.

Kate's Country Bread

Kate Almand is a very special lady to every cooking teacher who has had the pleasure to work with her at Rich's Cooking School in Atlanta. For many years she has been the right hand (and left hand too, if the truth be known) to Nathalie Dupree the founder of the cooking school. Ages ago when I was a scared student taking my first intensive cooking class away from home, it was Kate who first befriended me and set me at ease. I never told Nathalie, but I got double my money's worth at Rich's—because I learned about Southern cooking from Kate early in the mornings before class, and about French cooking from Nathalie during class!

Kate gave me the recipe for this bread on one of those mornings, and I know your family will love it as much as mine does. My daughter Cory eats it toasted almost every morning! I had better set the record straight before Kate writes to my publisher, though; she does not make it in the food processor as I do.

> **1/2 cup warm water (110F, 45C)**
> **2 tablespoons honey**
> **1 (1/4-oz.) package active dry yeast**
> **3 cups bread flour**
> **1/2 cup toasted wheat germ**
> **1 teaspoon salt**
> **1 tablespoon unsalted butter, room temperature**
> **1/2 cup milk, scalded, cooled**

❦ Grease bottom and sides of a large bowl; set aside. Lightly grease an 8" x 4" loaf pan; set aside. In a 1-cup glass measuring cup, combine water, honey and yeast; stir to blend. Set aside until yeast is dissolved and mixture is foamy on top. In a food processor fitted with the steel blade, combine flour, wheat germ, salt, butter and milk. Process to blend, using 3 or 4 on-off pulses. Add yeast mixture and process about 15 seconds to blend. Stop machine and check consistency of dough; it should be just slightly sticky. If dough is too wet, add more flour, a tablespoon at a time, processing just to blend after each addition, until consistency is correct. If dough is too dry, add more water, a tablespoon at a time, processing just to blend after each addition, until consistency is correct. Process 30 seconds longer to knead. Turn out dough into greased bowl and turn to coat all surfaces; cover bowl with plastic wrap. Let rise in a warm place until doubled in bulk (about 1-1/2 hours). Then punch down dough thoroughly with your fist, pressing out all air. Shape dough into a loaf; place in greased loaf pan. Cover loosely with a floured towel and let rise until doubled in bulk (about 1 hour). Preheat oven to 375F (190C). Remove towel from doubled loaf; bake loaf in preheated oven until it is golden brown and sounds hollow when tapped (30 to 35 minutes). Turn out onto a wire rack and cool completely. Makes 1 loaf.

Moravian Love Cake

The Moravians who came to the colonies in the 18th century belonged to a European religious sect, the Church of the Brethren. They established their first mission in Savannah in 1735; their largest mission, however, was established in what is now Winston-Salem, North Carolina, the location of their present-day Home Church. The Moravians stage celebrations of the unity of man, known as "lovefeasts," commemorating events in their lives. At each lovefeast, large or small, this traditional bread is served.

> 1 medium russet potato (about 1/2 lb.), peeled, quartered
> 1/4 cup warm water (110F, 45C)
> 1 teaspoon granulated sugar
> 1 (1/4-oz.) package active dry yeast
> 4 cups all-purpose flour
> 1 teaspoon salt
> 1/3 cup granulated sugar
> 1 egg
> 2/3 cup milk
> 3/4 cup unsalted butter or margarine, melted
> 2/3 cup firmly packed light brown sugar
> 1 teaspoon ground cinnamon

❧ Grease bottom and sides of a large bowl; set aside. Thoroughly grease a 15" x 10" jelly-roll pan and set aside. Place quartered potato in a small saucepan and cover with cold water. Bring to a boil, then reduce heat, cover and simmer until very tender (about 20 minutes). Drain, mash well and set aside. In a 1-cup glass measuring cup, combine warm water, 1 teaspoon granulated sugar and yeast; stir to blend. Set aside until yeast is dissolved and mixture is foamy on top. In a food processor fitted with the steel blade, combine flour, salt, 1/3 cup granulated sugar and egg. Process to blend, using 3 or 4 on-off pulses. Blend milk into mashed potato and add to flour mixture; process just to blend. Add yeast mixture and process about 15 seconds to blend. Stop machine and check consistency of dough; it should be just slightly sticky. If dough is too wet, add more flour, a tablespoon at a time, processing just to blend after each addition, until consistency is correct. If dough is too dry, add more warm water, a tablespoon at a time, processing just to blend after each addition, until consistency is correct. Process dough 30 seconds longer to knead. Turn out dough into greased bowl and turn to coat all surfaces; cover bowl with plastic wrap. Let rise in a warm place until doubled in bulk (about 1-1/2 hours). Then punch down dough thoroughly with your fist, pressing out all air. Roll out dough on a lightly floured work surface to a 15" x 10" rectangle and place in greased jelly-roll pan. Cover loosely with a floured towel and let rise again until doubled in bulk (about 45 minutes). Preheat oven to 375F (190C). Combine butter, brown sugar and cinnamon, stirring to blend. Remove towel from risen dough; with your thumb, make indentations in dough at 1-1/2-inch intervals, pressing about halfway through dough each time. Drizzle brown sugar mixture over dough, letting it seep into indentations. Bake in preheated oven until golden brown (20 to 25 minutes). Cool slightly and cut into squares to serve. Makes 1 coffee cake (6 to 8 servings).

Cream Cheese Coffee Ring

Visiting over coffee is a Southern tradition. In the South, you don't need an invitation to go have morning coffee or tea (or Coca-Cola if you live in Atlanta!). You just put on your clothes, comb your hair and go knock on the door. The only request is that you go home sometime before supper! This rich bread is a breakfast and morning coffee favorite at my house; I always like to have it on hand in the freezer for unexpected guests.

1/2 cup warm water (110F, 45C)
1/4 cup sugar
1 (1/4-oz.) package active dry yeast
4 cups bread flour
1/2 teaspoon salt
1/2 cup unsalted butter, room temperature
2 eggs
1/2 cup dairy sour cream
Cream Cheese Filling, see below
1 egg white, beaten until frothy
Orange Glaze, see below

Cream Cheese Filling:
2 (3-oz.) packages cream cheese, room temperature
1 egg yolk
1-1/2 tablespoons sugar
1/2 teaspoon almond extract
1/3 cup finely chopped pecans
1/3 cup raisins

Orange Glaze:
2/3 cup powdered sugar, sifted
3 tablespoons fresh orange juice

❦ Grease bottom and sides of a large bowl; set aside. In a 2-cup glass measuring cup, combine water, sugar and yeast; stir to blend. Set aside until yeast is dissolved and mixture is foamy on top. In a food processor fitted with the steel blade, combine flour, salt, butter, eggs and sour cream. Process to blend, using 3 or 4 on-off pulses. Add yeast mixture and process 15 seconds. Stop machine and check consistency of dough; it should be just slightly sticky. If dough is too wet, add more flour, a tablespoon at a time, processing just to blend after each addition, until consistency is correct. If dough is too dry, add more warm water, a tablespoon at a time, processing just to blend after each addition, until consistency is correct. Process 30 seconds longer to knead. Turn out dough into greased bowl and turn to coat all surfaces; cover bowl with plastic wrap. Let rise in a warm place until doubled in bulk (about 1-1/2 hours). Meanwhile, prepare Cream Cheese Filling; set aside. Punch down doubled dough thoroughly with your fist, pressing out all air. Roll out dough on a lightly floured work surface to a rectangle about 1/4 inch thick. Spread Cream Cheese Filling over rectangle, leaving a 1-1/2-inch border on all sides. Beginning at a long side, roll up rectangle jelly-roll style into a cylinder. Pinch seam together tightly. Join ends of cylinder together, forming a circle; pinch ends together. Place ring, seam side down, on a baking sheet. Using sharp scissors or kitchen shears, cut halfway through roll at 3/4-inch intervals all around ring. Spread slits open like a fan so filling shows. Cover ring loosely with a floured towel and let rise until doubled in bulk (about 1 hour). Preheat oven to 350F (175C). Remove towel from doubled ring; gently brush ring with egg white, being careful not to let any drip onto baking sheet. Bake in preheated oven until nicely browned (35 to 40 minutes). Cool on a wire rack. When ring is almost completely cool, prepare Orange Glaze and drizzle over top of ring. Makes 1 coffee cake (6 to 8 servings).

Cream Cheese Filling: Whisk together cream cheese, egg yolk, sugar and almond extract until light and fluffy. Stir in pecans and raisins.

Orange Glaze: Whisk together powdered sugar and orange juice until smooth and satiny.

Louisiana French Bread

Anyone visiting South Louisiana is always impressed by the region's marvelous French bread with its paper-thin, brittle-crisp crust and soft, airy inside texture. While no home oven can exactly duplicate the bread produced in bakery convection ovens, you can come mighty close—and a food processor makes the task even easier.

> **1-1/2 cups warm water (110F, 45C)**
> **1 teaspoon sugar**
> **1-1/2 (1/4-oz.) packages active dry yeast (about 4 teaspoons)**
> **4 cups bread flour**
> **2 teaspoons salt**
> **1 tablespoon solid vegetable shortening**
> **1/4 cup cornmeal**
> **1/2 cup water mixed with 1-1/2 teaspoons salt**

❡ Grease bottom and sides of a large bowl; set aside. In a 2-cup glass measuring cup, combine water, sugar and yeast; stir to blend. Set aside until yeast is dissolved and mixture is foamy on top. In a food processor fitted with the steel blade, combine flour, salt and shortening. Process to blend, using 3 or 4 on-off pulses. Add yeast mixture and process about 15 seconds to blend. Stop machine and check consistency of dough; it should be just slightly sticky. If dough is too wet, add more flour, a tablespoon at a time, processing just to blend after each addition, until consistency is correct. If dough is too dry, add more warm water, a tablespoon at a time, processing just to blend after each addition, until consistency is correct. Process 30 seconds longer to knead. Turn out dough into greased bowl and turn to coat all surfaces; cover bowl with plastic wrap. Let rise in a warm place until doubled in bulk (about 1-1/2 hours). Then punch down dough thoroughly with your fist, pressing out all air. Divide dough in half and roll out each half to a 15" x 10" rectangle. Beginning at a long side, roll up each rectangle jelly-roll style into a cylinder. Tuck ends under and pinch all seams together to seal well. Spread cornmeal on 2 baking sheets; place 1 shaped loaf on cornmeal on each baking sheet. Cut 3 or 4 diagonal slashes in surface of each loaf with a thin-bladed sharp knife or a razor blade. Cover loaves loosely with a floured towel and let rise until doubled in bulk (about 1 hour). Preheat oven to 400F (205C). Remove towel from doubled loaves; carefully brush loaves with water-salt mixture and bake in preheated oven 15 minutes. Reduce oven temperature to 350F (175C) and continue to bake until loaves are golden brown and sound hollow when tapped (about 20 minutes longer). Cool completely on wire racks before slicing. Makes 2 loaves.

Sally Lunn

Sally Lunn is a delightful tender bread that goes well with just about any meal. It is not Southern-born, to be precise, it is not even American born! The recipe is in fact a British one, reputed to be the creation of a young woman named Sally Lunn who baked and sold this bread in Bath, England. The formula came to America with the colonists and the loaf was prepared so extensively in the colonies that Southerners just sort of claimed it as their own.

> 3/4 cup milk
> 6 tablespoons unsalted butter
> 1/4 cup warm water (110F, 45C)
> 1 tablespoon sugar
> 1 (1/4-oz.) package active dry yeast
> 3-1/4 cups bread flour
> 3 tablespoons sugar
> 1-1/4 teaspoons salt
> 3 eggs

❦ Thoroughly butter a 10-inch kugelhopf pan or turk's head mold; set aside. Grease bottom and side of a large bowl; set aside. In a small saucepan, combine milk and butter. Heat just until small bubbles appear around side of pan. Cool until lukewarm. In a glass measuring cup, combine warm water, 1 tablespoon sugar and yeast until blended. Set aside until yeast is dissolved and mixture is foamy on top. In a food processor fitted with the steel blade, combine flour, 3 tablespoons sugar, salt and eggs. Process to blend, using 3 or 4 on-off pulses. Add yeast mixture and milk mixture; process 45 seconds. Dough will be very wet, almost batterlike. Turn out dough into greased bowl and cover bowl with plastic wrap. Let rise in a warm place until doubled in bulk (about 1-1/2 hours). Then stir dough with a wooden spoon and turn out into buttered baking pan. Cover pan loosely with a floured towel and let dough rise again until doubled in bulk (about 1 hour). Preheat oven to 350F (175C). Remove towel; bake risen loaf in preheated oven until it sounds hollow when tapped (45 to 50 minutes). Turn loaf out onto a wire rack and cool completely before slicing. Makes 1 loaf.

DESSERTS

Start a conversation in the South with one person on the subject of desserts and an amazing thing happens. Soon one other person has overheard and joined in the discussion, and then another and another—and quite soon, there's a full-scale seminar on Southern desserts in progress. To put it quite simply, everybody in the South has a lot to say about desserts. Sweets in general rank right up there with motherhood and, yes, apple pie in the hearts of Southerners. I'd be willing to bet that we have the greatest per capita consumption of sugar and chocolate in the country! Maybe it's the heat. Maybe it's the mosquitoes. Maybe over-indulging in desserts is our way of rewarding ourselves for surviving both the aforementioned Southern afflictions. If it should turn out to be a virus, I personally hope that no cure is found.

Southern cooks have always been able to pro-duce enticing desserts from whatever is on hand—sometimes from virtually nothing, it seems, when we consider such specialties as Vinegar Pie, page 160, Short'nin' Bread, page 174, and Buttermilk Pie, page 156. Indeed, cooks of modest means developed some of the South's best-loved desserts—humble pies filled with fresh fruits and vegetables, puddings made from leftover breads and rice, rich cobblers, pastries made from flour and lard with a little of what-ever sweetener was available. Many of our most celebrated sweets are based on the South's abun-dant fruits and berries—sometimes fresh, some-times dried.

The South has been involved in sugar produc-tion since the Spanish first introduced sugar cane cultivation in the early 1700s, and that may have something to do with our mania for sweets. But in the early years, sugar cane grown in the colonies and the Louisiana Territory had to be shipped to Europe for refining; it was then sold back to America as refined sugar, and the price was high. Most Southerners could not afford the costly sweetener—with the delicious result that many desserts were developed using corn syrup, maple syrup and honey. Wild honey in particular abounded in the South, and the locations of prolific "bee trees" were closely guarded family secrets.

When sugar-refining facilities were eventually built on Southern soil, molasses, an inexpensive by-product of the refining process, became a household staple. It too found its way into many Southern muffins and other breads, and classic desserts, such as gingerbread. And in south Louisiana and Mississippi, ribbon cane syrup was widely used as a sweetener in desserts, among them the Acadian Gâteau de Sirop, opposite.

Southern desserts are rich with butter, cream and milk, for any family that owned a cow had fresh dairy products on hand. Butter and cream were kept in springhouses—small, thick-walled stone buildings constructed above natural cold-water springs. The stones captured and held the chill from the water, and wept cooling moisture.

As the plantations began to prosper in those venerable regions of the Virginia Tidewater and the Low Country of South Carolina and Georgia, wines and imported liqueurs were added to desserts in emulation of the distinguished cuisines of Europe.

One of the best ways to sample Southern food—and desserts in particular!—is to attend a "progressive dinner," long a favorite form of entertainment in the South. Several friends get together and plan a fairly large and ambitious dinner; then break the meal up into courses; each course is assigned to a different cook and served in a different home. Such a dinner makes for a delightful evening, and one can really work up an appetite driving between courses! Naturally, the best is saved for last: the dessert course is usually a feast for the eyes as well as the palate. The buffet table is spread with pastries, fruits, and countless creations dripping with chocolate, caramel and rich icings. There is something for everyone, from gooey temptations for the chocoholics to light fruit tarts, brittles and small candies for those with restraint (or for those who have overindulged in the preceding courses). What a way to end the day!

Mississippi Mud Cake

Mississippi Mud Cake is probably one of the best-known desserts in the South, though its origin remains a mystery. The reason for the name is clear, though—just think of the dark, gooey mud on the bottom of the Mississippi River! There are dozens of versions of the cake, some fluffy and mousselike, others more like a dense chocolate fudge.

2 cups sugar
1 cup unsalted butter, room temperature
4 eggs
1-1/2 cups all-purpose flour
1/3 cup unsweetened cocoa powder
1/4 teaspoon salt
2 teaspoons vanilla extract
1 cup coarsely chopped pecans
1 (10-1/2-oz.) bag miniature marshmallows
Cocoa Icing, see below

Cocoa Icing:
1/2 cup unsalted butter, room temperature
1 (1-lb.) box powdered sugar, sifted
1/2 cup evaporated milk
1/3 cup unsweetened cocoa powder
1 teaspoon vanilla extract
1 cup coarsely chopped pecans

✤ Preheat oven to 300F (150C). Butter and flour a 13″ x 9″ baking pan; shake out excess flour. Set pan aside. In bowl of an electric mixer, cream sugar and 1 cup butter at medium speed until fluffy and light in color (about 4 minutes). Add eggs, 1 at a time, and beat until mixture is blended and light lemon-yellow in color (about 5 minutes). Add 1-1/2 cups flour, cocoa powder and salt and beat just to combine well. Add vanilla and pecans and beat just to combine. Pour batter into prepared pan; bake in preheated oven until a wooden pick inserted in center of cake comes out clean (about 30 minutes). Remove cake from oven and sprinkle marshmallows over top. Return to oven and continue to bake until marshmallows are melted (about 10 minutes longer). Watch closely to avoid burning. Cool in pan on a wire rack. Meanwhile, prepare Cocoa Icing. When cake is completely cool, spread icing on top; cut into squares and serve. Makes 12 to 15 servings.

Cocoa Icing: In bowl of an electric mixer, cream butter and powdered sugar at medium speed until fluffy and light in color (about 5 minutes). Add evaporated milk and beat to blend; add cocoa powder and beat to blend. Add vanilla and pecans and beat just to combine.

Acadian Gâteau de Sirop

Deep in the heart of Louisiana's sugar cane country, around the charming town of St. Martinsville, Cajun housewives learned long ago to make delicious use of the many by-products of sugar cane cultivation and sugar refining. The dark, gooey ribbon cane syrup used in this early 20th-century dessert is one of those products. The recipe below is my adaptation of a recipe developed by the C.S. Steen Company of Abbeville, Louisiana, producers of one of the state's tastiest products: Steen's Syrup, a pure and excellent ribbon cane syrup.

> **2-1/2 cups sifted all-purpose flour**
> **1 teaspoon ground cinnamon**
> **1 teaspoon ground ginger**
> **1/2 teaspoon ground cloves**
> **1/2 teaspoon salt**
> **1/2 cup vegetable oil**
> **1-1/2 cups ribbon cane syrup**
> **1 egg, beaten until frothy**
> **2/3 cup chopped pecans**
> **1-1/2 teaspoons baking soda**
> **3/4 cup hot water**
> **Vanilla ice cream**

✤ Preheat oven to 350F (175C.) Butter and flour a 13″ x 9″ baking pan; shake out excess flour. Set pan aside. Sift flour, cinnamon, ginger, cloves and salt into a bowl; set aside. In bowl of an electric mixer, combine oil, cane syrup and egg. Beat just to blend. Add pecans and beat to incorporate. Combine baking soda with hot water and stir to blend. Add flour mixture to oil-syrup mixture alternately with hot water mixture, adding each in 3 additions and stopping to scrape down side of bowl after each addition. Then beat just to smooth out batter (about 15 seconds longer). Pour batter into prepared pan. Bake in preheated oven until cake springs back when touched (about 45 minutes). Serve hot or warm; top each serving with a scoop of vanilla ice cream. Makes 8 to 10 servings.

Applesauce Cake with Praline Icing

Apples are getting a lot of press today as a remarkable source of fiber, but in the South they've been popular for decades—though probably more for their taste than for reasons of health! We like them crisp and juicy-fresh, just as they come from the tree, and made into pies and dumplings and certainly pureed into applesauce, which we sometimes eat for breakfast. This richly iced Kentucky-born cake is sure to boost the humble sauce's social standing a bit!

> 1 cup golden raisins
> 1/2 cup Calvados or Applejack
> 2-1/2 cups cake flour
> 1/4 teaspoon ground cloves
> 1/2 teaspoon ground cinnamon
> 1/4 teaspoon freshly grated nutmeg
> 2 teaspoons baking powder
> 1/2 teaspoon salt
> 1/2 cup unsalted butter or margarine, room temperature
> 1 cup sugar
> 1 cup unsweetened applesauce
> 2 tablespoons cake flour
> Praline Icing, see below
>
> *Praline Icing:*
> 1/4 cup unsalted butter or margarine
> 2/3 cup firmly packed light brown sugar
> 1/4 cup whipping cream
> 1 cup sifted powdered sugar
> 2 teaspoons vanilla extract
> 1 cup finely chopped pecans

❦ Place raisins in a small bowl; add Calvados or Applejack. Set aside to macerate overnight at room temperature. Preheat oven to 350F (175C). Butter and flour an 8-cup bundt pan; tap pan against edge of sink to shake out excess flour. Set pan aside. Sift 2-1/2 cups cake flour, cloves, cinnamon, nutmeg, baking powder and salt into a bowl; set aside. In bowl of an electric mixer, cream butter and sugar at medium speed until fluffy and light in color (about 4 minutes). Add flour mixture to creamed mixture alternately with applesauce, adding each in 3 additions and scraping down side of bowl after each addition. Drain raisins well, reserving liqueur for another use. Toss drained raisins with 2 tablespoons cake flour to coat well. Place raisins in a strainer and shake off excess flour, then fold raisins into batter. Pour batter into prepared pan; bake in preheated oven until a wooden pick inserted in center of cake comes out clean (about 45 minutes). Cool in pan 5 minutes, then turn out onto a wire rack and cool just slightly. Prepare Praline Icing; drizzle over warm cake, letting icing run down sides. Makes 10 to 12 servings.

Praline Icing: Melt butter in a medium saucepan over medium heat. Stir in brown sugar and cream. Cook, stirring, until mixture is smooth (about 3 minutes). Remove from heat and whisk in powdered sugar and vanilla; continue to whisk until mixture is glossy and holds stiff peaks. Fold in pecans.

Aunt Jessie's Sweet Potato Cake

Some of the very best dishes in the South were created by Blacks, and this cake is a delicious example. Aunt Jessie is the well-loved cook for a family I know, and she is amazing. She can cook anything and fry any critter better than the most highly paid chef; she can take whatever food comes her way and make something wonderful out of it. Starting with a few lowly sweet potatoes, Jessie produced a marvelous nut-studded cake flavored with spices, orange—and a healthy slug of whiskey.

> **4 medium sweet potatoes (about 2 lbs.** *total***), peeled, quartered**
> **3 cups all-purpose flour**
> **2 teaspoons baking soda**
> **2 teaspoons baking powder**
> **1 teaspoon ground cinnamon**
> **1/2 teaspoon ground allspice**
> **3/4 teaspoon salt**
> **1-1/2 cups granulated sugar**
> **1 cup firmly packed light brown sugar**
> **1 cup unsalted butter, room temperature**
> **4 eggs, beaten until frothy**
> **2 teaspoons grated orange zest**
> **1/3 cup good-quality Kentucky bourbon whiskey**
> **1/3 cup fresh orange juice**
> **1 cup finely chopped pecans**
> **Powdered sugar**

❦ Place sweet potatoes in a heavy 6-quart saucepan and cover with cold water. Bring to a boil, then reduce heat, cover and simmer until potatoes are very soft (about 25 minutes). Drain potatoes, mash thoroughly and cool completely. Preheat oven to 350F (175C). Butter and flour a 12-cup bundt pan; tap pan to shake out excess flour. Set pan aside. Sift flour, baking soda, baking powder, cinnamon, allspice and salt into a bowl; set aside. In bowl of an electric mixer, cream granulated sugar, brown sugar and butter at medium speed until fluffy and light in color (about 4 minutes). Add eggs and beat to blend. Add mashed sweet potatoes and orange zest; beat to incorporate well. Combine bourbon and orange juice; add to creamed mixture alternately with flour mixture, adding each in 3 additions and stopping to scrape down side of bowl after each addition. Add pecans and beat just to combine. Pour batter into prepared pan; bake in preheated oven until a wooden pick inserted in center of cake comes out clean (55 to 60 minutes). Cool in pan 5 minutes, then turn out onto a wire rack to cool completely. Sprinkle with powdered sugar before serving. Makes 12 to 15 servings.

TIP On those maddening occasions when a cake or loaf of bread absolutely refuses to come out of its baking pan without the promise of serious damage, try this technique to save your creation from ruin. Place the pan, right side up, on a heatproof surface, then completely wrap the pan in a very damp towel. Let stand 5 minutes, then remove the towel and try to unmold the cake or bread. Repeat, if necessary. The steam created by enclosing the hot pan in the damp cloth will usually loosen the stubborn offender!

Chocolate Voodoo Cake

Voodoo is still practiced today in many areas of the Caribbean and in the Deep South, particularly Louisiana. The practice settled early in New Orleans, arriving with the slaves brought to that busy port from Caribbean plantations; Marie Laveau, the greatest of all the Voodoo Queens, is said to be buried in one of the city's historic cemeteries. This impressive cake, sheathed in a dark, deep chocolate glaze, is easily as bewitching as any voodoo spell!

1-1/2 cups strong black coffee, preferably French dark roast
6 ounces bittersweet chocolate, grated
4 cups cake flour, sifted
1-1/2 teaspoons baking soda
1 teaspoon baking powder
1 teaspoon salt
3 cups firmly packed light brown sugar
1 cup unsalted butter, room temperature
4 eggs, beaten until frothy
2/3 cup buttermilk
1 tablespoon vanilla extract
Cream Cheese Filling, see below
Chocolate Glaze, see below

Cream Cheese Filling:
1/4 cup unsalted butter, room temperature
4 ounces cream cheese, room temperature
2 tablespoons dairy sour cream
1/2 (1-lb.) box powdered sugar (about 1-7/8 cups, unsifted), sifted
1 tablespoon vanilla extract
1/2 cup finely chopped pecans

Chocolate Glaze:
8 ounces bittersweet chocolate
1/2 pint (1 cup) whipping cream

❦ Preheat oven to 375F (190C). Butter and flour three 8-inch round cake pans; shake out excess flour. Line bottom of each pan with a circle of parchment paper; butter and flour parchment and again shake out excess flour. Set pans aside. Combine coffee and chocolate in a heavy saucepan and cook over medium heat until chocolate is melted, stirring often (5 to 6 minutes). Cool. Meanwhile, sift cake flour, baking soda, baking powder and salt into a bowl and set aside. In bowl of an electric mixer, cream brown sugar and butter at medium speed until fluffy and light in color (about 4 minutes). Add eggs and beat to incorporate. Add flour mixture to creamed mixture alternately with buttermilk, adding each in 3 additions and stopping to scrape down side of bowl after each addition. Add cooled coffee-chocolate mixture and vanilla; beat just to form a smooth, blended batter (about 1 minute). Divide batter equally among prepared pans. Bake in preheated oven until a wooden pick inserted in center of cakes comes out clean (35 to 40 minutes). Cool in pans 10 minutes, then turn out onto wire racks, peel off parchment and cool completely. Meanwhile, prepare Cream Cheese Filling. Place 1 cooled cake layer on an 8-inch cardboard cake round (available in cookware shops) and spread with half the filling. Add second layer and spread with remaining filling. Add third layer; carefully align all 3 layers. Gently press top layer into place. Place a wire rack over a sheet of foil; carefully lift cake by cardboard and place on rack. Prepare Chocolate Glaze and pour slowly over cake, allowing glaze to drizzle down sides of cake. Always pour from center of top of cake; do not spread glaze with a spatula. If there are unglazed gaps on cake, scrape up leftover glaze and re-pour; gently reheat if glaze has thickened too much. Let glaze firm up before slicing cake. Makes 12 to 15 servings.

Cream Cheese Filling: In bowl of an electric mixer, cream butter and cream cheese, blending well. Beat in sour cream until combined. Add powdered sugar in several portions, beating to blend after each addition. Add vanilla and pecans and stir to incorporate well. Use at room temperature.

Chocolate Glaze: Combine chocolate and cream in a heavy 2-quart saucepan. Cook over medium-low heat, stirring constantly, until chocolate is melted and mixture is smooth and creamy (7 to 8 minutes). Glaze should be easy to pour, with a consistency like that of unchilled pudding. Remove glaze from heat and use before it begins to thicken.

Apple Dapple Cake

A simple dessert with its sing-song name, this apple-nut cake comes from the rural regions of North Carolina. It's typical of the cakes you'll find at Southern covered-dish suppers.

> **3 cups all-purpose flour**
> **1 teaspoon salt**
> **1 teaspoon baking soda**
> **3 eggs**
> **2 cups sugar**
> **1-1/2 cups vegetable oil**
> **2 teaspoons vanilla extract**
> **1 cup finely chopped pecans**
> **4 cups peeled chopped apples (about 5 medium apples)**
> **Topping, see below**
>
> *Topping:*
> **1 cup firmly packed light brown sugar**
> **1-1/2 cups unsalted butter or margarine**
> **1/4 cup milk**

❦ Preheat oven to 350F (175C). Butter and flour a 13" x 9" baking pan; shake out excess flour. Set pan aside. Sift flour, salt and baking soda into a bowl; set aside. In bowl of an electric mixer, beat eggs and sugar at medium speed until thickened and light lemon-yellow in color (about 4 minutes). Add oil and beat to blend. Add flour mixture to egg mixture, 1/3 at a time, stopping to scrape down side of bowl after each addition. Add vanilla, pecans and apples and beat just to incorporate. Pour batter into prepared baking pan; bake in preheated oven until a wooden pick inserted in center of cake comes out clean (about 45 minutes). Remove from oven; prepare Topping and pour over hot cake. Cool before serving. Makes 10 to 12 servings.

Topping: Combine all ingredients in a 2-quart saucepan. Bring to a boil; boil, whisking vigorously, 2-1/2 minutes. Use while hot.

Burnt Sugar Cake

This unusual cake, sometimes called caramel cake, is an old, old favorite throughout the South. Sadly, the cake is not seen a great deal today, perhaps because its preparation involves several separate procedures and strikes many modern cooks as too time-consuming. I would love to encourage its revival, however: it is so delicious and different, with a delightfully light texture.

Burnt Sugar Syrup, see below
2-1/4 cups sifted cake flour
2 teaspoons baking powder
1 teaspoon baking soda
1/4 teaspoon salt
1/2 cup unsalted butter or margarine, room temperature
1 cup sugar
2 eggs, separated, room temperature
1 whole egg, beaten until frothy
1 cup water
2/3 cup chopped pecans
Burnt Sugar Icing, see below

Burnt Sugar Syrup:
1/4 cup sugar
1/4 cup boiling water

Burnt Sugar Icing:
2 egg whites, room temperature
1-1/2 cups sugar
1/8 teaspoon salt
1/3 cup water
2 teaspoons dark corn syrup
2 tablespoons (1/2 recipe) Burnt Sugar Syrup

❦ Preheat oven to 350F (175C). Butter and flour two 9-inch springform pans; shake out excess flour. Line bottom of each pan with a circle of parchment paper or wax paper; butter and flour paper and again shake out excess flour. Set pans aside. Prepare Burnt Sugar Syrup; set aside. (You will use 2 tablespoons syrup in cake, 2 tablespoons in icing.) Sift cake flour, baking powder, baking soda and salt into a bowl; set aside. In bowl of an electric mixer, cream butter and sugar at medium speed until fluffy and light in color (about 4 minutes). Beat 2 egg yolks until frothy and combine with whole egg; add to creamed mixture and beat to blend. Add flour mixture to creamed mixture alternately with water, adding each in 3 additions and stopping to scrape down side of bowl after each addition. Add pecans and beat just to incorporate. Turn out batter into a large bowl and set aside. In a separate bowl, beat 2 egg whites at medium speed until they hold soft peaks (about 2-1/2 minutes). With mixer running, slowly add 2 tablespoons Burnt Sugar Syrup. Continue to beat until mixture holds stiff peaks (about 2 minutes longer). Gently but thoroughly, fold egg white mixture into batter. Pour batter into prepared pans; bake in preheated oven until a wooden pick inserted in center of cakes comes out clean (30 to 35 minutes). Cool in pans

5 minutes, then remove sides of pans and place cakes on a wire rack. Remove bottoms of pans and carefully peel off parchment paper or wax paper. Cool cakes completely. Prepare Burnt Sugar Icing. To assemble cake, place 1 cooled layer on a platter and spread with some of icing. Carefully place second layer on top, aligning sides. Spread remaining icing on top and sides of cake. Makes 12 to 15 servings.

Burnt Sugar Syrup: Place sugar in heavy 2-quart saucepan and cook over medium heat, stirring often, until sugar has reached the light caramel stage. Slowly add boiling water and stir until sugar is dissolved. Cool before using. You should have 1/4 cup; use 2 tablespoons in cake batter, 2 tablespoons in icing.

Burnt Sugar Icing: Combine egg whites, sugar, salt, water and corn syrup in top of double boiler over gently boiling water. Beat with a hand-held electric mixer until mixture holds thick, soft peaks (about 7 minutes). Remove top of pan from boiling water and slowly add Burnt Sugar Syrup, continuing to beat until icing holds stiff peaks (about 2 minutes).

Wine Cake with Apricot Glaze

I have found variations of this delightfully moist, dense-textured cake all over the South. The recipes vary, but all are based on an egg- and butter-rich batter with dry white wine added. The cake is typically served during the holiday season. If you like, use another flavor of preserves in the glaze.

> **1-1/2 cups unsalted butter, room temperature**
> **3 cups sugar**
> **5 eggs**
> **3 cups sifted all-purpose flour**
> **3/4 cup dry white wine**
> **Apricot Glaze, see below**
>
> *Apricot Glaze:*
> **1 cup apricot preserves**
> **2 tablespoons brandy**
> **2 tablespoons sugar**

❦ Preheat oven to 350F (175C). Butter and flour a 10-cup bundt pan; tap pan against edge of sink to shake out excess flour. Set pan aside. In bowl of an electric mixer, cream butter and sugar at medium speed until fluffy and light in color (about 4 minutes). Beat in eggs, 1 at a time, stopping to scrape down side of bowl after each addition. Add flour, 3/4 at a time, again stopping to scrape down side of bowl after each addition. Beat just until flour is completely incorporated. Add wine and beat to blend (about 30 seconds). Pour batter into prepared pan; bake in preheated oven until a wooden pick inserted in center of cake comes out clean (about 1 hour). Cool in pan 10 minutes, then turn out onto a wire rack to cool completely. Place cooled cake on a platter. Prepare Apricot Glaze and brush over cake, covering thoroughly. Makes 12 to 15 servings.

Apricot Glaze: Place preserves in a heavy 2-quart saucepan and cook over medium heat until melted (about 6 minutes). Strain preserves through a fine strainer, stirring with a wooden spoon to remove all liquid. Discard solid portions remaining in strainer (or save to use on biscuits.) Combine strained preserves, brandy and sugar in a small saucepan and bring to a boil over medium heat. Use while hot.

Southern Jam Cake

Jam cakes are an institution in the South. The recipe was probably invented when some housewife wanted a nice fruit dessert in the dead of winter, and hit upon the idea of stirring some of her delicious homemade jam into a cake batter. The end product tasted so good that she shared the secret with her neighbors—and a Southern classic was born. You may substitute another fruit jam for blackberry jam, if desired.

3 cups sifted all-purpose flour
1 teaspoon baking soda
1/2 teaspoon salt
1/4 teaspoon ground cloves
1/4 teaspoon freshly grated nutmeg
1 teaspoon ground cinnamon
1 cup unsalted butter or margarine, room temperature
1-1/2 cups sugar
3 eggs, beaten until frothy
1-1/2 cups seedless blackberry jam
1 cup buttermilk
Icing, see below

Icing:
2 cups firmly packed light brown sugar
1 cup granulated sugar
1/2 cup water
1/2 cup whipping cream
3 tablespoons unsalted butter or margarine, room temperature

❦ Preheat oven to 350F (175C). Butter and flour a 10-cup tube pan; tap pan on edge of sink to shake out excess flour. Set pan aside. Sift flour, baking soda, salt, cloves, nutmeg and cinnamon into a bowl; set aside. In bowl of an electric mixer, cream butter and sugar at medium speed until fluffy and light in color (about 4 minutes). Add eggs and jam; beat to combine well. Add flour mixture to creamed mixture alternately with buttermilk, adding each in 3 additions and stopping to scrape down side of bowl after each addition. Pour batter into prepared pan; bake in preheated oven until a wooden pick inserted in center of cake comes out clean (55 to 60 minutes). Cool in pan 5 minutes, then turn out onto a wire rack to cool completely. Prepare icing. Place cooled cake on a serving platter and spread with Icing. Makes 12 to 15 servings.

Icing: Combine brown sugar, granulated sugar and water in a heavy 2-quart saucepan. Cook over medium heat, stirring gently, until syrup reaches the thread stage—234F (114C) on a candy thermometer. Remove from heat and add cream and butter. Beat with a hand-held electric mixer until thickened and creamy, with an icing-type consistency (3 to 4 minutes).

Upside-Down Apple Gingerbread
with Praline Cream

Gingerbread has long been a favorite Southern dessert, popular with rich and poor folks alike. This version is topped with tender sliced apples and served with praline-flavored whipped cream.

2-1/2 cups all-purpose flour
1 teaspoon baking soda
1/2 teaspoon salt
1-1/4 teaspoons ground ginger
1 teaspoon ground cinnamon
3 tablespoons unsalted butter or margarine, melted
6 tablespoons firmly packed dark brown sugar
3 medium apples (about 1-1/4 lbs. *total*), peeled, cored, quartered
1/2 cup unsalted butter or margarine, room temperature
1 egg
1 cup molasses
1 cup boiling water
Praline Cream, see below

Praline Cream:
1/2 pint (1 cup) whipping cream
2 tablespoons powdered sugar
2 teaspoons vanilla extract
2 tablespoons dairy sour cream
2 tablespoons praline liqueur or Frangelico

❦ Preheat oven to 350F (175C). Butter and flour an 8-inch-square baking pan; shake out excess flour. Set pan aside. In a bowl, combine flour, baking soda, salt, ginger and cinnamon. Set aside. Combine melted butter with 3 tablespoons brown sugar, stirring to blend. Spread mixture in bottom of prepared pan. Cut quartered apples into 1/4-inch-thick slices and scatter over butter mixture in baking pan. In bowl of an electric mixer, cream 1/2 cup butter or margarine and remaining 3 tablespoons brown sugar at medium speed until fluffy and light (about 4 minutes). Add egg and beat just to blend. In a separate bowl, combine molasses and boiling water. Add molasses mixture to creamed mixture alternately with flour mixture, adding each in 3 additions and stopping to scrape down side of bowl after each addition. Beat just until blended. Pour batter over apples in baking dish and bake in preheated oven until a wooden pick inserted in center comes out clean (about 35 minutes). Meanwhile, prepare Praline Cream; refrigerate as directed. Cool gingerbread in pan 10 minutes, then invert onto a platter. If any apple mixture sticks to baking dish, scrape it out with a spoon and gently spread back on top of gingerbread. Cut into squares and serve topped with Praline Cream. Makes 8 to 10 servings.
Praline Cream: Combine all ingredients in bowl of an electric mixer and beat at medium speed until mixture holds soft, floppy peaks (about 2 minutes). Cover tightly and refrigerate until ready to serve.

Sour Cream & Lemon Cake

A dense, moist cake with a crowd-pleasing not-too-sweet taste. It's easy to prepare and looks most impressive when baked in a kugelhopf pan.

> **2 cups all-purpose flour**
> **2 teaspoons baking powder**
> **1 teaspoon salt**
> **1 cup unsalted butter or margarine, room temperature**
> **2 cups sugar**
> **3 eggs**
> **Grated zest of 1 large lemon**
> **1/2 pint (1 cup) dairy sour cream**
> **Lemon Glaze, see below**
>
> *Lemon Glaze:*
> **1/4 cup unsalted butter, melted**
> **2 tablespoons fresh lemon juice**
> **2 cups powdered sugar, sifted**

❦ Preheat oven to 325F (165C). Thoroughly butter and flour a 10-inch kugelhopf or bundt pan; tap pan on edge of sink to shake out excess flour. Set pan aside. Sift flour, baking powder and salt into a medium bowl; set aside. In bowl of an electric mixer, cream butter and sugar at low speed until blended, then beat at medium until mixture is very fluffy (about 6 minutes). Beat in eggs, 1 at a time, scraping down side of bowl after each addition. Add lemon zest and blend. Add flour mixture to creamed mixture alternately with sour cream, adding each in 3 additions and scraping down side of bowl after each addition. Pour batter into prepared pan; bake in preheated oven until a wooden pick inserted in center of cake comes out clean (about 1 hour). Cool in pan 10 minutes. Meanwhile, prepare Lemon Glaze. Turn out cake onto a platter; drizzle evenly with glaze. Makes 12 to 15 servings.

Baked Custard Pie

A classic in the South, this pie is a fine example of rural Southern home cooking. Because everyone who lived out in the country had fresh eggs and fresh milk and cream to churn into butter, custard pies were always easy to whip up—and besides that, they were rich enough to satisfy the hungry household.

Pie Crust Dough, see below
1-1/2 cups milk
1/4 cup unsalted butter
7 eggs
1 cup sugar
1 tablespoon vanilla extract
Whole nutmeg

Pie Crust Dough:
3 tablespoons unsalted butter, room temperature
2 tablespoons lard or solid vegetable shortening
1/3 cup sugar
1 egg
About 3 tablespoons milk
1 teaspoon vanilla extract
1-1/2 cups all-purpose flour
1/4 teaspoon salt
1/2 teaspoon baking powder

❦ Prepare Pie Crust Dough and refrigerate as directed. Preheat oven to 425F (220C). Roll out chilled dough 1/16 inch thick on a generously floured work surface. Roll dough loosely around rolling pin and unroll over a 10-inch pie pan. Lift edges of dough to let it fall gently into bottom of pan; do not stretch dough. Pat dough gently into pan sides. Trim edges, leaving a 1-inch overhang. Fold overhang under; flute edges or crimp with tines of a fork. Refrigerate while you prepare filling. To prepare filling, combine milk and butter in a medium saucepan and heat over medium heat just until small bubbles appear around sides of pan (about 10 minutes). Do not boil. Set aside. In bowl of an electric mixer, beat eggs and sugar at medium speed until thickened and light and lemon-yellow in color (about 5 minutes). Then add scalded milk mixture, 1/4 cup at a time, beating constantly. Blend in vanilla. Strain mixture through a fine strainer and pour into prepared crust. Grate a fine sprinkling of nutmeg over top. Bake pie in preheated oven 10 minutes, then reduce oven temperature to 350F (175C) and continue to bake until a knife inserted in center of pie comes out clean (about 30 minutes longer). Remove pie from oven and cool completely before slicing. For best taste and texture, refrigerate until well chilled before serving. Makes 8 to 10 servings.

Pie Crust Dough: In bowl of an electric mixer, cream butter, lard and sugar at medium speed until fluffy and light in color (about 4 minutes). Add egg, 3 tablespoons milk and vanilla; mix well. (Mixture will appear curdled.) Set aside. In a separate bowl, combine flour, salt and baking powder. Using your fingertips and palms, combine creamed mixture with flour mixture to form a dough that holds together. If dough is too dry and crumbly, add more milk, 1 teaspoon at a time; if dough mixture is too sticky, add more flour, 1 tablespoon at a time. Flatten dough into a disc, wrap tightly in plastic wrap and refrigerate 1 hour.

Upside-Down Pear Pie
with Pear Custard Topping

I "borrowed" this recipe from one of my best friends—Christy Sheets Mull of Roswell, Georgia, a wonderful Southern cook born and bred. The first time she served me her sinfully gooey creation, I gained a profound new respect for plain old pears! It's an unforgettable dessert that's sure to impress your guests. (Christy's a talented artist as well as a superb cook, as evidenced by the illustrations throughout this book.)

6 medium pears, peeled, cored, coarsely chopped
1/2 cup golden raisins
1/2 cup Poire William (pear-flavored liqueur)
Pie Pastry, see below
5 tablespoons unsalted butter, melted
1/2 cup firmly packed dark brown sugar
2/3 cup chopped pecans
1 cup granulated sugar
3 tablespoons cornstarch
3/4 teaspoon ground cinnamon
1/4 teaspoon freshly grated nutmeg
1/8 teaspoon ground cloves
1/4 teaspoon salt
Pear Custard Topping, see below

Pie Pastry:
2-3/4 cups all-purpose flour
1 cup frozen unsalted butter, cut into 1-inch cubes
1 teaspoon salt
1 tablespoon sugar
1 egg yolk
1/2 cup ice water

Pear Custard Topping:
1/2 cup sugar
1 teaspoon cornstarch
1/4 teaspoon salt
5 egg yolks
1/2 cup milk
1 pint (2 cups) whipping cream
1/2 cup Poire William (pear-flavored liqueur)
2 teaspoons vanilla extract

❦ Place pears and raisins in a bowl and toss with liqueur. Set aside to macerate 2 hours at room temperature. Prepare pastry and refrigerate as directed. Preheat oven to 375F (190C). In bottom of a 10-inch deep-dish pie pan, combine melted butter, brown sugar and pecans, spreading evenly. Remove 1 pastry disc from refrigerator and roll out 1/16 inch thick on a lightly floured work surface. Ease pastry into pie pan over butter mixture and gently pat into pan sides, taking care not to stretch pastry. Trim edges, leaving a 1/2-inch overhang. Drain pears and raisins; scatter evenly over pastry. Combine granulated sugar, cornstarch, cinnamon, nutmeg, cloves and salt; sprinkle evenly over fruit. Roll out second pastry disc 1/16 inch thick and lay gently over filling. Trim edges, leaving a 1-inch overhang. Tuck edges of top crust under overhang of bottom crust; roll edges inward to secure. Seal edges with tines of a fork. Prick top crust 6 or 7 times with a fork. Place pie on a baking sheet and bake in preheated oven until crust is golden brown and filling is bubbly (about 50 minutes.) Meanwhile, prepare Pear Custard Topping; refrigerate. Remove baked pie from oven and loosen edges of pie with a metal spatula. Invert a large rimmed platter over pie; hold platter and pie pan together and quickly invert both. Let stand 5 minutes, then remove pie pan. Serve pie warm; generously top each serving with Pear Custard Topping. Makes 8 to 10 servings.

Pie Pastry: In a food processor fitted with the steel blade, combine flour, butter, salt, sugar and egg yolk. Process until butter is broken into pea-size bits. With machine running, pour ice water through feed tube and process just to form a dough that holds together; *do not* process until dough forms a ball. Turn out dough onto a work surface and gather together with your hands; pat into 2 flat discs. Wrap each disc in plastic wrap and refrigerate until ready to use.

Pear Custard Topping: Combine sugar, cornstarch and salt in a heavy small saucepan. Whisk in egg yolks, blending well. In a separate saucepan, heat milk and 1 cup cream over medium heat just until small bubbles appear around sides of pan (about 10 minutes); add to egg mixture, whisking constantly. Cook, whisking, over medium-low heat until thickened (about 8 minutes). Stir in liqueur and cook, whisking, until mixture thickens again (2 to 3 minutes longer). Remove from heat and whisk in vanilla. Transfer to a bowl, cover and refrigerate until chilled before serving. When ready to serve, beat remaining 1 cup cream until it holds medium-stiff peaks; fold into custard.

Pecan Chess Pie

Chess pie is an old-time dessert that you'll encounter in any number of variations—cornmeal chess pie, lemon chess pie, apple chess pie, plain chess pie. All feature a rich, custard-type filling baked in a flaky pastry crust. My favorite version is made with pecans, the South's number one nut.

> 1/2 recipe Basic Southern Pie Pastry, page 165, chilled
> 1/2 cup unsalted butter, room temperature
> 1 cup sugar
> 1/4 cup all-purpose flour
> 1/4 teaspoon salt
> 3 egg yolks
> 1/2 cup evaporated milk
> 2 teaspoons vanilla extract
> 1 cup chopped pecans

❦ Preheat oven to 425F (220C). Roll out pastry and fit into a 9-inch pie pan as directed on page 164. Refrigerate while you prepare filling. To prepare filling, in bowl of an electric mixer, cream butter and sugar at medium speed until fluffy and light in color (about 4 minutes). Add flour, salt and egg yolks; beat until blended (about 2 minutes). Add evaporated milk and vanilla; beat 2 minutes to form a smooth blended mixture. Pour into pastry-lined pie pan and sprinkle pecans over top, distributing evenly. Bake in preheated oven 10 minutes. Reduce oven temperature to 300F (150C) and continue to bake until a knife inserted in center of pie comes out clean (35 to 40 minutes longer). Cool to room temperature, then refrigerate until well chilled before slicing. Makes 8 to 10 servings.

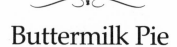

Buttermilk Pie

Buttermilk pie is a perfect example of the South's wonderful "down-home style cookin'." It's especially good if made from fresh buttermilk, though you'll only get fresh buttermilk if you churn your own butter! (Buttermilk is the liquid left in the churn after the butter solidifies on the dasher; it tastes very much like liquid cottage cheese.)

> 1/2 recipe Basic Southern Pie Pastry, page 165, chilled
> 3/4 cup firmly packed light brown sugar
> 3/4 cup granulated sugar
> 1/2 cup unsalted butter, room temperature
> 1 tablespoon all-purpose flour
> 3 eggs
> 1/3 cup buttermilk
> 1-1/2 teaspoons vanilla extract
> 1/4 teaspoon salt

✤ Preheat oven to 350F (175C). Roll out pastry and fit into a 9-inch pie pan as directed on page 164; refrigerate while you prepare filling. To prepare filling, in bowl of an electric mixer, cream brown sugar, granulated sugar and butter until fluffy and light in color (about 4 minutes). Add flour and beat just to blend. Beat in eggs, 1 at a time, stopping to scrape down side of bowl after each addition. Add buttermilk, vanilla and salt; beat just to blend. Pour mixture into pastry-lined pan; bake in preheated oven just until filling is set (30 to 35 minutes). Do not overbake or the pie will be watery. Refrigerate until well chilled before slicing. Makes 8 to 10 servings.

Rum-Tum Pie

This rum-heady South Florida treat is, pardon the pun, as easy as pie to prepare. For the best flavor, be sure to use dark Jamaican rum.

> **Chocolate Crust, see below**
> **26 large marshmallows**
> **1/2 cup milk**
> **3 tablespoons unsalted butter, room temperature**
> **1/3 cup dark rum**
> **2 teaspoons vanilla extract**
> **1/2 pint (1 cup) whipping cream**
>
> *Chocolate Crust:*
> **1-1/4 cups fine chocolate wafer crumbs**
> **1 tablespoon sugar**
> **3 tablespoons unsalted butter, melted**

✤ Prepare Chocolate Crust and refrigerate as directed. To prepare filling, combine marshmallows and milk in top of a double boiler over rapidly simmering water. Cook until marshmallows are melted (10 to 12 minutes). Remove from heat and stir in butter. Cool completely. Stir in rum and vanilla, blending well. Whip cream until it holds stiff peaks; fold into cooled mixture. Pour mixture into prepared crust. Refrigerate until completely set (about 3 hours). Makes 8 to 10 servings.

Chocolate Crust: Combine all ingredients in a medium bowl; toss with a fork to moisten crumbs well. Pour mixture into a 9-inch pie pan and pat into bottom and sides of pan. (The bottom and sides of a small juice glass work well for this purpose.) Refrigerate at least 1 hour before filling.

Black Bottom Pie

Black bottom pie is another classic Southern dessert. Appearance alone could explain the name: the pie is dark and chocolaty on the bottom, light and whiskey-flavored on top. There's a second explanation, though: this dessert was created by Blacks, who, in years past, often lived in low-lying marshy areas known as bottoms.

 Ginger Crust, see below
 2 cups milk
 4 eggs, separated, room temperature
 1 cup granulated sugar
 1-1/2 tablespoons cornstarch
 2 ounces bittersweet chocolate, melted, cooled
 1 teaspoon vanilla extract
 1-1/2 tablespoons unflavored gelatin
 2 tablespoons cold water
 1/2 teaspoon cream of tartar
 2 tablespoons good-quality Kentucky bourbon whiskey
 1/2 pint (1 cup) whipping cream
 2 teaspoons vanilla extract
 2 tablespoons powdered sugar
 2 tablespoons dairy sour cream
 Grated bittersweet chocolate

 Ginger Crust:
 1 cup fine gingersnap crumbs
 5 tablespoons unsalted butter or margarine, melted

❦ Prepare crust and chill as directed. To prepare filling, heat milk in a medium saucepan over medium heat just until small bubbles appear around sides of pan (about 10 minutes). Do not allow milk to boil. In bowl of an electric mixer, beat egg yolks, 1/2 cup granulated sugar and cornstarch at medium speed until thickened and light lemon-yellow in color (about 2 minutes). Place egg mixture in top of a double boiler over simmering water and slowly add the scalded milk, whisking egg mixture vigorously. Cook, whisking often, until custard coats a spoon (about 9 minutes). Remove custard from heat and measure out 1 cup; cover remaining custard and set aside. Fold melted chocolate and 1 teaspoon vanilla into the 1 cup custard, pour into chilled pie crust and spread evenly. Refrigerate until set (about 1 hour). Then stir gelatin into cold water in a heatproof bowl and set aside until all liquid is absorbed and gelatin feels spongy to the touch. Set over hot water and stir until completely dissolved, then stir into reserved custard. Cool at room temperature 20 minutes. In bowl of an electric mixer, beat egg whites at medium speed until they begin to stiffen (about 1 minute). Add remaining 1/2 cup granulated sugar, cream of tartar and bourbon and beat at medium speed until mixture holds medium-stiff peaks (about 2 minutes). Do not overbeat. Fold cooled custard into beaten whites gently but thoroughly; spread over chocolate custard. Refrigerate until completely set (about 3 hours). Beat whipping cream with 2 teaspoons vanilla, powdered sugar and sour cream until stiff. Spread mixture over pie and sprinkle with grated chocolate. Makes 8 to 10 servings.

Ginger Crust: Combine gingersnap crumbs with butter in a medium bowl; toss with a fork to moisten crumbs well. Turn out into a 9-inch pie pan and pat into bottom and sides of pan. (The bottom and sides of a small juice glass work well for this purpose.) Place crust in freezer to chill while you prepare filling.

Peanut Pie

The peanut is a staple in the South, with dozens of cooking uses; it even plays an important role as the hog feed that gives Virginia country hams their uniquely wonderful flavor! But like sesame seeds, eggplant, and a number of other Southern favorites, peanuts are not native to North America. They came to the U.S. from Africa.

Credit for peanut pie, one of the best-known Southern desserts, goes to George Washington Carver, founder of Tuskegee Institute. In the late 1800s, when the boll weevil threatened the cotton crop and with it the entire Southern economy, Carver encouraged increased cultivation of peanuts as a replacement crop. His research teams developed recipes for peanut soups, stews, pies and cookies—and peanut pie in particular gained quick and lasting popularity. With the introduction of creamy peanut butter in 1912, it acquired the smooth texture for which it is known today.

> 1 recipe Cream Cheese Pie Pastry, page 166, chilled
> 3 eggs
> 1 cup dark corn syrup
> 1/2 cup sugar
> 1/2 cup creamy peanut butter
> 1 teaspoon vanilla extract
> 1 cup salted peanuts
> Whipped cream

❦ Preheat oven to 400F (205C). Roll out pastry and fit into a 9-inch pie pan as directed on page 164. Refrigerate while you prepare filling. To prepare filling, in bowl of electric mixer, beat eggs, corn syrup, sugar, peanut butter and vanilla at medium speed until mixture is smooth and thickened (about 4 minutes). Stir in peanuts and beat just to blend. Pour filling into pastry-lined pie pan; bake in preheated oven 15 minutes. Reduce oven temperature to 350F (175C) and continue to bake until filling is set and a knife inserted in center of pie comes out clean (30 to 35 minutes longer). Cool completely before serving; top each slice with a dollop of whipped cream. Makes 8 to 10 servings.

Green Tomato Pie

When tomatoes were first introduced to Europe, many believed them to be poisonous, probably because these native Central and South American fruits belong to the same botanical family as deadly nightshade. In the American colonies, the plant was initially grown exclusively as an ornamental shrub—but eventually, a few brave souls risked eating the colorful fruit. Thomas Jefferson cultivated tomatoes at Monticello in the early 1800s, but it wasn't until around 1900 that consumption of tomatoes really took off in the South. Once it did, though, we made up for lost time! We use tomatoes ripe or green, raw or cooked, at breakfast, lunch and dinner. This delicious and very different pie is a fine example of Southern country-style food.

> 1 recipe Boiling Water Method Pie Pastry, page 165
> 3 cups sliced green tomatoes (about 1-3/4 lbs.)
> 1-1/2 cups sugar
> 1/4 teaspoon salt
> 5 teaspoons grated lemon zest
> 1/4 teaspoon ground cinnamon
> 5 tablespoons fresh lemon juice
> 1/4 cup unsalted butter or margarine, melted

❦ Preheat oven to 350F (175C). Roll out bottom crust and fit into a 9-inch pie pan as directed on page 164. Arrange a layer of tomatoes in bottom of pastry-lined pie pan. In a bowl, combine sugar, salt, lemon zest, cinnamon, lemon juice and butter; tossing with a fork to blend. Sprinkle about 1/3 of sugar mixture over tomatoes. Add another layer of tomatoes and sprinkle with half the remaining sugar mixture. Layer on remaining tomatoes and sprinkle with remaining sugar mixture. Roll out top crust and place on filling. Flute edges, then cut steam vents in top crust. Bake in preheated oven until crust is golden brown and filling is bubbly (35 to 40 minutes). Cool slightly before serving. Makes 8 to 10 servings.

Vinegar Pie

Vinegar Pie is as Southern as apple pie is American. The recipe was concocted years ago by country cooks, who rarely had fancy store-bought seasonings or "exotic" fruits, and had to make do with what was on hand in the farm kitchen. For example, fresh lemons were seldom available, so bottled lemon extract was used in their place. Another popular flavoring was homemade cider vinegar, brewed up from apple peels and cores, fresh rainwater, and a touch of honey or molasses.

Today, of course, fresh lemons aren't the least bit hard to come by. In testing this old recipe, though, I found that the highly concentrated lemon extract actually produced a better-tasting pie than did fresh lemon juice—proof that it's often best to leave well enough alone, especially in regard to recipes that have already stood the hard test of time.

1/2 recipe Basic Southern Pie Pastry, page 165, chilled
1 cup water
1/4 cup all-purpose flour
1 cup sugar
1 egg, beaten until frothy
3 tablespoons apple cider vinegar
1 teaspoon lemon extract

❦ Roll out pastry, fit into a 9-inch pie pan and bake "blind" as directed on page 164. Cool baked pastry shell completely. In a heavy 2-quart saucepan, bring water to a boil. In a small bowl, combine flour and sugar, tossing with a fork to blend. Add flour-sugar mixture to boiling water and cook, whisking often, until thickened (about 5 minutes). Remove from heat and slowly add egg, whisking vigorously. Return to medium-low heat and cook, whisking, until smooth and velvety (about 2 minutes). Add vinegar and lemon extract and whisk just to blend. Turn out into cooled pastry shell and refrigerate until set (about 2 hours). Makes 8 to 10 servings.

Osgood Pie

No one seems to know the origin of this yummy raisin- and pecan-studded custard pie. It's just one of those Southern desserts that has always been around—and wherever it came from, it is certainly here to stay. A little old lady described Osgood pie to me as "one of my favorites for carrying to suppers at the church."

1 recipe Cream Cheese Pie Pastry, page 166, chilled
4 eggs
2 cups sugar
1/4 cup milk
3 tablespoons unsalted butter or margarine, melted
1/2 teaspoon ground cinnamon
1 cup raisins
1 cup chopped pecans
2 teaspoons vanilla extract

❦ Preheat oven to 450F (230C). Roll out pastry and fit into a 9-inch pie pan as directed on page 164. Refrigerate while you prepare filling. To prepare filling, in bowl of an electric mixer, beat eggs and sugar at medium speed until thickened and light lemon-yellow in color (about 4 minutes). Add milk, butter, cinnamon, raisins, pecans and vanilla; beat just to blend. Pour mixture into pastry-lined pie pan; bake in preheated oven 10 minutes. Reduce oven temperature to 350F (175C) and continue to bake until filling is set and a knife inserted in center of pie comes out clean (about 30 minutes longer). Refrigerate until well chilled before slicing. Makes 8 to 10 servings.

Key Lime Pie

Delicate, pleasantly tart key lime pie is one of Florida's best-known desserts. The authentic pie gets its truly wonderful flavor from fresh key limes, grown only in South Florida. These yellow fruit look for all the world like lemons, but their flesh is an unmistakable lime-green. If you cannot get key limes, you may use regular limes in their place. Either way, the pie filling will be a sort of nondescript pale yellow in color; many restaurants add green food coloring to give the pie a more "limelike" hue, but this is a purely optional step.

1/2 recipe Basic Southern Pie Pastry, page 165, chilled
1 (1/4-oz.) envelope unflavored gelatin
1/4 cup water
1 cup sugar
1/4 teaspoon salt
4 eggs, separated, room temperature
2 teaspoons grated lime zest
1/2 cup fresh key lime juice (about 3 large key limes)
2 drops green food coloring, if desired
1/2 pint (1 cup) whipping cream
Meringue, see below

Meringue:
2/3 cup sugar
4-1/2 tablespoons lukewarm water
6 egg whites, room temperature

❡ Roll out pastry, fit into a 9-inch pie pan and bake "blind" as directed on page 164. Cool baked pastry shell completely. To prepare filling, in a small bowl, stir gelatin into water and set aside until all liquid is absorbed and gelatin feels spongy to the touch. Turn out softened gelatin into top of double boiler over gently simmering water and stir until completely dissolved. In a medium bowl, combine 1/2 cup sugar, salt, egg yolks, lime zest and lime juice; whisk until frothy. Slowly add egg mixture to dissolved gelatin, whisking constantly. Cook, whisking constantly, just until mixture comes to a low boil (3 to 4 minutes). Immediately remove from heat and whisk in food coloring, if desired. Refrigerate mixture until it will mound slightly when dropped from a spoon (about 1 hour). In bowl of an electric mixer, beat egg whites at medium speed until they hold soft peaks (about 2-1/2 minutes). Gradually add remaining 1/2 cup sugar, beating until whites hold medium-stiff peaks (about 1-1/2 minutes longer). Using a rubber spatula, fold chilled gelatin mixture into beaten whites. In a separate bowl, beat cream at medium speed until it holds medium-stiff peaks (about 3 minutes). Fold whipped cream into filling, then spoon into cooled pastry shell and spread evenly. Refrigerate until filling is completely set (about 3 hours). Then preheat oven to 350F (175C). Prepare Meringue and spread evenly over pie. Bake in preheated oven until peaks of Meringue are lightly browned (10 to 12 minutes). Refrigerate until well chilled before serving. Makes 8 to 10 servings.
Meringue: Combine sugar and lukewarm water in a heavy 2-quart saucepan. Cook over medium heat until mixture reaches the thread stage. Meanwhile, in bowl of an electric mixer, beat egg whites at medium speed until they hold soft peaks (about 2-1/2 minutes). Slowly add hot sugar syrup to whites, beating until mixture holds medium-stiff peaks (about 2 minutes longer). Use at once.

Caramel Pie

Like Southern Jam Cake, page 150, caramel pie is practically a Southern institution, a wonderful, down-home sweet that stands in open opposition to modern trends toward lighter desserts. I first tasted the pie in a restaurant in Bolivar, Tennessee, where the cook kept his recipe a closely guarded secret. The version below is adapted from the pie served at the Mendenhall Hotel in Mendenhall, Mississippi, an old-fashioned hotel-boarding house famous far and wide for its good old everyday Southern fare. All meals at the hotel are served family style, at large round tables centered with revolving "trays" that hold the food.

> 1/2 recipe Boiling Water Method Pie Pastry, page 165
> 1-1/2 cups sugar
> 3 tablespoons plus 1 teaspoon cornstarch
> 1/4 teaspoon salt
> 3 egg yolks
> 2 cups milk, warmed
> 1/4 cup unsalted butter or margarine, room temperature
> 2 teaspoons vanilla extract
> Meringue, opposite

❦ Prepare pastry, roll out, fit into a 9-inch pie pan and bake "blind" as directed on page 164. Cool baked pastry shell completely. To prepare filling, place 1/2 cup sugar in a heavy 4-quart saucepan and cook over medium heat, stirring often, until sugar has reached the light caramel stage. Meanwhile, in bowl of an electric mixer, beat remaining 1 cup sugar, cornstarch, salt and egg yolks at medium speed until thickened and light lemon-yellow in color (about 4 minutes). Slowly add milk and beat to blend. Whisk milk mixture into caramelized sugar in saucepan and stir in butter. (Mixture will "clump," but soon dissolve.) Cook, whisking constantly, until mixture is thickened (about 3 minutes). Remove from heat; whisk in vanilla. Continue to whisk about 2 minutes longer. Strain mixture through a fine strainer into cooled pastry shell. Refrigerate until well chilled. Then preheat oven to 350F (175C) and prepare Meringue; spread over pie. Bake in preheated oven until peaks of Meringue are lightly browned (10 to 12 minutes). Cool completely before serving. Makes 8 to 10 servings.

Southern Pie Pastry

Southern pie pastry is known far and wide for its wonderful flavor and light, flaky texture. To create the same special pastry in your own kitchen, you need two "secret" ingredients—lard and Southern soft wheat flour. The most traditional method of making Southern pastry was rubbing a mixture of lard and freshly churned butter into flour, then adding just enough water to hold the dough together. Another favorite technique, first popular in the Carolinas, was beating lard, boiling water and milk until fluffy, then mixing in the flour. After the introduction of commercial cream cheese in the 1920s, Southern housewives grew fond of a rich pie crust made with cream cheese and butter.

To roll out pastry for a bottom crust or single-crust pie, lightly flour a work surface and roll pastry gently, but with pressure, into a circle about 1/16 inch thick. Loosely roll pastry around rolling pin, then unroll it over pie pan. Lift edges of pastry all around pan, allowing pastry to slide into bottom of pan; do not stretch or force pastry into pan bottom. Gently pat pastry into sides of pan. Using kitchen shears, trim off excess pastry at pan rim, leaving a 1-inch overhang. If preparing a single-crust pie, tuck overhang under, pressing it lightly against pan rim; flute edges, if desired, or press with tines of a fork. Fill and bake as directed in pie recipe.

To roll out pastry for a double-crust pie, roll out bottom crust as directed above, then add filling. Reflour work surface and roll out top crust 1/16 inch thick. Loosely roll pastry around rolling pin and unroll carefully over filled pie. Using kitchen shears, trim off excess pastry at pan rim, leaving a 1-inch overhang. Press edges of top and bottom crusts together and tuck overhang under, even with pan. Flute edges, if desired, or press with tines of fork. Cut several steam vents in an attractive pattern in top crust. Bake as directed in pie recipe.

To bake a single pie crust "blind" (without filling), prick bottom all over with a fork. Preheat oven to 400F (205C). Carefully line bottom and sides of crust with foil, then fill with dried beans or rice. Bake in preheated oven 25 to 30 minutes. Remove foil and beans carefully and return crust to oven. Continue to bake until bottom of crust is browned (7 to 8 minutes longer). Remove from oven; cool before filling.

Basic Southern Pie Pastry

2 cups Southern soft wheat flour, see pages 122
1-1/2 teaspoons salt
1/3 cup unsalted butter, room temperature
1/3 cup lard
4 to 6 tablespoons ice water

❦ Combine flour, salt, butter and lard in a large bowl. With your fingertips, work fat into flour until mixture resembles coarse meal. Add 4 tablespoons ice water and toss together with your fingers just to moisten flour and form a cohesive dough. Do not knead; handle dough as little as possible. If dough is too dry and crumbly, add more ice water, a teaspoon at a time. Divide dough in half and flatten each half into a disc. Wrap tightly in plastic wrap and refrigerate 1 hour before rolling. (See opposite page.) Makes enough pastry for 1 (9-inch) double-crust pie.

Boiling Water Method Pie Pastry

3/4 cup lard or solid vegetable shortening
1/4 cup boiling water
1 tablespoon milk
2-1/2 cups Southern soft wheat flour, see pages 122
1 teaspoon salt

❦ Place lard or shortening in a large bowl. Add boiling water and milk. Working quickly, break up lard or shortening with a fork, then whisk vigorously until mixture is smooth, thickened and fluffy. Mixture should hold soft peaks. Sift flour and salt into lard mixture. Stir vigorously and quickly to form a mass that cleans side of bowl. Turn out onto a work surface and lightly knead into a smooth ball. Divide in half and use as needed. Makes enough pastry for 1 (9-inch) double-crust pie.

Cream Cheese Pie Pastry

> 1 cup Southern soft wheat flour, see pages 122
> 1/2 cup unsalted butter, cut into 1-inch cubes
> Dash of salt
> 1 teaspoon sugar
> 1 (3-oz.) package cream cheese, room temperature

❦ Combine all ingredients in a food processor fitted with the steel blade. Process to blend all ingredients and form a smooth dough. Turn out dough onto a work surface and gather together; gently knead 3 or 4 times to form a smooth ball. Wrap tightly in plastic wrap and refrigerate 1 hour before rolling. Makes enough pastry for 1 (9-inch) single-crust pie.

Peach Half-Moon Pies

Generally called "fried pies" today, these crisp and delicious morsels are still very popular in the South, especially among children. In the Old South, they were often called "preaching pies": they were given to children during church services to keep them quiet and content during long sermons! For the most authentic flavor, fry the pies in lard.

> 3 cups peeled, diced (1/2-inch dice) fresh peaches (4 or 5 medium peaches)
> 2 teaspoons fresh lemon juice
> 1/2 cup firmly packed light brown sugar
> 1/2 teaspoon ground cinnamon
> 1/4 teaspoon freshly grated nutmeg
> 1 recipe Basic Southern Pie Pastry, page 165, chilled
> 2 eggs, beaten until frothy
> Lard or vegetable oil for deep-frying
> Powdered sugar

❦ Place peaches in a large bowl; add lemon juice and toss to coat well. Add brown sugar, cinnamon and nutmeg and stir to blend. Set aside. Roll out pastry 1/16 inch thick on a lightly floured work surface and cut into 24 rounds, using a 4-inch cutter. To shape each pie, place a heaping tablespoon of peach filling in center of a pastry round. Brush edges of pastry with beaten eggs, using a pastry brush. Fold pastry over to form a half-circle, lining up edges evenly. Press edges together with tines of a fork to seal; invert pie and repeat sealing on other side. In a heavy 12-inch skillet, heat 2 inches of melted lard over medium heat to 360F (180C) or until a 1-inch bread cube turns golden brown in 60 seconds. Add pies to hot fat, 4 or 5 at a time, being careful not to crowd skillet. Deep-fry, turning once, until golden brown on both sides (4 to 5 minutes). Drain on paper towels, sprinkle with powdered sugar and serve hot, at room temperature or cold, as desired. Makes 24 pies.

Fresh Peach Cobbler

Peach cobbler. Now doesn't the mere mention of it make your mouth water? Peach cobbler and summer are synonymous in the South, and this dessert is often on the table in humble cypress shacks and grand mansions alike. Some folks like to pour a little cream over cobbler, while others (myself included) like to put a big scoop of vanilla ice cream on top of the hot cobbler, then let it melt a little bit before digging in.

5 cups peeled, sliced fresh peaches (about 7 medium peaches)
1-1/2 teaspoons fresh lemon juice
1/2 cup sugar
1/2 teaspoon ground cinnamon
1/2 teaspoon freshly grated nutmeg
3 tablespoons all-purpose flour
2 tablespoons unsalted butter, cut into 1/2-inch cubes
1/4 cup whipping cream
Pastry, see below

Pastry:
2 cups all-purpose flour
2 teaspoons baking powder
1/4 teaspoon salt
1/2 cup solid vegetable shortening
About 5 tablespoons cold milk

❖ Preheat oven to 350F (175C). Butter a 13″ x 9″ baking dish and set aside. Place peaches in a large bowl, sprinkle with lemon juice and toss to coat well. Add sugar, cinnamon, nutmeg and flour; toss to blend. Turn out peach mixture into buttered baking dish, spreading evenly. Scatter butter cubes over top and drizzle with cream. Prepare Pastry, then roll out 1/4 to 3/8-inch thick on a lightly floured work surface. Place on top of peach mixture. Cut several steam vents in crust. Bake in preheated oven until crust is golden brown and filling is bubbly (35 to 40 minutes). Makes 8 to 10 servings.
Pastry: In a medium bowl, combine flour, baking powder and salt. Cut in shortening with a pastry blender or 2 knives until mixture resembles coarse meal. Add 5 tablespoons milk and stir just to form a dough that holds together; if necessary, add more milk, a teaspoon at a time.

Deep-Dish Apple Crisp

Hearty, homey deep-dish desserts such as this one are hard to beat. Generally made from apples, peaches or pears, they are simple to prepare: the sliced fruit is placed in a deep baking pan, sprinkled with sugar and spice, covered with pastry or other topping and baked.

> **6 medium apples, peeled, cored, quartered**
> **2 teaspoons fresh lemon juice**
> **1-1/4 cups sugar**
> **1/2 teaspoon ground cinnamon**
> **2 eggs**
> **2 tablespoons unsalted butter or margarine, melted**
> **1 cup sifted all-purpose flour**
> **1/2 teaspoon salt**
> **1 teaspoon vanilla extract**
> **Whipped cream**

❦ Preheat oven to 350F (175C). Slice apple quarters and place in a medium bowl. Sprinkle with lemon juice and toss to coat well. Combine 1/4 cup sugar and cinnamon, tossing with a fork to blend; sprinkle sugar mixture over apples and toss to coat well. Turn out apple mixture into a 9-inch deep-dish pie pan; set aside. In bowl of an electric mixer, beat eggs and remaining 1 cup sugar at medium speed until thickened and light lemon-yellow in color (about 3 minutes). Beat in butter. Sift flour with salt; add to egg mixture, 1/3 at a time, stopping to scrape down side of bowl after each addition. Add vanilla and beat just to blend. Spread mixture evenly over apple mixture and bake in preheated oven until apples are bubbly and topping is crisp and golden brown (about 45 minutes). Serve with whipped cream. Makes 8 to 10 servings.

Almond Crème Brûlée

Crème Brûlée—"burnt cream"—is a marvelous baked custard topped with a thin crust of lightly caramelized sugar. Now enjoying increased popularity in much of the country, it has long been a very traditional dessert in the South. The almond-flavored version served at Arnaud's Restaurant in New Orleans makes a perfect ending for any meal—it's rich, light as a feather and very hard to beat indeed.

> **1 cup firmly packed light brown sugar**
> **1-1/2 pints (3 cups) whipping cream**
> **1/4 teaspoon salt**
> **8 egg yolks**
> **1/2 cup granulated sugar**
> **1 tablespoon vanilla extract**
> **1/4 cup amaretto or other almond-flavored liqueur**

❦ Spread brown sugar on a baking sheet in a thin layer and let dry out (about 1 hour). When dry, process in a food processor fitted with the steel blade until pulverized (sugar should have a powdery consistency). Set aside. Preheat oven to 350F (175C). Lightly butter eight 4-ounce ramekins; set aside. Combine cream and salt in a 3-quart saucepan and heat over medium heat just until small bubbles appear around sides of pan. Meanwhile, in bowl of an electric mixer, beat egg yolks and granulated sugar at medium speed until thickened and light lemon-yellow in color (about 4 minutes). With mixer running, slowly add scalded cream to egg mixture. Add vanilla and liqueur and beat just to blend. Strain through a fine strainer, then pour equally into buttered ramekins. Place ramekins in a large, deep baking dish and place in preheated oven. Add boiling water to the large baking dish to come halfway up sides of ramekins. Place a large sheet of buttered parchment paper over tops of all ramekins. Bake until custards are set (35 to 40 minutes). Position oven rack 4 inches below heat source and preheat broiler. Remove custards from oven and place on a baking sheet. Sprinkle an equal portion of the brown sugar over each. Place under preheated broiler just until sugar is melted and lightly caramelized (about 1-1/2 minutes). Serve at once. Makes 8 servings.

Gingerbread Pudding with Whiskey Sauce

Southern women, rich and poor alike, have always been known for their ability to make a little bit of food go a long way. This satisfying dessert is adapted from one served at The Settlement, a 19th-century living project of the Tennessee Valley Authority. It's a delicious illustration of the "waste not, want not" philosophy that has kept Southerners well fed even in lean times.

>2 eggs, beaten until frothy
>2 cups milk
>3 tablespoons firmly packed dark brown sugar
>1 tablespoon apple cider vinegar
>Dash of salt
>3 cups crumbled leftover Upside-Down Apple Gingerbread, page 151
>1 large apple, peeled, cored, diced
>Whiskey Sauce, see below
>
>*Whiskey Sauce:*
>1 cup sugar
>2 tablespoons cornstarch
>2 cups boiling water
>2 tablespoons unsalted butter, room temperature
>1/2 teaspoon freshly grated nutmeg
>1/4 cup good-quality Kentucky bourbon whiskey

❦ Preheat oven to 350F (175C). Butter an 8-inch-square baking dish and set aside. In a bowl, combine eggs, milk, brown sugar, vinegar and salt; stir to blend. Stir in gingerbread and apple. Spoon into buttered baking dish and bake in preheated oven until a knife inserted in center of pudding comes out clean (about 40 minutes). Prepare Whiskey Sauce; serve pudding warm, topped with sauce. Makes 8 to 10 servings.

Whiskey Sauce: Combine sugar and cornstarch in a 2-quart saucepan; stir in water. Bring mixture to a boil and boil 1 minute, stirring constantly. Remove from heat and whisk in butter, nutmeg and bourbon. Serve hot.

Jambalaya's Bread Pudding with Bourbon Sauce

Bread pudding is offered in Cajun-Creole and Southern-style restaurants all over the country, but one of the best I've tasted was on the menu at Jambalaya, a charming restaurant in Austin, Texas serving excellent and authentic New Orleans-style foods. This recipe is a variation on Jambalaya's great, easy-to-prepare version of the classic dessert.

1 (1-lb.) loaf French bread (about 18 inches long)
1 quart (4 cups) milk
3 tablespoons unsalted butter or margarine
3 eggs, beaten until frothy
2 cups sugar
2 tablespoons vanilla extract
1 teaspoon ground cinnamon
1 cup golden raisins
Bourbon Sauce, see below

Bourbon Sauce:
1/2 cup unsalted butter
1 cup sugar
1 egg, beaten until frothy
1/4 cup good-quality Kentucky bourbon whiskey

❦ Tear bread into small bite-size pieces, dropping pieces into a large bowl. Pour milk over bread and let soak until very soft (about 1 hour), then stir mixture well. Set aside. Preheat oven to 375F (190C). Melt butter in a 13" x 9" baking dish and swirl to coat bottom and sides. Add eggs and sugar to bread mixture; stir to mix well. Stir in vanilla, cinnamon and raisins. Pour mixture into buttered baking dish. Bake in preheated oven until pudding is set (about 1 hour). Prepare Bourbon Sauce; serve pudding warm or at room temperature, topped with sauce. Makes 10 to 12 servings.

Bourbon Sauce: Combine butter and sugar in top of a double boiler over simmering water. Whisk until butter is melted and sugar is dissolved; gradually whisk in beaten egg. Cool slightly, then whisk in bourbon. If not serving sauce at once, reheat gently before serving, whisking constantly.

Bourbon Balls

During the Christmas season, I make hundreds of these addictive little confections. They are the perfect hostess gift to take to holiday parties; I like to pack them in small white Chinese take-out food containers lined with red and green tissue paper. The containers hold only about 10 pieces each, though—so if the hostess sets the goodies out for the party, you'll probably have to go home for more. (Nobody can eat just one!)

1-1/2 cups vanilla wafer-type cookie crumbs
1 cup powdered sugar
1 cup finely chopped pecans
2 tablespoons unsweetened cocoa powder
2 tablespoons light corn syrup
1/4 cup good-quality Kentucky bourbon whiskey
Powdered sugar

❦ Combine cookie crumbs, 1 cup powdered sugar, pecans, cocoa powder, corn syrup and bourbon in a medium bowl. Roll into 24 balls and dredge in powdered sugar to coat well; shake off excess sugar. Cover and refrigerate until ready to serve. Makes 24 bourbon balls.

English Raspberry & Peach Trifle

Even after settling in America, the colonists of course continued to prepare some of the foods they had enjoyed in England—and trifle was one of them. This version layers fresh raspberries and peaches with cake fingers, custard and a whipped cream topping flavored with raspberry liqueur. It can be prepared in advance and refrigerated to provide a luxurious yet hassle-free ending to your meal.

Custard, see below
1 pint (2 cups) whipping cream
1/3 cup dairy sour cream
3 tablespoons powdered sugar
2 tablespoons Chambord, Framboise or other raspberry-flavored liqueur
10 (2-inch thick) slices Sour Cream & Lemon Cake, page 152, or purchased
    pound cake
1 (12-oz.) jar red raspberry jam, melted
6 medium, ripe peaches, peeled, pitted, chopped
1 pint fresh raspberries
Fresh mint sprigs

Custard:
2-1/2 cups milk
5 eggs
1 cup sugar
1/2 cup all-purpose flour
2 teaspoons vanilla extract
1/2 pint (1 cup) whipping cream

❦ Prepare Custard and refrigerate as directed. In a medium bowl, beat together whipping cream, sour cream, powdered sugar and liqueur until mixture holds medium-stiff peaks. Cover and refrigerate. To assemble trifle, break cake slices into bite-size chunks. Divide half the chunks equally among 8 brandy snifters, placing a layer of cake in bottom of each. Next, drizzle half the melted jam evenly over cake. Spoon half the Custard over jam; add a layer of peaches (using all), then half the whipped cream mixture. Repeat layering, this time substituting raspberries for peaches and again ending with a layer of whipped cream mixture. Cover with plastic wrap and refrigerate until ready to serve. Garnish with mint sprigs before serving. Makes 8 servings.

Custard: In a medium saucepan, heat milk over medium heat just until small bubbles appear around sides of pan (about 10 minutes). Set aside. In bowl of an electric mixer, beat eggs, sugar and flour at medium speed until very smooth and creamy (about 5 minutes). Transfer mixture to a separate heavy saucepan; whisk in scalded milk and cook over medium-low heat until thickened (4 to 5 minutes), whisking constantly. Remove from heat and whisk in vanilla. Transfer custard to a bowl and place a sheet of plastic wrap directly on surface; refrigerate until well chilled. Beat cream until it holds medium-stiff peaks; fold into chilled custard, incorporating thoroughly. Cover bowl with plastic wrap and keep refrigerated.

Variation To serve trifle as a buffet-style dessert, assemble the ingredients as directed above in a single large, footed trifle bowl. Cover tightly and refrigerate until ready to serve.

Fennel Seed Tea Cakes

These delightfully different-tasting little cakes with their sweet-tart glaze are perfect for afternoon tea or coffee with friends or neighbors. They are even good for solitary munching as you watch the world go by from your rocking chair on the veranda!

1/2 cup unsalted butter or margarine, room temperature
1/2 cup sugar
2 eggs, beaten until frothy
1 teaspoon fennel seeds
3-1/4 cups all-purpose flour
1/2 teaspoon salt
2 teaspoons baking powder
1/2 teaspoon baking soda
1/2 cup dairy sour cream
Lemon Glaze, see below

Lemon Glaze:
1-1/2 cups powdered sugar, sifted
1/3 cup fresh lemon juice

In bowl of an electric mixer, cream butter and sugar at medium speed until light and fluffy (about 3 minutes). Add eggs and fennel seeds; beat until blended (about 2 minutes). Sift flour, salt, baking powder and baking soda into a separate bowl. Then add flour mixture to egg mixture alternately with sour cream, adding each in 3 additions and stopping to scrape down side of bowl after each addition. Preheat oven to 375F (190C). Lightly grease 2 large baking sheets; set aside. Turn out dough onto a generously floured work surface; roll out dough 1/4 inch thick and cut into rounds with a 2-inch cutter. Reroll and cut scraps; repeat until all dough has been used. Place rounds on greased baking sheets; bake in preheated oven until lightly browned (15 to 18 minutes). Remove from oven and cool on wire racks. Prepare Lemon Glaze. When cakes are cool, spread tops with glaze. Makes about 36 tea cakes.
Lemon Glaze: Whisk together powdered sugar and lemon juice vigorously until smooth and satiny.

Short'nin' Bread

"Put on de skillet, put on de lid. Mammy's little baby wants short'nin' bread." Everybody's heard the old song about this Southern classic, but how many people have ever tasted it? When I began to ask that question in various parts of the country, I found that most people didn't even know exactly what short'nin' bread was! Let me say that short'nin' bread is a wonderful cookie-type concoction made from a butter- (or often lard-) rich dough containing no liquid. The resultant pastry is dense and crumbly—the texture commonly known as "short." In times past, the dough was often patted into a cast-iron skillet and baked in one big round, right in the skillet, to provide a quick treat for children hungry for a sweet.

> 1 cup unsalted butter, room temperature
> 1 cup sugar
> 2-1/2 cups Southern soft wheat flour, see pages 122

❦ In bowl of an electric mixer, cream butter and sugar at medium speed until fluffy and light in color (about 4 minutes). Add flour and beat just until blended (about 2 minutes), stopping to scrape down side of bowl once or twice. Turn out onto a floured work surface and knead 3 or 4 times to form a dough that holds together. Pat dough into a 10-inch disc, wrap in plastic wrap and refrigerate 1 hour. Preheat oven to 325F (165C). Lightly flour work surface and roll out dough 1/2 inch thick. Cut into rounds with a 3-inch biscuit cutter; reroll scraps (reflouring work surface as needed) and cut. Repeat until all dough has been used. Place cookies on baking sheets and bake in preheated oven until light golden brown (about 25 minutes). Cool on baking sheets 10 minutes, then transfer to wire racks to cool completely. (If cooling on baking sheets is omitted, cookies will literally fall apart.) Makes about 24 cookies.

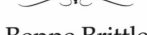

Benne Brittle

Cookie type wafers and candies flavored with benne (sesame) have long been popular in the Low Country regions of the Carolinas and Georgia. Benne brittle packaged in a small, colorful tin and tied with a ribbon makes a nice hostess gift.

> 2 cups sugar
> 1 cup lightly toasted sesame seeds
> 1/4 teaspoon salt

❦ Oil a marble slab or large baking sheet. Place sugar in a heavy 3-quart saucepan and cook over medium heat, without stirring, just until sugar begins to melt. Then cook, stirring, until mixture has reached the light caramel stage—about 320F (160C) on a candy thermometer. Remove from heat and stir in sesame seeds and salt. Pour mixture onto oiled slab or baking sheet and spread into a thin, even layer with an oiled spatula. Set aside until completely hardened. Break candy into pieces to serve. Store airtight. Makes about 1 pound.

BREAKFAST & BRUNCH

reakfast has always been a very important meal in largely agrarian societies, and the South is no exception. "Working the land" is hard physical labor requiring a heavy, energy-building diet, with a good portion of it at the day's beginning. Today, lavish breakfasts consisting of many dishes have largely been relegated to weekend brunch in the South, but breakfast is still an important part of everyday life. It is a family time, a time to chat and relax before we scatter our separate ways, perhaps not to meet again until the next morning. The breakfast table is often set in the dining room, with good china, linen napkins and fresh flowers or other flourish. It's a lovely way to begin each day.

Fresh, seasonal fruits are an important part of the Southern breakfast. Assorted fruits may simply be placed in the middle of the table in a big bowl, but fried fruits—green tomatoes, plantains, apples—are popular as well. Berries and sliced peaches are topped with sugar and double cream, a sumptuous delight. Fruit juices are served, too, though these are a modern-day addition to the menu.

Corn and rice have always played just as big a role at breakfast as they do at lunch and dinner. Corn breads, cornsticks, corn muffins, cornmeal griddle cakes topped with butter and syrup—all are enjoyed at the morning meal. And no Southern breakfast would be complete without grits. They may be slow-cooked and topped with butter, fried to produce the Cajun "coush-coush" or even cut into squares when cold, then battered and fried for a Southern version of hash-browns. Rice is eaten as a breakfast cereal, with butter and sugar and a little cream; in the Deep South, it is folded into a rich egg batter and deep-fried to make the fritters known as *calas* (See page

128). Delightful and nutritious pancakes are created from leftover rice combined with pecans and a little Southern soft wheat flour.

Southern breakfasts feature meats in abundance: fried country ham with dark, rich "red-eye" gravy made from the pan drippings and strong black coffee; pan-fried calves' brains served with fluffy scrambled eggs; bacon and sausage patties or links; and small game birds such as dove, quail, jacksnipe, woodcock or coot, fried and presented on large platters. In parts of Tennessee, even fried catfish and fried chicken are breakfast fare! Fried chicken livers, still served today at restaurant brunches, were a favorite in many regions of the Deep South.

Southern breakfast breads are legendary. Lighter-than-air biscuits, fruit- and nut-filled muffins, deep-fried squares of rich dough folded over fresh fruit ("fried pies") and of course the mouthwatering beignets of Louisiana—triangles of rich yeast dough deep-fried and sprinkled with powdered sugar—grace breakfast tables across the South. As accompaniment for these heavenly breads, crocks and jars of rich preserves prepared from the freshest of fruits and berries in season are Southern tradition.

Some say that "brunch," most often defined as a combination of breakfast and lunch eaten in one late morning meal, did not become an American custom until the 1930s. Perhaps the rest of the country did not know the pleasures of the leisurely brunch until then, but the South had been perfecting the custom for decades. As plantation life evolved, friends and families often lived many miles apart; going to visit meant making a considerable journey, and guests would generally stay for several days. On these occasions, breakfast was a relaxed, easy-going sort of meal, with brandy milk punch and mint juleps enjoyed on the veranda as family and guests slowly gathered together late in the morning.

In Kentucky and Virginia, fox-hunting became a popular sport among the wealthy. Extravagant brunches were presented at the estates where the hunts took place, and the Kentucky bourbon and branch water flowed. The grand and ceremonious hunt breakfasts of Lexington, Kentucky and Albemarle County, Virginia are cherished reminders of these elegant occasions.

The first Saturday in May each year finds kitchens in Louisville, Kentucky abustle with preparations for the South's most legendary brunch day—the Kentucky Derby. Bountiful brunches are served in opulent clubs and gracious homes before the famous Run for the Roses, with a copious supply of mint juleps adding a decidedly heady aura to the day's events.

Whatever your lifestyle or budget, breakfast or brunch with family or friends can really make your day. And I can't think of any better breakfast dishes than those from the Southern cook's repertoire. Who knows, maybe you'll get an addictive dose of the slow-paced, laid-back Southern style of living along with those grits!

Ginger-Mango Butter

Grown extensively in Florida, mangoes are available fresh from midwinter until autumn. This exotic-tasting spread does something decidedly wonderful to the breakfast biscuit and is always on hand at my house.

    4 cups peeled, chopped mangoes
    1/2 cup chopped gingerroot
    2-1/2 cups sugar

❦ Combine mangoes and gingerroot in a heavy 4-quart saucepan; add enough cold water to cover. Bring to a boil, then reduce heat and simmer, uncovered, until mangoes are very tender (about 10 minutes). Drain well, then puree by putting through a food mill fitted with the fine blade. Discard leftover pulp. Return puree to heavy 4-quart saucepan, add sugar and cook over medium-low heat, stirring often, until very thick (15 to 20 minutes); frequently skim away any foam that rises to surface of fruit mixture. Meanwhile, sterilize three 1/2-pint canning jars. Pour hot mango butter into sterilized canning jars, leaving 1/2 inch head space. Seal jars according to manufacturer's directions. Process 5 minutes in a boiling water bath canner to seal. Cool jars completely before storing. Makes 1-1/2 pints.

Peach & Cantaloupe Preserves with Pecans

July and August are canning months in Southern households. Everything in the garden is proliferating, and every family shares their fresh fruits and vegetables with friends, neighbors and relatives until each kitchen resembles a small produce market! When Southern women go to visit, they often take along a jar of something home-canned as a hostess gift. And if they visit often enough, their pantrys are empty by the following July!

Peaches are one of the true loves of all Southerners, and their taste is treasured throughout the year. This rich and delicious preserve pairs them with cantaloupe and toasted pecans for a combination of flavors that's mighty pleasing on a biscuit.

> 3 cups peeled, chopped fresh peaches (about 4 or 5 medium peaches)
> 3 cups peeled, chopped cantaloupe (about 1 medium melon)
> 4-1/4 cups sugar
> 3 tablespoons fresh lemon juice
> 3/4 cup toasted chopped pecans
> 1/2 teaspoon freshly grated nutmeg
> 1/4 teaspoon salt
> 1 teaspoon grated orange zest

❦ Sterilize seven 1/2-pint canning jars; set aside. In a heavy 8- to 10-quart Dutch oven, combine peaches and cantaloupe. Bring to a full rolling boil over medium-high heat, stirring constantly. Add sugar and lemon juice. Bring to a full boil again, then continue to boil gently, uncovered, stirring often, 12 minutes. Stir in pecans, nutmeg, salt and orange zest. Boil rapidly 5 minutes longer. Remove pan from heat; quickly skim foam from surface with a metal spoon. Immediately pour preserves into sterilized jars, leaving 1/2 inch head space. Seal jars according to manufacturer's directions. Process 5 minutes in a boiling water bath canner to seal. Cool jars completely before storing. Makes 3-1/2 pints.

Strawberries in Double Cream

When strawberry season begins in the South, nothing is better than berries and cream on the table surrounded by blooming azaleas on the patio.

Double cream—*crème fraîche*—is a thick, rich, tangy cream widely used in French cooking. It cannot be made just from the ultra-pasteurized whipping cream sold in the United States, since pasteurization destroys the enzymes responsible for fermentation. But by blending a bit of sour cream with the whipping cream, then letting the mixture stand for a day or so, you can produce a reasonable facsimile of double cream.

> **Crème Fraîche, see below**
> **2 cups sliced strawberries**
> **2 teaspoons vanilla extract**
> **1/4 cup powdered sugar**
> **2 tablespoons white creme de cacao**
> **Fresh mint sprigs**
>
> *Crème Fraîche:*
> **1 pint (2 cups) whipping cream**
> **1/2 pint (1 cup) dairy sour cream**

❦ Prepare Crème Fraîche. Place strawberries in a medium bowl; set aside. In bowl of an electric mixer, combine Crème Fraîche, vanilla, powdered sugar and crème de cacao. Beat at medium speed until mixture holds soft, floppy peaks (about 2 minutes). Fold cream into berries, blending well. Spoon into individual fruit bowls or brandy snifters, garnish with mint sprigs and serve. Makes 4 servings.

Crème Fraîche: In a non-metal bowl, whisk together whipping cream and sour cream. Cover with plastic wrap and let stand 24 hours in a warm place. Ideal temperature is around 75F (27C); do not expose mixture to temperatures over 80F (27C) or the enzymes which cause fermentation will be destroyed. After 24 hours, cream should be thickened and have a slightly acidic taste. Cover tightly and store in refrigerator up to 1 week. Makes 3 cups.

Rum-Broiled Grapefruit

One taste will tell you that this is no ordinary grapefruit! Give your breakfast or brunch a lift with the divinely delicious ruby-red fruit from Florida, topped with rum, brown sugar and spice and broiled till warm and golden.

> **2 ruby-red grapefruit**
> **2 tablespoons unsalted butter, melted**
> **1/2 cup dark rum**
> **2/3 cup firmly packed light brown sugar**
> **1/2 teaspoon ground cinnamon**
> **Fresh mint sprigs and maraschino cherries**

✿ Position oven rack 8 inches below heat source and preheat broiler. Cut each grapefruit in half and loosen segments with a grapefruit knife. Place halves in a 13″ x 9″ baking pan; set aside. In a small bowl, combine butter, rum, brown sugar and cinnamon. Drizzle mixture equally over grapefruit halves. Place baking pan under preheated broiler; broil until grapefruit halves are golden brown on top (about 15 minutes). Transfer grapefruit halves to individual bowls; spoon juices from pan over fruit. Place a small mint sprig and a cherry in center of each grapefruit half for garnish. Serve hot. Makes 4 servings.

Turkey Hash

Turkey hash is an institution for breakfast or brunch in all parts of the South. Sort of a pot pie without the pastry, it is a delicious example of the Southern cook's artistry with leftovers. You may substitute chicken for turkey, if you like.

> 1/2 cup unsalted butter or margarine
> 1 medium onion, chopped
> 1 small green bell pepper, chopped
> 2/3 cup sliced mushrooms
> 1/4 cup chopped leafy celery tops
> 2 large russet potatoes (about 1-1/4 lbs. *total*), unpeeled, halved lengthwise, thinly sliced
> 1/4 cup all-purpose flour
> 3 cups heated Poultry Stock, page 38, or canned chicken broth
> 2-1/2 cups diced cooked turkey
> 2 tablespoons minced parsley, preferably flat-leaf
> 6 green onions (including tops), chopped
> 1 tablespoon Worcestershire sauce
> 1/4 teaspoon dried leaf thyme
> 1/8 teaspoon dried leaf marjoram
> 1/2 teaspoon freshly ground black pepper
> 1/2 teaspoon Tabasco sauce
> Salt to taste
> 2/3 cup fine dry bread crumbs

✿ Preheat oven to 350F (175C). Melt butter or margarine in a heavy 12-inch skillet over medium heat. Add onion, bell pepper, mushrooms, celery tops and potatoes. Cook until potatoes are lightly browned (about 15 minutes). Add flour all at once; stir to combine. Cook, stirring, 3 to 4 minutes. Slowly stir in heated stock. Boil, stirring, until thickened. Stir in turkey, parsley, green onions, Worcestershire sauce, thyme, marjoram, black pepper, Tabasco sauce and salt. Spoon into a 3-quart baking dish. Sprinkle with bread crumbs; bake in preheated oven until golden brown and bubbly (about 30 minutes). Serve hot. Makes 4 servings.

Crabmeat Omelet
with Ginger-Mushroom Sauce

This Caribbean-inspired masterpiece is an entree worthy of your most regal brunch. The sauce may be prepared ahead and gently reheated before serving. When preparing the omelets in quantity, cook them one at a time, slide onto serving plates and keep them hot in a warm oven while preparing the remaining omelets. Nap with sauce just before serving.

Ginger-Mushroom Sauce, see below
2/3 cup plain white crabmeat
3 tablespoons unsalted butter or margarine
1/4 cup chopped green bell pepper
1/4 cup chopped green onions (including tops)
3 eggs
3 tablespoons lukewarm water
1/4 teaspoon salt

Ginger-Mushroom Sauce:
1-1/2 cups milk
1/4 cup chopped onion
3 medium garlic cloves, smashed
1 bay leaf
1 teaspoon whole black peppercorns
Pinch of freshly grated nutmeg
1/4 cup unsalted butter or margarine
1 tablespoon grated gingerroot
1 cup sliced mushrooms
2 tablespoons all-purpose flour
1/4 cup dry sherry
1/4 teaspoon Tabasco sauce
Salt to taste

❦ Prepare Ginger-Mushroom Sauce; keep hot over low heat. To prepare omelet, carefully pick through crabmeat and remove any bits of shell and cartilage; set aside. Melt 2 tablespoons butter or margarine in a heavy 10-inch skillet over medium heat. Add bell pepper and green onions; cook until vegetables are slightly wilted (about 5 minutes). Remove from heat and set aside. In a bowl, whisk together eggs, lukewarm water and salt until frothy. Melt remaining 1 tablespoon butter or margarine in a 10-inch non-stick omelet pan over medium heat. When butter begins to bubble and sizzle, add egg mixture and stir until just beginning to set. Continue to cook until eggs are almost completely cooked (about 2 minutes), running a thin spatula around edges of pan to prevent sticking. Spread crabmeat and cooked vegetables down middle of omelet and cook 1 minute longer. Slide omelet onto a plate, folding half of omelet over filling. Top with some of Ginger-Mushroom Sauce and serve hot. Makes 1 omelet.

Ginger-Mushroom Sauce: Combine milk, onion, garlic, bay leaf, peppercorns and nutmeg in a 1-quart saucepan. Bring to a boil; then reduce heat, cover and simmer 10 minutes. Remove from heat and strain; discard seasonings. Set aside. Melt butter or margarine in a heavy 12-inch skillet over medium heat. Add gingerroot and mushrooms and cook, stirring often, until mushroom liquid has evaporated (about 10 minutes). Add flour all at once; stir until blended. Cook, stirring, 2 to 3 minutes. Slowly stir in strained seasoned milk. Boil until thickened, then reduce heat and add sherry, Tabasco sauce and salt. Cook just until heated through. Serve hot. Makes enough sauce for 2 omelets.

Strawberry Soufflé Omelet

This lighter-than-air omelet is a stunning dish that's sure to impress your brunch guests. Substitute other berries or fruits for the strawberries, if desired.

> **3/4 cup thinly sliced strawberries**
> **1 tablespoon powdered sugar**
> **3 eggs, separated, room temperature**
> **2 teaspoons granulated sugar**
> **3 tablespoons lukewarm water**
> **1/4 teaspoon salt**
> **2 tablespoons unsalted butter or margarine**
> **1 unhulled strawberry, cut in half lengthwise**

❦ Position oven rack 4 inches below heat source and preheat broiler. In a small bowl, toss sliced strawberries with powdered sugar to coat well; set aside. In a large bowl, whisk egg yolks with granulated sugar, lukewarm water and salt until frothy. Set aside. In bowl of electric mixer, beat egg whites at medium speed until they hold medium-stiff peaks (about 3 minutes). Gently but thoroughly, fold whites into yolk mixture. Melt butter in a 10-inch non-stick omelet pan with a heatproof handle. When butter begins to bubble and sizzle, pour egg mixture into pan and smooth it out with a spatula. Cook until edges of omelet are dry (about 2 minutes); run a thin spatula around edges of pan to prevent sticking. Bottom of omelet should be golden brown. Place pan under preheated broiler 30 to 45 seconds to firm up surface of omelet. Then spoon strawberries down center of omelet; using a thin, flexible spatula, fold omelet in half over filling, pressing edges together. Slide onto a serving plate and serve hot; garnish top with halved strawberry. Makes 1 omelet.

Eggs Portuguese

This brunch favorite makes no secret of its ethnic roots! The dish is based on a spicy, tomato-laden sauce, typical of the early Portuguese- and Spanish-inspired Creole sauces that came to the South via Spain and the Caribbean. The sauce may be prepared ahead of time and even freezes well up to 2 months.

> 4 to 6 frozen dinner-size patty shells
> Portuguese Sauce, see below
> Easy Hollandaise Sauce, page 192
> 6 crisp-cooked bacon slices, crumbled
> 4 to 6 poached eggs
> Hungarian paprika
>
> *Portuguese Sauce:*
> 2 (16-oz.) cans stewed tomatoes
> 1/3 cup bacon drippings or vegetable oil
> 1 medium green bell pepper, chopped
> 1 medium onion, chopped
> 2 celery stalks, chopped
> 2 medium garlic cloves, minced
> 2 teaspoons Hungarian paprika
> 1 bay leaf
> 1/2 teaspoon dried leaf thyme
> 1/4 to 1/2 teaspoon red (cayenne) pepper
> 3 cups Poultry Stock, page 38, or canned chicken broth
> Salt to taste

❡ Bake patty shells according to package directions. Meanwhile, prepare Portuguese Sauce and Easy Hollandaise Sauce. Remove center circle from each baked shell and spoon in Portuguese Sauce to fill by about 2/3. Sprinkle tops of sauce equally with bacon, then place a poached egg on each serving. Top with Easy Hollandaise Sauce and a dusting of paprika. Serve hot. Makes 4 to 6 servings.

Portuguese Sauce: Drain tomatoes, reserving liquid; chop tomatoes and set aside. Heat bacon drippings or oil in a heavy 12-inch skillet over medium heat. Add bell pepper, onion, celery and garlic; cook, stirring often, until vegetables are slightly wilted and onion is transparent (about 5 minutes). Add chopped tomatoes and reserved liquid, paprika, bay leaf, thyme and red pepper. Stir to combine. Cook, stirring occasionally, until all liquid has evaporated (15 to 20 minutes). Stir in stock and salt. Simmer briskly until slightly thickened (about 10 minutes). Discard bay leaf.

Eggs Gautier

Gautier (*GO-tee-ay*) is a charming, tiny little town on a finger of land extending into a bay off the Southern coast of Mississippi. Some noteworthy and stately antebellum homes still stand in this region, and the entire area almost seems to have been plucked from another time. The coastal waters teem with both fish and shellfish, and in fact provide a large percentage of the country's shrimp. This elegant and impressive brunch dish combines classic seasonings with the downright sensuous sweetness of fresh lump crabmeat.

> **1/2 pound backfin lump crabmeat**
> **4 to 6 (4-inch-diameter) rounds cut from commercial frozen puff pastry**
> **Easy Béarnaise Sauce, page 192**
> **1 large tomato, cut into 6 slices**
> **Olive oil**
> **Salt and freshly ground black pepper to taste**
> **3 tablespoons unsalted butter or margarine**
> **3 tablespoons finely chopped green bell pepper**
> **2 tablespoons minced parsley, preferably flat-leaf**
> **4 to 6 poached eggs**
> **Hungarian paprika**

❦ Carefully pick through crabmeat and remove any bits of shell and cartilage. Refrigerate until ready to use. Preheat oven to 425F (220C). Place pastry rounds on a baking sheet and place in preheated oven. Immediately reduce oven temperature to 400F (205C); bake until pastry circles have risen and are golden brown (15 to 20 minutes). Set aside. Prepare Easy Béarnaise Sauce; set aside. Reduce oven temperature to 375F (190C). Brush tomato slices with oil, sprinkle with salt and black pepper, place on a baking sheet and bake in pre-heated oven 4 minutes. Set aside. Melt butter or margarine in a heavy 12-inch skillet over medium heat. Add bell pepper and parsley and cook just until heated through (about 3 minutes). Add crabmeat and stir to blend, taking care not to break up lumps of meat. Cook just until heated through (about 3 minutes). To assemble each serving, place a baked pastry round on a serving plate. Top with a baked tomato slice, then with 1/4 to 1/6 of crabmeat mixture. Nest 1 poached egg in crabmeat mixture. Nap servings equally with Easy Béarnaise Sauce. Garnish with a dusting of paprika and serve hot. Makes 4 to 6 servings.

Eggs Benedict

So many stories have been told about the origin of this legendary brunch dish! It has been attributed to everyone from St. Benedict to Pope Benedict XIV to Benedict Arnold—and before researching the subject, I must admit that I firmly believed it to have been created at Brennan's, New Orleans's famous bastion of brunch. After receiving a letter from a Mr. John C. Benedict, though, I believe I have the true story of Eggs Benedict. Mr. Benedict sent me a copy of an interview with his great-uncle which appeared in the December 19, 1942 issue of *The New Yorker*. The article reads in part:

> Forty-eight years ago a young blade named Lemuel Benedict came into the dining room of the old Waldorf for a late breakfast. He had a hangover, but his brain was clicking away in high gear. He ordered some buttered toast, crisp bacon, two poached eggs, and a hooker of Hollandaise sauce, and then and there proceeded to put together the dish that has, ever since, borne his name. Oscar of the Waldorf got wind of this unorthodox delicacy, tested it, and put it on his breakfast and luncheon menus, with certain modifications. Oscar's version of Eggs Benedict substituted ham for bacon and a toasted English muffin for toasted bread.

This article dates the dish's origin at around 1894, and I certainly have found no record of it before that time. I do hope that the Benedict family will indulge Southerners, however, in our claims for Eggs Benedict. When enjoying brunch in charming old Savannah, in elegant and stately Charleston or in the timeless Vieux Carré of New Orleans, it seems that the dish must always have been part of those idyllic scenes!

Easy Hollandaise Sauce, page 192
Unsalted butter or margarine, room temperature
2 English muffins, halved
3 tablespoons unsalted butter or margarine
8 thin Canadian bacon or cooked ham slices
3 tablespoons dry sherry
4 poached eggs
Hungarian paprika
Curly-leaf parsley sprigs

❦ Prepare Easy Hollandaise Sauce and set aside. Lightly butter halved muffins and toast them until golden brown. Melt 3 tablespoons butter or margarine in a heavy 12-inch skillet over medium heat. Add Canadian bacon and cook, turning once, until golden brown on both sides (4 to 5 minutes). Add sherry and swirl skillet to distribute. Cook until sherry has evaporated (about 2 minutes). Remove from heat. To assemble each serving, place a toasted muffin half on a serving plate and top with 2 Canadian bacon slices. Place a poached egg atop bacon and ladle a portion of Easy Hollandaise Sauce over top. Garnish with a dusting of paprika and parsley sprigs. Serve hot. Makes 4 servings.

Crabmeat Brunch Puffs

These rich, scrumptious little "soufflés" are bound to please the crowd at your next seated brunch. They can even be assembled ahead of time, then baked after your guests arrive.

1 pound plain white crabmeat
24 (1/2-inch-thick) stale French bread slices
1/2 pound mushrooms, sliced
8 green onions (including tops), chopped
1/2 pound Monterey Jack cheese, shredded
3 cups milk
4 eggs
1/2 teaspoon salt
1/2 teaspoon freshly ground black pepper
1/2 teaspoon red (cayenne) pepper

❦ Preheat oven to 350F (175C). Butter six 12-ounce ramekins and set aside. Carefully pick through the crabmeat and remove any bits of shell and cartilage. Place 2 French bread slices in a single layer in bottom of each buttered ramekin. Top bread in ramekins equally with crabmeat, mushrooms, green onions and cheese. Finally, top each ramekin with 2 more bread slices in a single layer. Press down with the palm of your hand to compact ingredients. In a bowl, beat together milk, eggs, salt, black pepper and red pepper; pour equal portions over ramekins. Bake in preheated oven until puffy and golden brown (about 45 minutes). Serve hot. Makes 6 servings.

Kentucky-Style Scrambled Eggs

A favorite in Kentucky, this hearty dish of eggs, bacon and corn is typical of the rich, energy-building foods served for breakfast throughout the Old South.

    8 meaty bacon slices
    1 (8-oz.) can whole-kernel corn, drained well
    1 medium green bell pepper, chopped
    4 green onions (including tops), chopped
    10 eggs
    1/4 cup lukewarm water
    1/2 teaspoon freshly ground black pepper
    1/2 teaspoon dry mustard
    Salt and Tabasco sauce to taste

❦ Cook bacon in a heavy 12-inch skillet over medium heat until golden brown and crisp (7 to 8 minutes). Remove from skillet (reserve drippings), drain on paper towels, crumble and set aside. Add corn, bell pepper and green onions to drippings and cook over medium heat until vegetables are wilted (about 10 minutes). In a large bowl, whisk together eggs, lukewarm water, black pepper, mustard, salt and Tabasco sauce until frothy. Add egg mixture and crumbled bacon to skillet and cook, stirring often, until eggs are almost completely set but still slightly creamy (about 4 minutes). Serve hot. Makes 4 to 6 servings.

Virginia Country Ham with Red-Eye Gravy

Skillet-fried country ham topped with rich, dark red-eye gravy is doubtless the South's most famous breakfast dish. Mark Twain is reputed to have named the coffee-based gravy when dining with a friend one morning. It seems that the cook, an unkempt and sottish man, delivered the plates to Mr. Twain's table personally. Looking up, the great humorist commented, "That cook's eyes are as red as this gravy is black"—and the gravy was known as "red-eye" from that point on! The dish is usually served with hot buttered grits and biscuits.

    1-1/2 pounds country ham, cut 1/4 inch thick
    1/3 cup bacon drippings or lard
    Freshly ground black pepper to taste
    2 tablespoons all-purpose flour
    2/3 cup strong black coffee
    1 cup Brown Stock, page 38, or canned beef broth

Score fat edges of ham slices at several points to prevent curling. Heat bacon **drippings or lard** in a heavy 12-inch skillet over medium heat. Add ham slices and sprinkle **liberally with pepper**; cook, turning often, until golden brown on both sides (about 10 **minutes).** Remove ham from skillet; keep warm. Add flour to skillet all at once and stir to blend **with drippings.** Cook, stirring constantly, 2 to 3 minutes. Stir in coffee, scraping up all **browned bits** from bottom of skillet. Boil over medium-high heat until reduced to a thick **glaze** (about 5 minutes). Add stock and again cook until thickened (5 minutes longer). To **serve,** top hot ham slices generously with gravy. Makes 4 servings.

Apple & Sausage Casserole

This easy-to-prepare dish may be assembled in advance, then baked before serving. It's great for a company buffet brunch or a plain old family breakfast.

> 1 pound bulk-style pork sausage
> 2 cups stale French bread cubes
> 6 ounces Cheddar cheese, shredded
> 3 medium Granny Smith apples (about 1-1/4 lbs. *total*), peeled, cored, chopped
> 6 eggs
> 2 cups milk
> 1/2 teaspoon salt
> 1 teaspoon dry mustard

❦ Preheat oven to 350F (175C). Butter a 13" x 9" baking dish and set aside. In a 12-inch skillet, cook sausage until browned; turn out into a fine strainer and press out all fat. Combine sausage, bread cubes, cheese and apples in a bowl; toss to blend and turn out into buttered baking dish, spreading evenly. In a separate bowl, whisk together eggs, milk, salt and mustard; pour over sausage mixture. Bake in preheated oven until golden brown and set in center (45 to 50 minutes). Makes 4 to 6 servings.

Pan Sausage Patties in Caul Fat

Sausage is an important part of breakfast in Southern homes, and every small neighborhood grocery with its own butcher counter features a "house" version. My very favorite sausages are the highly seasoned "pan patties" wrapped in caul fat. This lacy-looking fat, also known as lace fat or *crepine,* is the mesentery of the hog (the membrane that holds the "innards" in place); it has a delicious taste when fried. Small butcher shops, which cut their pork from whole carcasses will probably be able to sell you caul fat, but if you cannot find it, simply fry the sausages without a covering.

        1-1/2 pounds medium-lean ground pork
        1 medium onion, finely chopped
        2 medium garlic cloves, minced
        1 tablespoon crushed red pepper flakes
        1/4 to 1/2 teaspoon red (cayenne) pepper
        1-1/4 teaspoons salt
        1/2 teaspoon dried leaf thyme
        1 tablespoon minced parsley, preferably flat-leaf
        2 bay leaves, minced
        1 teaspoon freshly ground black pepper
        1/4 teaspoon freshly ground allspice
        3 tablespoons port wine
        Caul fat
        1/2 cup vegetable oil for frying

☙ Combine all ingredients except caul fat and oil in a large bowl. Using your hands, work mixture together, blending all ingredients thoroughly. Pat mixture into patties about 1/2 inch thick and 3 inches in diameter; set aside. Using scissors, cut fat into 7-inch squares and wrap each sausage patty in a square of fat. (At this point, you may wrap sausages tightly and freeze up to 2 months.) To cook sausage, heat oil in a heavy 12-inch skillet over medium heat. Add patties and cook, turning as needed, until well browned on both sides and cooked through (about 6 minutes per side). Drain on paper towels and serve hot. Makes about 2 pounds sausage.

Southern Breakfast Grits

A breakfast in the South without grits is simply not a real breakfast. Grits are a coarse meal ground from the dried corn kernels called hominy (see page 111). Like most breakfast cereal grains, they are available today in a quick-cooking "instant" variety, but quick grits don't even come close to matching the taste and texture of the old-fashioned slow-cooking type. To serve grits the traditional way, spoon them onto the serving plate and make a little well in the center with the back of a spoon, then place a chunk of butter in the well and let it melt.

> **4 cups water**
> **1 teaspoon salt**
> **1 cup slow-cooking grits**
> **1 cup milk**
> **1/4 cup unsalted butter or margarine, room temperature**

❧ Combine water and salt in a heavy 3-quart saucepan. Bring to a full boil over high heat; stir in grits. Boil, stirring often, 5 minutes. Reduce heat to lowest setting; stir in milk. Cover and cook until all liquid is absorbed and grits are thick and creamy (45 to 60 minutes). Remove from heat, add butter or margarine and stir until melted. Serve hot. Makes 4 to 6 servings.

Fried Green Tomatoes

Southerners love tomatoes, and just about everybody grows them—even on apartment balconies, you'll often see big pots holding a fruit-laden plant or two. We even like to pick them green, slice them and fry them up in a cornmeal coating for breakfast! They're a perfect complement to Southern Breakfast Grits, above, and Pan Sausage Patties in Caul Fat, opposite.

> **2 medium, green tomatoes**
> **1/3 cup bacon drippings or vegetable oil**
> **1 cup yellow cornmeal, preferably stone-ground**
> **3/4 teaspoon salt**
> **3/4 teaspoon finely ground black pepper**
> **3/4 teaspoon sugar**
> **2 eggs beaten with 1-1/2 cups milk**

❧ Cut tomatoes into 1/4- to 1/2-inch-thick rounds. Heat bacon drippings or oil in a heavy 12-inch skillet over medium heat. Meanwhile, in a medium bowl, combine cornmeal, salt, pepper and sugar, tossing with a fork to blend. Dip tomato slices in egg-milk mixture to coat well; then dip in cornmeal mixture, turning to coat well. Shake off excess cornmeal mixture and place slices in hot fat. Cook, turning once, until golden brown on both sides (about 6 minutes). Serve hot. Makes 4 servings.

Rice & Pecan Griddle Cakes

Rice and corn are the South's staple grains and they appear in various forms at almost every meal—sometimes even in every course. These tasty and truly Southern pancakes, made with leftover rice, are a favorite with children. Top them with white corn syrup or ribbon cane syrup for a very Southern touch.

> 1 cup cooked white rice
> 2 cups buttermilk
> 3 tablespoons unsalted butter or margarine, melted
> 1/2 teaspoon salt
> 1 teaspoon vanilla extract
> 1 tablespoon sugar
> 2/3 cup finely chopped pecans
> 4 eggs, separated, room temperature
> 1/3 cup sifted Southern soft wheat flour, see page 122
> Unsalted butter or margarine
> Syrup of your choice

❦ Grease a heavy griddle or 12-inch skillet with oil. Meanwhile, in a large bowl, stir together rice, buttermilk, 3 tablespoons melted butter or margarine, salt, vanilla, sugar and pecans. In bowl of an electric mixer, beat egg yolks at medium speed until thickened and light lemon-yellow in color (about 4 minutes). Blend in flour, then stir into rice mixture. In a separate bowl, beat egg whites at medium speed until they hold medium-stiff peaks (about 3 minutes). Fold whites into rice mixture gently but thoroughly. Meanwhile heat griddle. Drop 2 tablespoons batter onto hot griddle or skillet for each pancake. Cook pancakes until golden brown on bottom and bubbly on top (about 2 minutes). Flip and cook just until brown on other side (about 1 minute). Serve hot with butter or margarine and your choice of syrup. Makes about 24 pancakes.

Cornmeal Batter Cakes with Honey Butter

Thin cornmeal pancakes are a Southern favorite. Slather them with Honey Butter and stack them up for a truly soul-satisfying breakfast.

> Honey Butter, opposite
> 1 cup yellow cornmeal, preferably stone-ground
> 2 teaspoons sugar
> 1 teaspoon salt
> 2 eggs, beaten until frothy
> 1-1/3 cups buttermilk
> Melted bacon drippings or vegetable oil

Honey Butter:
3/4 cup unsalted butter, room temperature
1/4 cup honey

❦ Prepare Honey Butter and set aside. In a medium bowl, combine cornmeal, sugar and salt. Combine beaten eggs and buttermilk; add to dry ingredients and beat until smooth. Place a heavy (preferably cast-iron) 12-inch skillet over medium heat. When skillet is hot, pour in enough bacon drippings to coat pan with a thin film of fat; swirl to coat bottom evenly. Spoon about 2 tablespoons batter into skillet for each pancake; you can cook 4 at a time. Cook pancakes until golden brown on bottom and bubbly on top (about 3 minutes). Flip and cook just until brown on other side (about 30 seconds). Keep warm while cooking remaining batter. Serve hot with Honey Butter. Makes about 24 pancakes.
Honey Butter: Whisk butter and honey in a medium bowl until blended and fluffy. Place in a small bowl or crock; serve at room temperature.

Buckwheat Yeast Pancakes

Buckwheat is used—most often in pancakes—in the rural and mountainous areas of Virginia, Kentucky, Tennessee and North Carolina. This recipe follows a method popular in Virginia: you begin by making a starter which is allowed to ferment overnight.

Buckwheat flour has an earthy, slightly musky taste; it is available at health food and specialty food stores.

1 (1/4-oz.) package active dry yeast (about 1 tablespoon)
2 cups warm water (110F, 45C)
2 cups buckwheat flour
1 tablespoon dairy sour cream
1 cup all-purpose flour
1 cup lukewarm water
1 teaspoon salt
1/2 teaspoon baking soda
2 tablespoons molasses
Unsalted butter or margarine
Syrup of your choice

❦ To make starter, in a large bowl, stir yeast into 2 cups warm water. Stir in buckwheat flour and sour cream. Cover bowl tightly with plastic wrap; set aside in a warm place overnight. Then stir down starter and add all-purpose flour, 1 cup lukewarm water, salt, baking soda and molasses. Blend well. Cover with plastic wrap and let rest 30 minutes. Liberally grease a heavy griddle or 12-inch skillet and heat. Ladle 2 tablespoons batter onto hot griddle for each pancake; cook until golden brown on bottom and bubbly on top (3 to 4 minutes). Flip and cook just until brown on other side (1 to 2 minutes). Serve hot with butter or margarine and your choice of syrup. Makes about 24 pancakes.

Easy Béarnaise Sauce

Richly aromatic béarnaise sauce is a cousin of classic hollandaise and made in much the same way, but with one extra step: the addition of aromatic seasonings and vinegar greatly reduced to intensify the flavor. Like hollandaise, béarnaise sauce cannot be served hot.

> 1/3 cup tarragon-flavored vinegar
> 2 tablespoons finely chopped shallots
> 1 tablespoon dried leaf tarragon
> 1 tablespoon dried leaf chervil
> 3 egg yolks
> 1 cup unsalted butter, melted
> 1/2 teaspoon salt
> Dash of red (cayenne) pepper

❦ Combine vinegar, shallots, tarragon and chervil in a heavy 1-quart saucepan over medium heat. Boil until liquid is reduced to about 2 tablespoons (about 7 minutes). Set aside. Place egg yolks in a food processor fitted with the steel blade; process until thickened and very light in color (about 1-1/2 minutes). With machine running, pour melted butter through feed tube in a very slow, steady stream. When all butter has been incorporated, transfer sauce to a medium bowl and whisk in reduced vinegar mixture, salt and red pepper until blended. Run warm water through a fine strainer or chinois, then strain sauce through it. Makes about 1-1/2 cups.

Easy Hollandaise Sauce

By preparing this sauce in the food processor, you can save yourself much frustration, though you will sacrifice a bit of the silken texture attained by the classic method.

Always remember that emulsified egg sauces cannot be served hot: egg yolks curdle and break down at 180F (80C), far below the boiling temperature of 212F (100C). To keep such sauces warm, hold them over warm water (never above 140F, 60C). The temperature of the food over which the sauces are served will gently warm them.

> 3 egg yolks
> 3 tablespoons lukewarm water
> 3/4 cup unsalted butter, melted
> 1/4 cup fresh lemon juice
> 1/2 teaspoon salt
> 1/4 teaspoon red (cayenne) pepper

Combine egg yolks and lukewarm water in a food processor fitted with the steel blade; process until thickened and very light in color (about 1-1/2 minutes). With machine running, pour melted butter through feed tube in a very slow, steady stream. When all butter has been incorporated, transfer sauce to a medium bowl. Whisk in lemon juice, salt and red pepper until blended. Makes about 1-1/2 cups.

BEVERAGES

The settlers of our country endured many hardships in establishing their foothold in the New World, but one of those hardships has perhaps been less publicized than most: the acute shortage of the brandy, wine and ale to which the colonists were accustomed. The only beverage was water. The rest of the diet was scarcely less spartan; in 1607, conditions in Jamestown were so bleak that the daily ration was "1 pint of wheat and barley boiled." Indeed, one early settler commented, "Had we been as free as from all other sins as from gluttony and drunkenness, we might have been canonized for saints."

The lack of alcohol was clearly a problem to be remedied with all due expediency! Brewmasters were brought in from England and other European countries, and soon the colonists were producing beer from persimmons, pumpkins, Jerusalem artichokes, green cornstalks and doubtless many other native plants. Wines were made from native grapes such as scuppernong and muscadine; other fruits and berries yielded more wines, cordials and ratafias. In addition, the colonists imported fine brandy and wine from Europe and heady rum from Jamaica; arrack, a liqueur produced in the East Indies, was a popular punch ingredient.

By the end of the 17th century, the cellars of the great plantations were well stocked with wines, liqueurs and homemade beer, and it had become customary to provide various dignitaries with plenty of spirits: in 1676, the justices of the court sessions in Virginia were allotted a daily ration of one gallon of brandy. (One can only hope that no decisions rendered by this court are used as precedents today!)

Alcoholic beverages were a household staple

in the colonies, used as pain-killers and tranquilizers, as protection from such maladies of the day as "fever and flux," and even as a morning tonic for the plantation master. Wine was drunk with every meal, and in wealthy homes, a different one might be served with each course.

Punch in various guises became a specialty of Tidewater Virginia. Kept chilled with molded ice rings in huge sterling silver bowls, it was served with great fanfare at weddings and other celebrations and even at funerals. The original punch recipe came to the colonies with the British, who in turn had picked up the idea in their dealings with the Far Eastern countries on the spice trade route. The very word "punch" comes from *pauch*, the Hindustani word for "five," in this case referring to the five traditional punch ingredients: spirits, water or other liquid, sliced fruit, sugar and spices. In the colonies, West Indian rum was the spirit most often used in punches, though brandy was also popular. Later on, champagne became a punch favorite throughout the South.

As the South grew, so did its appetite for newer and more exotic beverages. In 1793, a Frenchman named Antoine Amdee Peychaud fled the slave uprisings of Santo Domingo for New Orleans, bringing with him a secret formula for a concoction he called "bitters." Peychaud opened an apothecary shop in the Vieux Carré and began serving the drink by small shots in egg cups—called *coquetiers* in French. *Coquetier* was eventually anglicized to "cocktail," and came to refer to the mixed drinks we know today.

Though Southerners brewed homemade beer and wine aplenty in colonial times, by far the greatest and most lasting achievement of the early South was the creation of bourbon whiskey. Elijah Craig, a pioneer Baptist preacher, distilled the first American corn whiskey in 1789 and baptized his creation "bourbon," after the county where it was produced. Bourbon County was originally in Virginia, but the territory was later ceded to Kentucky; today, 70% of all the bourbon consumed in the United States is produced in that state, by great families who fiercely guard their generations-old formulas. The distillation process is strictly regulated, and the word "bourbon" even has a legal definition.

Lest the South's reputation be totally undone, let me point out that we have some famous non-alcoholic beverages too. Louisiana is known far and wide for its inky black, drip-pot coffee with chicory. Tourists are sometimes appalled by this hair-raising brew—said to be so strong that a spoon will stand alone in it!—but the natives can't wake up without it. Chicory coffee came into use during the Civil War, when the stores of coffee beans dwindled. Louisianians found that they could double their coffee supply by mixing it half and half with the dried, ground root of the chicory plant. By the end of the war, they had acquired a real preference for the sweet, pungent flavor of chicory coffee, and it is still popular today in Louisiana and many other parts of the South.

Whatever your pleasure in imbibing, lift your glass or cup or mug and join me in a Southern toast. "Let's drink to our gracious friend and host. May his generous heart, like his good wine, only grow mellower with the passing of the years."

Hot Spiced Apple Cider

Just right for a chilly winter evening. Serve beside a roaring fire, with plenty of buttery popcorn.

> **8 cups natural-style apple cider**
> **1/3 cup firmly packed light brown sugar**
> **2 (2-inch-long) cinnamon sticks**
> **1 teaspoon whole allspice berries**
> **1 teaspoon whole cloves**
> **1/4 teaspoon freshly grated nutmeg**

❦ Pour cider into a 4-quart saucepan and add remaining ingredients. Bring to a boil, then reduce heat, cover and simmer 30 minutes, stirring to dissolve sugar. Strain out and discard spices. Serve hot in mugs. Makes 8 cups.

Cafe au Lait

Made famous in the coffeehouses of New Orleans, this wonderful coffee tastes just as good on your patio at home as it does in the French Quarter. Serve with Croquignolles, page 130, for a perfect breakfast or late-night snack.

> **1 pint (2 cups) half and half**
> **1/3 cup firmly packed light brown sugar**
> **2 cups very hot dark-roast coffee with chicory**

❦ Place half and half in a 2-quart saucepan and bring just to the boiling point. Add brown sugar and stir until dissolved. Pour into a pot. To serve, pour equal amounts of coffee and half and half mixture into coffee mugs. Serve hot. Makes 4 (8-oz.) servings.

Southern Christmas Punch

If you need a non-alcoholic beverage for your next holiday get-together, think first of this delicious, easy-to-prepare hot punch. I often serve it at club meetings or on similar occasions calling for a beverage and a light snack.

> **8 cups natural-style apple cider**
> **2 cups fresh orange juice**
> **2 cups unsweetened pineapple juice**
> **1/2 cup fresh lemon juice**
> **1/2 cup sugar**
> **1 tablespoon whole cloves**
> **2 (2-inch-long) cinnamon sticks**

❦ Combine all ingredients in a 4-quart saucepan over medium heat. Bring to a boil, then reduce heat and simmer 15 minutes, stirring to dissolve sugar. Strain out and discard spices. Serve hot in mugs. Makes about 3 quarts.

Fruit Shrubs

Before the days of soft drinks and iced tea, frosty fruit shrubs were a favorite thirst-quencher during hot Southern summers. Even today, a tall, chilly glass of shrub is as good and refreshing as it was 100 years ago! The Old Southern Berry Shrub below follows the original recipe: you make a highly concentrated syrup from fresh berries, vinegar and sugar, then dilute the syrup with water and serve it over ice. More modern fruit shrubs are often prepared from ice cream or sherbet. Either way, the drink is mighty tasty.

Old Southern Berry Shrub

1 pound fresh blackberries or raspberries
2 cups apple cider vinegar
2 cups sugar
Ice water
Crushed ice or ice cubes

❦ Place berries in a non-metal bowl; add vinegar. Cover tightly with plastic wrap; set aside to macerate 3 days. Then strain mixture through a fine strainer into a medium saucepan, pressing down on berries to extract all liquid. Discard pulp. Stir in sugar; boil 2 to 3 minutes, then remove from heat and cool. Store in a jar with a tight-fitting lid. To prepare each serving, combine 1/4 cup berry concentrate with 1 cup ice water; pour over ice in tall glasses and serve. Makes about 3 cups concentrate (enough for 12 servings).

Raspberry-Grapefruit Shrub

1/3 cup frozen grapefruit juice concentrate, thawed
1 cup red raspberry jam
2 cups raspberry sherbet, softened
3 cups club soda, chilled
Crushed ice or ice cubes
Fresh mint sprigs

❦ Combine grapefruit juice concentrate, jam and sherbet in a blender; blend at high speed until liquefied and smooth. Pour into a pitcher and stir in club soda, blending well. Pour over ice in tall glasses and garnish with mint sprigs. Makes about 8 servings.

Pineapple-Grapefruit Shrub

1 (6-oz.) can frozen grapefruit juice concentrate, thawed
2 cups ice water
1/4 teaspoon Angostura bitters
1/2 cup Grenadine syrup
2 cups pineapple sherbet, softened
Crushed ice or ice cubes
Fresh mint sprigs

❦ In a pitcher, combine thawed grapefruit juice concentrate with ice water; stir to dissolve concentrate. Then add bitters, Grenadine syrup and sherbet, stirring until smooth. Pour over ice in tall glasses and garnish with mint sprigs. Makes about 8 servings.

Orange-Apricot Shrub

1 (6-oz.) can frozen orange juice concentrate, thawed
2 cups ice water
2 cups orange sherbet, softened
1/4 cup apricot preserves
Crushed ice or ice cubes
Orange slices

❦ Combine orange juice concentrate, ice water, sherbet and preserves in a blender; blend at high speed until liquefied and smooth. Serve over ice in tall glasses; garnish each serving with an orange slice slit to center and fitted on rim of glass. Makes about 8 servings.

Coconut-Orange Shrub

1 quart (4 cups) half and half
2 cups sweetened flaked coconut
1 (6-oz.) can frozen orange juice concentrate, thawed
3 cups orange sherbet, softened
Crushed ice or ice cubes
Orange slices and maraschino cherries on wooden picks

❦ Combine half and half, coconut, orange juice concentrate and sherbet in a blender; blend at high speed until liquefied and smooth. Pour over ice in tall glasses; garnish each serving with an orange slice and a maraschino cherry on a wooden pick. Makes about 8 servings.

Southern Eggnog

Eggnog was a favorite holiday punch in the early Virginia colonies and was served each Christmas at Mount Vernon. In England, the drink was made with red Spanish wine, but the colonists used a headier combination of liquors, including Jamaican rum. There are two secrets to achieving a perfectly thick, smooth consistency. First, you must beat the egg yolks and sugar until thickened and light in color. Then, you must add the liquor a drop at a time, whisking all the while.

> **2 cups brandy**
> **1 cup rye whiskey**
> **1/2 cup dark rum**
> **1/2 cup dry sherry**
> **12 eggs, separated, room temperature**
> **3/4 cup sugar**
> **2 quarts (8 cups) half and half**

❦ Combine brandy, whiskey, rum and sherry, stirring to blend; set aside. In a large bowl, combine egg yolks and sugar; beat with a hand-held electric mixer until thickened and light lemon-yellow in color (about 4 minutes). Add combined liquors, drop by drop, whisking to blend. Add half and half very slowly, whisking constantly to form a velvety smooth mixture. Cover and refrigerate until well chilled. When ready to serve, beat egg whites until they hold medium-stiff peaks; slowly fold into chilled eggnog. Pour into a punch bowl and serve in punch cups. Makes about 16 (8-oz.) servings.

Champagne Punch

The South consumes more champagne per capita than any other region in the world—including France—and champagne punch is one of our favorite ways of drinking it. You will find it served at weddings, all kinds of parties, bon voyage to-dos and probably even a few funerals! There are as many recipes for champagne punch, I am quite sure, as there are Southern hostesses, but this one is delightfully different and really stands out from the rest.

> **8 cups dry champagne, chilled**
> **1 cup fine cognac, chilled**
> **1 cup Triple Sec, chilled**
> **1 quart (4 cups) club soda, chilled**
> **Ice ring**
> **4 medium oranges, cut into thin rounds**

❦ Combine champagne, cognac, Triple Sec and club soda in a large punch bowl. Add a molded ice ring and orange slices. Serve in punch cups. Makes about 15 (8-oz.) servings.

Chatham Artillery Punch

The Chatham Artillery is a Georgia military organization, founded in Chatham County by veterans of the Revolutionary War. This punch, perfected over many years of being served at various regimental functions, has gained fame as a "heavy gun" party punch.

8 cups strong tea
1 cup fresh lemon juice (about 5 large lemons)
5 cups firmly packed light brown sugar
8 cups Catawba wine
8 cups dark rum
4 cups brandy
4 cups rye whiskey
2 cups pitted fresh red cherries
2 cups diced fresh or canned pineapple
10 cups dry champagne, chilled
Ice ring

❡ Combine tea, lemon juice and brown sugar in a 4-quart saucepan. Heat over medium heat, stirring often, until sugar is dissolved (about 6 minutes). Cool. In a 10- to 12-quart container, combine cooled tea mixture, wine, rum, brandy, whiskey, cherries and pineapple. Stir to blend. Cover and refrigerate 1 week. When ready to serve, pour tea mixture into a large punch bowl and stir in champagne. Add a molded ice ring and serve in punch cups. Makes about 50 (7-oz.) servings.

Cherry Bounce

Popular in colonial Virginia, this rich, mellow after-dinner liqueur is similar to the home-made ratafias and cordials which stocked the cellars of fine homes throughout the South. Many Southerners still prepare liqueurs, and cherry bounce is one of the best.

4 pounds pitted fresh Bing cherries
2 cups sugar
1 teaspoon crushed mace blades
1 teaspoon whole allspice berries
1 cup dark rum
1 cup fine cognac

❡ In a 6-quart saucepan, combine cherries, sugar, mace and allspice. Bring to a boil, then reduce heat and simmer, uncovered, stirring often, until cherries are very soft and pulpy (about 20 minutes). Increase heat; boil, skimming foam from surface, 3 minutes. Pour into a large crock or tempered bowl. Cool completely. Stir in rum and cognac. Cover and let stand 48 hours at room temperature. Strain well, pressing on cherry pulp to extract all liquid. Place in a decanter or jar with a tight-fitting lid; store at room temperature. Makes 4 cups.

Syllabub

Syllabub is a rich and frothy drink, enjoyed as a punch in the colonies but generally served as a dessert today. The origin of the word is uncertain, but here is one possible explanation: The colonists originally used a wine imported from Sillery, France to prepare the drink; the word "bub" was a 17th-century slang term for "drink"—and this popular "bub" from Sillery became *sillabub!*

> 1/2 cup fine cognac, chilled
> 1/3 cup superfine sugar
> 1 cup dry white wine such as Chardonnay, chilled
> 2 tablespoons fresh lemon juice
> 1 pint (2 cups) whipping cream, chilled
> Fresh mint sprigs

❦ Combine cognac, sugar, wine and lemon juice in a large bowl; whisk until sugar is dissolved. Add cream; beat with an electric mixer until mixture holds soft peaks (4 to 5 minutes). Spoon into parfait glasses; garnish with mint. Serve at once. Makes 6 to 8 servings.

The Old Southern Tea Room 24-Hour Cocktail

Founded in 1941 by Mary McKay, The Old Southern Tea Room in Vicksburg, Mississippi is one of the South's legendary restaurants. The delicious food served there has delighted guests from all over the world. What cuisine could inspire so much excitement for so many years, you ask? Nothing but plain old Southern home cooking—the best fried chicken anywhere, served with rice and pan gravy, the crispest fried shrimp, the most flavor-packed tomato aspic and desserts that could make you cry, but only if you were deprived of them! This cocktail, at its best after a 24-hour sit in the refrigerator, is a long-time Tea Room favorite.

> 1/4 cup fresh lemon juice
> 1 quart (4 cups) orange juice
> 2 cups unsweetened pineapple juice
> 2 cups unsweetened grapefruit juice
> 2/3 cup Grenadine syrup
> 3 cups good-quality Kentucky bourbon whiskey
> Crushed ice

❦ Combine all ingredients except ice in a 3- to 4-quart container. Cover and refrigerate 24 hours. To serve, shake well and serve over ice. Makes 3 quarts.

Virginia Sherry Cobbler

Sherry cobbler is a delightful "ladies' drink" that was popular throughout the South many years ago: I have found it in old recipe files and cookbooks from Virginia to New Orleans. The following recipe was adapted from one in a Richmond recipe file dated 1894; I find it perfect for sipping before dinner.

> 1 canned pineapple slice
> 1 orange slice
> 4 maraschino cherries
> 2 teaspoons powdered sugar
> 1 cup dry sherry
> 1/4 cup ice water
> Crushed ice

❧ Place pineapple, orange and cherries in a cocktail shaker and add powdered sugar. Muddle fruit and sugar in bottom of shaker. Add sherry and ice water and shake vigorously about 30 seconds. Strain into a 12-ounce highball glass filled with ice. Makes 1 serving.

Absinthe Cocktail

Absinthe is a greenish liqueur with a licoricelike flavor, made from wormwood, anise seeds, fennel, star anise, coriander seeds, hyssop and 190-proof alcohol. Though produced in Switzerland, it became very popular in the saloons of 19th-century New Orleans, and the Old Absinthe House in the Vieux Carré was, for a time, the city's busiest watering hole. Unfortunately for its devotees, the liqueur's wormwood content proved devastatingly addictive—and those who became addicted often died or went mad.

The United States banned absinthe from its wormwood formula in 1912, but several wormwood-free anise-flavored liqueurs are widely available today, including Pernod, anisette, Ojen and Herbsaint. The last-named is my favorite, thanks to its very nice, mellow taste, but the others work equally well in this bracing cocktail.

> 1 tablespoon Herbsaint
> 1 tablespoon gin
> 1 egg white
> 1 teaspoon powdered sugar
> 1/2 cup crushed ice

❧ Combine all ingredients in a cocktail shaker and shake vigorously until very frothy (about 2 minutes). Strain into a chilled wine glass. Makes 1 serving.

Planter's Punch

Heady Jamaican rum was unlike any liquor the colonists had known in England, but they soon became fond enough of it to import sizable quantities. Rum's mellow flavor lends itself to stout fruity concoctions like this one, once a favorite of the gentleman plantation master.

> **3 tablespoons dark rum**
> **2 tablespoons white crème de cacao**
> **1 tablespoon fresh lime juice**
> **1 tablespoon fresh orange juice**
> **Crushed ice**
> **Orange slice**

❦ Stir together rum, crème de cacao, lime juice and orange juice. Half-fill an old-fashioned glass with ice; add rum mixture. Garnish with an orange slice. Makes 1 serving.

Southern Comfort Sparkle

Southern Comfort was born and bred in the South, with a mellow, sweet flavor that comes from the addition of caramel. Originally produced in New Orleans, the liqueur is now made in Louisville, Kentucky, in the heart of bourbon country.

> **1/4 cup Southern Comfort**
> **1/2 cup unsweetened pineapple juice**
> **1 tablespoon fresh lime juice**
> **Crushed ice**
> **Ginger ale**
> **Lime slice**

❦ Combine Southern Comfort, pineapple juice and lime juice. Pour over ice in a highball glass and fill glass with ginger ale. Stir to blend, then garnish with a lime slice and serve. Makes 1 serving.

Hot Buttered Rum

Summer is not the only time to enjoy rum! Nothing beats a steaming mug of hot buttered rum on chilly winter evenings. The batter keeps indefinitely in the refrigerator; a small jar of it with the drink recipe attached, makes a very nice hostess gift.

1 tablespoon Hot Buttered Rum Batter, see below
2-1/2 tablespoons dark rum
1 cup boiling water
1-1/2 teaspoons unsalted butter

Hot Buttered Rum Batter:
1/2 cup unsalted butter, room temperature
1 (1-lb.) box dark brown sugar
1/2 teaspoon ground cinnamon
1/4 teaspoon ground allspice
1/4 teaspoon ground cloves

❦ Prepare the Buttered Rum Batter and refrigerate. To prepare each drink, place rum and 1 tablespoon batter in a mug. Add boiling water and stir to dissolve batter. Float butter on top. Serve hot. Makes 1 serving.

Hot Buttered Rum Batter: In bowl of an electric mixer, cream butter and brown sugar at medium speed until light and fluffy (about 4 minutes), stopping to scrape down side of bowl 2 or 3 times. Add cinnamon, allspice and cloves; beat 1 minute longer to blend. Pack batter into jars with tight-fitting lids and store in refrigerator. Makes about 2 cups batter (enough for 32 servings).

Cold Buttered Rum

This smooth and creamy drink will positively make your day—especially if the day is one of those hot, lazy days of a Southern summer. (For a non-alcoholic cooler, simply omit the rum.)

1 cup firmly packed butter pecan ice cream, softened slightly
2 tablespoons dark rum
3 tablespoons whipping cream
1 teaspoon vanilla extract
Crushed ice or ice cubes

❦ Combine all ingredients except ice in a blender and blend until smooth. Pour over ice in a 12-ounce highball glass. Makes 1 serving.

Mint Julep

The mere mention of mint juleps brings to mind magnolias and hoop-skirted Southern belles. No Southerner with any sense really wants to discuss recipes for the legendary drink, though, because the discussion might lead to a fight! Everybody has his own formula, and where juleps are concerned, Southerners are very opinionated. The key issues are these: Do you bruise the mint? Do you use simple syrup or powdered sugar? How much bourbon do you use? (Early juleps were made with brandy or rum, but once bourbon whiskey was formulated, it became the only acceptable choice.) Even the origin of the drink provides grounds for dispute, since both Virginia and Kentucky claim to have invented it.

The writings of an early Virginia traveler tell us that for a plantation owner, a typical day began with a julep upon rising; and when overnight guests were visiting, juleps in frosty sterling silver tankards were brought to them in their rooms each morning. What a way to start the day!

We may no longer have our juleps before our feet touch the floor in the morning, but we still take them very seriously in the South. Mint juleps are a tradition at the Kentucky Derby—served each year at Churchill Downs on the first Saturday in May, they are considered part of the Southern rites of spring!

> 8 fresh mint leaves
> 1 tablespoon Bar Syrup, below
> Crushed ice
> 1/4 cup good-quality Kentucky bourbon whiskey
> Ice water
> Fresh mint sprigs

❧ In bottom of a 12-ounce glass, combine mint leaves and Bar Syrup. Using a wooden spoon, muddle mint and syrup to bruise mint thoroughly. Fill glass with ice and add bourbon. Fill glass with ice water and stir to blend. Garnish with mint sprigs and serve. Makes 1 serving.

Bar Syrup (Simple Syrup)

Bar syrup keeps indefinitely when refrigerated in a jar with a tight-fitting lid. It's handy to have on hand for sweetening various drinks as the need arises.

> 2-2/3 cups sugar
> 1-1/3 cups water

❧ Combine sugar and water in a heavy medium saucepan. Boil 5 minutes, stirring until sugar is dissolved. Remove from heat; cool before using. Makes about 4 cups.

INDEX

MAIL-ORDER SOURCES

Cajun Sausages & Seasoning Meats

Poche's Meat Market
Route 2, Box 415
Breaux Bridge, LA 90517
Tasso, pickled marinated pork, andouille, smoked Cajun sausage, pork sausage, boudin. Chaurice in winter only. Will ship fastest and best way for area.

Coffee

Neighbors Coffee Company
P.O. Box 46
Covington, LA 70434
(504) 892-2741
Dark Roast Coffee with Chicory, Special Blend Dark Roast, Dark Roast Decaffeinated. Uniquely packaged in amounts to make 8 and 12 cups. Eliminates the guesswork.

Community Kitchen
Box 3778
Baton Rouge, LA 70821-3778
(504) 381-3900
Community Dark Roast Coffee, New Orleans Blend with Chicory. Write or call for catalog.

Corn Flour

Louisiana Fish Fry Products
5267 Plank Road
Baton Rouge, LA 70805
(504) 356-2905
Corn flour (unseasoned fish fry). Write or call for prices.

Cornmeal

War Eagle Mill
Route 6, Box 127
Rogers, Arkansas 72756
(501) 789-5343
Stone-ground cornmeal, white and yellow. Write or call for catalog and price list.

Country Hams

S. Wallace Edwards and Sons, Inc.
Box 25
Surrey, Virginia 23883
1-800-222-4267
Virginia country hams. Write or call for catalog and price list.

Herb Plants

Taylors Herb Gardens, Inc.
1535 Lone Oak Road
Vista, California 92084
(619) 727-3485
Many varieties of herb plants. Call or write for catalog and price list.

Seafood

Harlon's Old New Orleans Seafood
126 Airline Highway
Metairie, LA 70001
(504) 831-4592
All types of Gulf Coast fish and shellfish, including turtle meat, frog legs, crabmeat and many others. Will air freight and arrange for delivery to your door. Accepts all major credit cards.

Southern Soft Wheat Flour

White Lily Flour Company
Box 871
Knoxville, TN 37901
Unbleached soft wheat flour, all-purpose and self-rising. Also bread flour. Write for prices.